"*Unapologetic* offers the philosophy of religion the swift, ugly end it has long deserved. This single book will cause the death of a discipline. "

—Dr. Peter Boghossian, Assistant Professor of Philosophy, Portland State University, and author of *A Manual for Creating Atheists*

"As an introduction to the ever-growing frustration with so-called Christian philosophy among many secular ex-Christian authors, *Unapologetic* is invaluable reading material for any reader interested in the wide variety of polemical issues it deals with."

—Dr. Jaco Gericke, Associate Research Professor, Department of Theology and Philosophy, North-West University

"*Unapologetic* is probably my favorite monograph by John Loftus. It deserves a gold medal for undertaking the Olympian task of explaining in clear and accessible prose why the area known as philosophy of religion should be ejected from modern academia and our intellectual life. Pretending that we have good arguments for God is about as useless as pretending we have good arguments for Zeus."

—Dr. Hector Avalos, Professor of Religious Studies, Iowa State University, and author of *The End of Biblical Studies*

"*Unapologetic* is a wonderfully entertaining read. With masterful erudition, John Loftus presents a compelling case for why the philosophy of religion contains nothing but sophistry and illusion and should, therefore, be committed to the flames. It has no more right to exist than the philosophy of fairies, or the study of Superman. One might be skeptical of this claim— as I was before starting the book—but the arguments are so well-crafted and persuasive that I bet you'll walk away nodding your head in agreement. Of Loftus's many critiques of Christianity, this is the best yet. I highly recommend it to anyone with a fondness for great writing and the truth!"

—Phil Torres, author of *The End: What Science and Religion Tell Us About the Apocalypse* and founder of the X-Risks Institute

UNAPOLOGETIC

Why Philosophy of Religion Must End

JOHN W. LOFTUS

Foreword by David Eller

Pitchstone Publishing
Durham, North Carolina

Pitchstone Publishing
Durham, North Carolina
www.pitchstonepublishing.com

10 9 8 7 6 5 4 3 2 1

Library of Congress Cataloging-in-Publication Data

Names: Loftus, John W., author.
Title: Unapologetic : why philosophy of religion must end / John W. Loftus ; foreword by David Eller.
Description: Durham, North Carolina : Pitchstone Publishing, 2016. | Includes bibliographical references.
Identifiers: LCCN 2016035263 (print) | LCCN 2016035641 (ebook) | ISBN 9781634310987 (pbk. : alk. paper) | ISBN 9781634310994 (mobi) | ISBN 9781634311007 (epub) | ISBN 9781939578266 (epdf)
Subjects: LCSH: Religion—Philosophy. | Religion—Controversial literature. | Apologetics.
Classification: LCC BL51 .L579 2016 (print) | LCC BL51 (ebook) | DDC 210—dc23
LC record available at https://lccn.loc.gov/2016035263

CONTENTS

Foreword *by David Eller*   7

Introduction   11

1. My Intellectual Journey   19

2. Anselm and Philosophy of Religion   41

3. Case Studies in Theistic Philosophy of Religion   63

4. Case Studies in Atheistic Philosophy of Religion   85

5. Why Philosophy of Religion Must End   111

6. How to Effectively Deal with Faith-Based Claims   139

7. Answering Objections and Other Practical Concerns   167

8. It's Enough to Be Right!   189

9. On Justifying Ridicule, Mockery, and Satire   211

Appendix A: My Interview with Keith Parsons   237

Appendix B: Robert Price's Rebuttal to William Lane Craig   250

Appendix C: The Demon, Matrix, Material World,
and Dream Possibilities   257

About the Author   272

FOREWORD

There is no greater threat to any group or cause than the defector, the turncoat, the apostate. Islam, for instance, does not compel anyone to join the religion but decrees death for anyone who would leave, and we all know how Scientology pillories and intimidates former members. And groups have good reason to fear the escapee and traitor, because that person knows their secrets, sees through their errors and lies, and, most devastating of all, is evidence of a happy life after and without the group.

John Loftus is philosophy of religion's—or what we would both probably prefer to call "Christian philosophy's"—worst nightmare. He was inside of the whole bankrupt enterprise, earning a Master of Theology degree and studying toward a PhD under august teachers like William Lane Craig. He has since converted (or deconverted) from insider to outsider, even punishing theology with his "outsider test for faith." He has written or edited powerful texts on the failings of Christianity and theism more generally, using philosophy of religion's own tools against it. In honor of the recent decision of British voters to secede from the European Union, we might dub this new book his Apologexit.

Loftus is not the first to urge a rethinking if not a total abandonment of philosophy of religion, but he is probably the first to do so after emerging from the cocoon of religious education (if that oxymoron does not make us too dizzy). A few years ago, philosopher Keith Parsons announced that he was jumping from the sinking ship of philosophy of religion because he recognized "the case for theism" as fraudulent. That it is. But such a critique misses the bigger and deeper point: philosophy, even philosophy of religion, is not supposed to be about "the case for theism." In fact, it should not give theism preferential treatment at all. The *Stanford Encyclopedia of Philosophy* defines philosophy of religion as "the philosophical examination of the central themes and concepts involved in religious traditions," but— and this will come as a surprise to many philosophers and religionists— *most religions never had a concept of god(s) and therefore had no theism and cannot be subsumed under the category of theology.*

In the present book, Loftus takes apologetics as his prime adversary within the philosophy of religion. And for good reason: apologetics is the poorest kind of philosophy of religion. In fact, apologetics masquerades as philosophy of religion when it is not. The aforementioned *Stanford Encyclopedia of Philosophy* contains no entry for apologetics, *because it is not philosophy.* The *Catholic Encyclopedia* (http://www.newadvent.org/cathen/01618a.htm) is honest when it explains that apologetics is "a theological science which has for its purpose the explanation and defense of the Christian religion" (except of course it is not a "science" at all: what experiments does it conduct, and what new knowledge and theories does it generate?). The Christian Apologetics & Research Ministry (https://carm.org/apologetics) is clearer still: "Apologetics is the branch of Christianity that deals with the defense and establishment of the Christian faith." In a word, apologetics is not philosophy of religion, *it is religion.* It does not analyze, let alone critique, religion but aims to propagate it: as another page on the Christian Apologetics & Research Ministry site proclaims, apologetics "is similar to preaching because its goal is ultimately the defense and presentation of the validity and necessity of the gospel."

An internal problem for apologetics, however, is that it can only defend and present *one* religion and not all, since religions so dramatically differ and disagree in their doctrines. For instance, the Catholic version of apologetics inevitably represents and defends not Christianity but *Catholic Christianity* specifically. *The Catholic Encyclopedia* emphasizes that apologetics begins with "the study of religion in general and the grounds of theistic belief" before proceeding to "the study of revealed religion and the grounds of Christian belief" and finally "the study of the true Church of Christ and the grounds of Catholic belief." Baptist or Methodist or Mormon apologists, *ad infinitum*, would not accompany Catholic apologists on this journey and would even reject its destination. And then there are the rest of the world's religions, which could and sometimes do indulge in their own defenses—Muslim apologetics, Jewish apologetics, Buddhist apologetics, Hindu apologetics, and (why not?) Norse and ancient Greek apologetics.

None of this has anything to do with philosophy of religion. It simply wraps itself in the cloak of philosophy to lend itself legitimacy and (superficial) sophistication. It is pure partisanship, as Loftus demonstrates, a total betrayal of the aspirations of philosophy. Non-Christians, and serious philosophers of religion, should simply dismiss it, sweep it off the table. If apologists want to do their work—and we can hardly stop them—they should do it within the confines of theology programs (which, in a better world, would not exist either, because they teach fantasy) without the endorsement or justification of philosophy.

But even if philosophy were to repudiate apologetics, there is still much rotten in the state of philosophy of religion. Almost from its inception, it has been too narrow—it has essentially been philosophy of Christianity—and has asked the wrong (exclusively Christian) questions: look at the chapter titles in any textbook of philosophy of religion and you will see "god" and "miracles" and "resurrection," which, as we have already said, *have no place in most of humanity's religions*. This Christianity-saturated worldview is observable in other disciplines as well, particularly the psychology of religion and the sociology of religion, although my own anthropology of religion has come the farthest in escaping the gravitational pull of Christianity, in *provincializing* Christianity as just one religion among many and by no means typical of religions.

That philosophy of religion is blatantly partisan and Christian is manifest, but some of what passes as professional scholarship in philosophy of religion is offensive nonsense. I offer three examples. In the *International Journal for Philosophy of Religion*, the June 2010 issue contained an article by T. J. Mawson titled "Praying to Stop Being an Atheist," which argued that atheists "are under a *prima facie* epistemic obligation to pray to God that He stop them being atheists," and the February 2016 issue contained an article by Travis Dumsday titled "Divine Hiddenness and the One Sheep," which insisted that "God refrains from revealing Himself in a rationally indubitable manner" because, for people who "resist" God's existence, "having God's reality forced upon them unwillingly might result in significant spiritual/moral harm." Meanwhile, a 2015 issue of the journal *Sophia* featured G. R. McLean's "Antipathy to God," which suggested seriously that "we ought to be ashamed of our antipathy to God, which reflects badly upon us." What is shameful is that academic resources are squandered on such absurd projects: does Mawson also contend that nonbelievers should pray (or maybe sacrifice a chicken) to Osiris or Mama Loa to stop disbelieving in those entities? Should Christians, Professor McLean, regret their antipathy to Zeus and Odin, not to mention Allah? And Dr. Dumsday, this god hides himself from us for our own good yet does not refrain from forcing his will and eternal punishment upon us?!

It is possible that there is a valid philosophy of religion to be done. There are certainly philosophical questions to ask about religion. But what parades as philosophy of religion today is a dismal and embarrassing abdication of intellectual discipline. No other scholarly field falls as short of its calling, and no one is more qualified than that turncoat Loftus to induce philosophers of religion to snap out of their dogmatic slumber or else shut the whole business down.

—**David Eller, author of** *Introducing Anthropology of Religion*

INTRODUCTION

This book reflects a change in my approach to religion in two ways. First there is a change of tone. If there is any other person beside myself who has read all of my books, beginning with the first edition of *Why I Became an Atheist*, there is something noticeable in the trajectory of my tone. Over the years I have been jaded by pseudo-theologians and pseudo-philosophers who don't bat an eye when the light of convincing evidence-based logic has shown their faith is delusional. Like a deer caught in the headlights they are unmoved. They don't care about objective evidence. They are indoctrinated, deluded, and brainwashed to believe. Since most were not reasoned into belief, most cannot be reasoned out of belief either. Nothing can cause them to walk away from their faith. They are closed-minded to objective evidence, preferring instead private subjective states of the mind that we know are misleading about the nature of nature and its workings. They resemble a person who shuts his eyes, plugs his ears, and shouts out loud so as not to hear what is being said. They turn a deaf ear to atheists by pretending they're listening, nodding their heads as we speak, but they're not listening. They're really thinking of what to say before we're even finished. So at this point I'm not all that interested in trying to convince them wrong. Others can do that, or they can read my earlier works that have a more respectful tone to them.

These Christian pseudo-intellectual apologists have a vested interest in defending their faith. I think I have a right to say this after nearly a decade of trying to communicate with them. But then I haven't really cared to try for some time. I haven't cared for the same reasons I wouldn't care to convince Scientologist pseudo-scholars or Mormon pseudo-scholars or Hindu pseudo-scholars or Muslim pseudo-scholars, or any other religionist pseudo-scholars—and they're all pseudo-scholars. Talking to them is like talking to a wall, all of them. Don't get me wrong. Talking to a wall or out loud isn't always an entirely bad thing, since hearing the sound of our own voice can help as a sounding board. I'm not saying we don't learn from discussions with pseudo-scholars either. I have most definitely learned a thing or two, if sometimes just how to spot obfuscationism or psychological defense mechanisms or logical fallacies. It's just that nothing seems to change their minds. Plus, I've said about all I wanted to say to them.

I thus have a new target audience, which is the second change in my approach. In this book it's largely reflected in a change of subject matter. Up until now I've targeted the university student and educated person in the pew. I've done so in hopes I might convince a few rare intellectually honest believers who were merely misinformed and looking for answers about their faith. And I have found a modicum of success. It was my focus. I'll still try to communicate to this same audience. But in this book the subject matter is focused more on the nonbelieving intellectuals and the believing pseudo-intellectuals who teach (or who want to teach) philosophy of religion in secular universities. They will be the ones more likely to be interested in what I say, although my usual target audience will certainly be interested as well.

This book is a call for atheist philosophers of religion to end their own discipline by being brutally honest about it. That about sums it all up in a nutshell. They just have to ask themselves how they would treat a deity if he was believed to be Baal, Ishtar, Hathor, Zeus, Odin, or any number of other dead gods and goddesses. How seriously would they consider them? Would they push for a subdiscipline of philosophy classes to discuss the attributes, abilities, and existence of these deities? *What if the history of the philosophy of religion was little more than a history of discussing the rationality, existence, attributes, and actions of fairies?* What if it was about the attributes, abilities, and existence of Superman? What if one day as a philosopher you awoke from your dogmatic slumber and realized this is what you have been teaching for decades in your classes? Well then, this book is a call for you to wake up and smell the roses. For the truth is that the history of philosophy of religion is little more than a history of discussing the rationality, existence, attributes, and actions of fairies. Fairies don't exist.

Neither do Baal, Ishtar, Hathor, Zeus, or Odin. Neither does Yahweh, the supposed Father-god of Jesus.

Just consider what the philosophy of religion would be like if no "revealed" religion ever existed. No written revelation was compiled either. No scriptures were ever written down. There never was a Bible, or a Koran, or a Bhagavad Gita, or a Book of Mormon. The only god worthy of being discussed in philosophy of religion classes would be a philosopher's god—one that was uninformed by the content of any ancient prescientific "sacred" text or current religion. What would there be to discuss? What would a class on the history of philosophy of religion look like if that was the only god to discuss? In our scientific era what could justify having a whole subdiscipline on such a god or goddess when there are other disciplines we could look to for answers? Well then, here too, this book is a call to wake up. There really are no sacred scriptures. They do not exist. No deity inspired anything because no deity exists. All so-called revealed religions are false.

So upon the reasonable overwhelmingly probable evidence-based supposition that the philosophy of religion is little more than a history of discussing the rationality, existence, attributes, and actions of fairies, and that there never was, is, or will be any sacred scriptures or revealed religions, what should atheist philosophers of religion think about their own discipline? What are they doing in their classes? What should be the objectives or aims of a philosopher teaching classes about the rationality, existence, attributes, and actions of fairies? In a syllabus for any college class the professor must state his or her objectives, or aims. What are they? That is the question I am raising. If you share my conclusion you should agree with me that the philosophy of religion must end.

Philosophy of religion must end because there is no truth to religion. Religion must end because it isn't based on evidence, but rather on faith. Faith must end because it is the antithesis of an intellectual virtue. Faith has no objective method and solves no problems. Faith-based belief processes are unreliable. Faith cannot tell us anything about matters of fact like the nature of nature, its workings, or even its origins. If faith is trust then there is no reason to trust faith.

Applying this line of argument specifically to the various sects within Judeo-Christianity, the philosophy of religion must end because biblical studies must end. Biblical studies must end because the evidence is decisive:

the bible god, his wife, sons, and daughters, angels, demons, and other superhuman entities originated in the ancient prescientific superstitious past by mythmakers who were clueless about reality.

The precise nature of my call is to end the philosophy of religion discipline in secular universities. It basically follows the same strategy Dr. Hector Avalos advocates in his book titled *The End of Biblical Studies*. Avalos argues that religion professors and those teaching in biblical studies departments should tell their students the truth about the Bible even though it's considered sacred to many of them. Essentially his call is to debunk the Bible for the good of any future society we might have. So similarly, I'm calling upon philosophy of religion professors to do likewise with the arguments to the existence of God. They should essentially try to put themselves out of a job by arguing against faith, even though the philosophy of religion discipline may not go away anytime soon. In its place philosophy proper can take over the relevant discussions, as can scientific fields that teach us about evolution, the human mind, and the universe. Religion-focused subdisciplines in other academic fields that treat all religious faith-based claims equally should continue, such as comparative religion, anthropology of religion, and psychology of religion.

If subjects such as biology, chemistry, physics, and geology are taught without relying on faith-based superhuman forces as explanations, then using these faith-based explanations isn't legitimate in the secular university in any other discipline either. Just as creationism isn't a legitimate subdiscipline of biology, neither should the philosophy of religion be a legitimate subdiscipline of philosophy. Philosophy of religion is pseudo-philosophy since it isn't dealing with any objective evidence.

I'm sure this will be my most controversial book. Who dares to call for the end of the philosophy of religion, anyway? Me. Believing philosophers will rip it to shreds. Deistic and agnostic philosophers will do likewise. Atheist philosophers like Keith Parsons, Graham Oppy, J. L. Schellenberg, or Paul Draper may do likewise. Amateurs and students currently in philosophy of religion programs from both sides will join in the slugfest. The best and the brightest philosophers, intellectuals, experts, thinkers, and teachers will object to what I have to say, especially since for many of them this is not only about their livelihood but also their life's work. I expect this although I don't look forward to it.

I don't expect believers to agree with any of my proposals. The dividing line is between atheist philosophers who think faith has some epistemic warrant and those who don't. I don't. Faith has no method, solves no problems, and is an utterly unreliable guide for knowing anything objective about the nature of nature. The arguments on behalf of religion have no merit either. All of them have been soundly refuted. All of them are based on special pleading and begging the question. So to the degree secular philosophers agree with this they can agree with my proposals, especially since we're talking specifically about teaching the philosophy of religion in secular universities, where no other intellectual discipline of learning can appeal to faith as an explanation or as a justification.

Most committed atheists shouldn't find this book all that controversial though. It's saying little that's different than what Friedrich Nietzsche said in 1882, when he proclaimed the death of God: "Where is God gone? I mean to tell you! We have killed Him—you and I! God is dead! God remains dead! And we have killed Him!"[1] He elaborated on this same theme later: "God is dead: but given the way people are, there may still for millennia be caves in which they show his shadow. —And we—we must still defeat his shadow as well!"[2] This book is about beating back God's ever-receding shadow over us and escaping from Plato's cave of superstition into the light of reason and science.

Skeptics Society director Michael Shermer disagrees with Nietzsche's pronouncement though. After sharing several polls and indicators that a great many people still believe in God, he wrote, "God is alive and well at the end of the second millennium—and likely will be at the end of the third. It would appear that news of God's death will always be premature."[3] This isn't the point though. It isn't that there aren't still many believers, nor that they won't continue to flourish into the distant future, which is probably true. It's rather that with the rise of science, the method of science, the progress of science, and the spread of science around the globe, it's all but a foregone conclusion that faith won't survive critical scrutiny. Doubt, or nonbelief, is the wave of the future, even if that wave started out being small. One merely needs to look at how unbelief has grown since the beginning of the scientific revolution in the sixteenth century CE. That wave of unbelief has recently increased in strength much more with the rise of the so-called new atheists and the success of New York Times best-selling books by Sam Harris, Richard Dawkins, Christopher Hitchens, Daniel Dennett, and Victor Stenger. They helped create an opening through which growing numbers of people are coming out as atheists and propelling the reach of several different atheist activist organizations.

I'll hitchhike on Nietzsche's claim then. If God is dead, then the philosophy of religion is also dead. She has had an exceedingly long life in the limelight and outlived all reasonable expectations of her life expectancy. It's time for the coroner to sign her death certificate and for the undertaker to bury her deep in the ground. Let's move on. Good riddance. Sayonara.

She cannot exist where religion doesn't exist. They are inextricably entangled. One can have religion without her, but for her to be alive religion must first exist. There just isn't any credible evidence she's alive. Without sufficient evidence it's time we laid her to rest along with the philosophical refutations against her. Philosophical refutations are no longer needed when the overwhelming evidence is against religious castles built in the sky. Refuting them is a waste of time, a waste of talent, and a financial drain on resources. She is dead. She is irrelevant to the needs of the world too. The amount of time wasted on thinking and writing and debating her down through the millennia could have been better used to solve poverty, improve the lives of all living things on earth, and perhaps even help bring peace to the people on earth.

Usually when someone dies a loved one who knows the deceased will offer the eulogy. The word eulogy means "to speak well of" coming from *eu* "well" and *-logia* "speaking." Even though I knew her well, and used to love her, I cannot speak well of her now. Yet, as one of her closest of kin I should say something now that she's dead. So I'll offer a dyslogy instead. By adding the prefix *dys* or "bad" to *-logia* we get the following definition of dyslogy from the Urban Dictionary—and I choose this definition on purpose—"an unfavorable speech wherein one publicly talks shit about another." ;-)

Unfortunately, there are many pseudo-philosophers who want to prop her corpse up in a rocking chair like Norman Bates did to his dead mother in Alfred Hitchcock's 1960 thriller *Psycho*. And like Bates they continue talking to her as if she's alive, asking her questions and believing she's providing answers too. These people are deluded in a similar way as Bates. What he needed was an intervention. He needed a good strong dosage of reality and truth based on empirical facts. They do too. These are the facts upon which I base this book. I do so because of all that I know, and I know more than I can manage to tell in one book. I do so in hopes I can help persuade philosophers to give her a proper burial, since there's no longer any reason to pretend she's still alive and still talking to people.

* * * * *

I am very thankful for Kurt Volkan, who works tirelessly on behalf of Pitchstone Publishing. He's turned his publishing company into a major force on behalf of atheism, with many top atheist authors. He has been responsive to my queries, patient with my edits, and a complete joy to work with as well. I rate his company with an enthusiastic 5 stars!

Notes

1.   Friedrich Nietzsche, *The Gay Science*, ed. Bernard Williams (Cambridge: Cambridge University Press, 2001), Book III, Aphorism 125.

2.   Friedrich Nietzsche, *The Gay Science*, Book III, Aphorism 108.

3.   Michael Shermer, *How We Believe: The Search for God in an Age of Science* (New York: W. H. Freeman and Company, 2000), p. 29.

1

MY INTELLECTUAL JOURNEY

Alvin Plantinga is a fundamentalist Christian philosopher of religion held in high esteem among like-minded Christians. Upon his appointment as the John O'Brien Professor of Philosophy at the University of Notre Dame in 1983, he gave an inaugural lecture titled "Advice to Christian Philosophers." Before he gave his advice he prefaced it by saying this:

> I propose to give some advice to the Christian or theistic philosophical community: some advice relevant to the situation in which in fact we find ourselves. "Who are you," you say, "to give the rest of us advice?" That's a good question to which one doesn't know the answer: I shall ignore it.[1]

Of course by this time in his life he had already become an accomplished philosopher of religion. Besides, he had just been introduced to the audience. They already knew of his credentials. So he could get away with appearing humble.

Me not so much. I don't have Plantinga's credentials. So I cannot ignore this same question when I'm proposing the philosophy of religion must end. It's a very bold claim. Who do I think I am? What do I know such that philosophers of religion should take me seriously? Why should anyone listen to me? I'll confess when it comes to these sorts of questions I wonder myself.

What I can do is share my intellectual journey. I do so in hopes readers can understand what happened to me in the last decade or so. People had previously asked why I became an atheist. So I wrote an encyclopedic counterapologetics book to answer that question titled *Why I Became an Atheist*,[2] which I consider my magnum opus. As a philosophically minded atheist myself, with three master's degrees and doctoral work in related fields, people will ask how I can defend the religious perspectives of new atheists like Richard Dawkins, Sam Harris, Christopher Hitchens, and Victor Stenger. After all, they aren't known for being philosophically sophisticated to say the least. Why do I take a dismal view of a discipline I once majored in under Drs. James D. Strauss, at Lincoln Christian University, and William Lane Craig, at Trinity Evangelical Divinity School? This chapter will answer these kinds of questions. Hopefully they will satisfy.

Richard Dawkins, P. Z. Myers, and Philosophy of Religion

After evolutionary biologist Richard Dawkins published what came to be the best-selling atheist book of all time, *The God Delusion*, many theists wrote responses to it. These responses all argued that Dawkins was neither biblically nor philosophically informed. Well, what do you do when you have no regard at all for the God delusion, like Dawkins? What do you do when deluded pseudo-intellectuals came out in force with what I call *obfuscationist theology*? Do you study up on it? Do you try to match wits with these theologians and philosophers who have been at this kind of stuff for most of their lives? Do you commit yourself to years of study to show them wrong? No. I don't think that's required. Dawkins simply called these theological responses fleas. He responded correctly by ignoring their criticisms. Fleas are parasites and pests. You simply swat them away.

In 2006 biologist P. Z. Myers wrote a celebrated blog post in response to the critics of Dawkins titled "The Courtier's Reply,"[3] which was inspired by Hans Christian Andersen's "The Emperor's New Clothes." For those not familiar with the Andersen story, here is a brief summary:

> Andersen's tale involves a vain king who was preoccupied with his appearance and his wardrobe. A pair of swindlers took advantage of this by pretending to be able to weave the finest cloth, which couldn't be seen by people who were either unfit for office or were particularly stupid.

The king decided to have a suit of clothes made from the fabric in order to test which of his courtiers was unfit for office. As he didn't want to appear stupid or unfit for rule himself, he pretended to be able to see the new clothes, as did all of his courtiers. He paraded the "new clothes" through the streets and the onlookers, also not wishing to appear stupid, all admired them. A small child, who didn't understand the apparent necessity for pretence, piped up "But he has nothing on!". The bubble of pretence burst and soon all the onlookers were repeating what the child had said, whilst the king continued the procession, attempting to maintain his dignity by pretending that nothing had happened.[4]

Putting Dawkins in the position of the child who interpidly spoke the obvious, Myers satirized the demand made by obfuscationist theologians and philosophers that Dawkins learn more before he dare to criticize their religious beliefs.

I have considered the impudent accusations of Dawkins with exasperation at his lack of serious scholarship. He has apparently not read the detailed discourses of Count Roderigo of Seville on the exquisite and exotic leathers of the Emperor's boots, nor does he give a moment's consideration to Bellini's masterwork, *On the Luminescence of the Emperor's Feathered Hat*. We have entire schools dedicated to writing learned treatises on the beauty of the Emperor's raiment, and every major newspaper runs a section dedicated to imperial fashion; Dawkins cavalierly dismisses them all. He even *laughs* at the highly popular and most persuasive arguments of his fellow countryman, Lord D. T. Mawkscribbler, who famously pointed out that the Emperor would not wear common cotton, nor uncomfortable polyester, but must, I say *must*, wear undergarments of the finest silk.

Dawkins arrogantly ignores all these deep philosophical ponderings to crudely accuse the Emperor of nudity … Until Dawkins has trained in the shops of Paris and Milan, until he has learned to tell the difference between a ruffled flounce and a puffy pantaloon, we should all pretend he has not spoken out against the Emperor's taste. His training in biology may give him the ability to recognize dangling genitalia when he sees it, but it has not taught him the proper appreciation of Imaginary Fabrics.

There are two matters to note about Myers' post, a reply that Dawkins himself praised. The first is that it represents a good case of ridicule or mockery, something we'll come back to in a later chapter. The most important thing to note is that obfuscationist theology doesn't change a thing with regard to the lack of evidence for a particular deity's religion. What matters is the evidence, sufficient objective evidence, evidence that convinces others. That's the only thing, the only requirement reasonable people who want to know the truth need. It's also the one thing lacking, for if it existed obfuscationist theology wouldn't need to be invented in order to defend the indefensible.

P. Z. Myers, like other scientists, will accept only empirical evidence for a religion. If it's not found, that's the end of it. He recommended a parable about sausages in which a philosopher and a scientist discuss a sausage machine. It starts as it ends like this:

> A philosopher designs a marvelous sausage machine. A scientist comes to marvel at this wonderful creation, and raises an eyebrow. The philosopher says, "Ah, behold the wonderful cogs and sprockets and temperature-controlled mixing chambers in my wonderful machine—surely you can see how it must produce the most fantastic sausages!" The scientist says "Yes, that is all very interesting. "Show me the sausages."[5]

To understand my previous views on the philosophy of religion, I'll quote what I earlier wrote about the courtier's reply on my blog:

> There are different types of critiques of Christianity. Each one of them stresses something different coming from different areas of expertise. Some of the major areas of criticism come from 1) The sciences, especially evolution and brain science; 2) Biblical and historical criticism; 3) Philosophy, especially the philosophy of religion; 4) Archaeology; 5) Cultural anthropology; 6) Psychology; and, 7) Social and moral criticism of the Bible and the church. There are others. What atheists think is a more effective criticism is not always the same as what Christians think is more effective.
>
> I suspect we won't all agree. Without the sciences (#1) we probably don't have much of a critique at all, at least no reasonable alternative to a creator God, so that has got to be the highest on the list. But here's the problem. Christians denigrate the sciences in favor of their holy book. In every era Christian believers have repeatedly said that reason must bow down before faith, you see. That's the problem when using the sciences in getting Christian believers to change their minds. We must first help

believers see that their holy book has holes in it. To do that we must speak to them in their language by critiquing their beliefs in terms they will understand and appreciate. Otherwise we're preaching to the choir.

While I see the value of ridicule, the most effective critique of the Christian faith will be one that can best be described as a counter-apologetic. An apologetic offers reasons from several different areas of expertise on behalf of the Christian faith. A counter-apologetic does the opposite. A counter-apologetic must take believers where they are and move them (or push them) in the right direction, the direction that the sciences have shown us. But since believers usually denigrate the sciences (#1) I start with the other areas of criticism (#'s 2–7), especially biblical and historical criticism (#2), and philosophy, especially the philosophy of religion (#3).[6]

I was thinking that believers can always reject most any scientific evidence, if doing so was required to maintain one's faith. So we needed other arguments, including those grounded in the philosophy of religion, to help them see their faith is false. Those other arguments are indeed helpful of course, if done in the right way, as I'll show in chapter 6 later. But I have come to think that since believers can always reject most any objective evidence, scientific evidence, or empirical evidence to maintain their faith, they can also reject any philosophical arguments. So why shouldn't we just focus on the evidence against faith and the corresponding lack of sufficient evidence for any extraordinary miraculous claims? It is the better route to take, since the lack of evidence is the Achilles' heel to all faith-based explanations and justifications. It's the best we can do. If appealing to the evidence doesn't convince believers then I see no reason to think mere philosophical argumentation will do any better. It's the evidence that can convince the believer, if anything can do so. Scientifically based reasoning is the best we've got. Logical reasoning based on the evidence can convince. Consistent reasoning based on the evidence can convince. Coherent reasoning based on the evidence can convince. But the evidence is paramount.

Victor Stenger and Philosophy of Religion

Around the time I first started blogging at Debunking Christianity, I posted a review on Amazon of Victor Stenger's New York Times best-selling book

God: The Failed Hypothesis: How Science Shows That God Does Not Exist, which had just come out. My comments, dated April 15, 2007, reveal how I thought at the time.

Stenger's argument [in his book] is that science has progressed to the point that it can now make "a definitive statement" on the existence of a God who has the attributes "traditionally associated with the Judeo-Christian-Islamic God." (p. 11). His conclusion is that the existence of this God "is not only missing from but also is contradicted by the empirical data." (p. 231).

In Stenger's previous book, *Has Science Found God?* he argued that the evidence for God is "inadequate." In this book he wants to say something more. Here he claims that the evidence is actually against the existence of God. (p. 17).

Stenger begins by basing his argument "on the contention that God should be detectable by scientific means simply by virtue of the fact that he is supposed to play a central role in the operation of the universe and the lives of humans." (p. 13) To those who disagree with this contention, he refers the reader to Theodore Drange's argument from non-belief, and to John L. Schellenberg's argument with regard to the problem of divine hiddenness. Drange has argued that since God wants people to believe and since he has the power to help them to believe, the reason why a majority of people don't believe in the Christian God is probably because God doesn't exist. Schellenberg has argued that since there are people who are open to believe in God who still don't believe, it means that a perfectly loving God probably doesn't exist.

Both Drange and Schellenberg's philosophical arguments form the basis of Stenger's whole argument, and I find them very persuasive. Stenger, however, seems to have a low view of philosophical arguments in general when it comes to solving the debate over the existence of God. He thinks science can step in where philosophical arguments only seem to lead to further debates, as both sides define and redefine the terms used in the arguments themselves. (p. 34). According to Stenger, "Arguments for and against God have been largely confined to philosophy and theology," while "science has sat on the sidelines and quietly watched this game of words march up and down the field." (p. 9).

The most charitable way to read Stenger is that scientific evidence is the way to tip the scales in favor of atheism, not that philosophy isn't useful in doing so, since two philosophical arguments form the basis of his whole argument. But I'm not so sure such a charitable interpretation is justified, given what he said, and given that many scientific minded people eschew philosophical argumentation.

Stenger proceeds from here by arguing there is scientific evidence against the existence of God, in so far as "absence of evidence" is "evidence of absence." (p. 18) "If we have no evidence or other reason for believing in God, then we can be pretty sure that God does not exist." (p. 18). He claims that if there is a failure with the evidence, "the argument may be made that a hidden God still may exist," but only if the believer can adequately deal with Drange and Schellenberg's arguments.

After this introductory material Stenger argues that "design is an illusion," simply because "earth and life look just as they can be expected to look if there is no God." (p. 71). He argues that brain science shows us that "thought processes are accompanied by localized physical activity in the brain." (p. 83) He argues there is no credible evidence for "out of body experiences," for psychics who claim to contact the dead, for ESP, or for the efficacy of petitionary prayer.

In his most unique scientific argument he claims that since the existence of "nothing" is fundamentally unstable, "only by the constant action of an agent outside the universe, such as God, could a state of nothingness be maintained. The fact that we have something [rather than nothing at all] is just what we would expect if there is no God." (p. 133).

Stenger moves on to the evidential failures with regard to religious experience, unfulfilled prophecies, Messianic and otherwise, and the lack of archaeological evidence for the Israelite Exodus. With regard to the Exodus, Stenger quotes former believer turned agnostic, William Dever, who said, "Absolutely no trace of Moses, or indeed of an Israelite presence in Egypt, has ever turned up." (p. 186).

Stenger argues we don't need the Bible for morality, and that at times the church has used it to justify horrendous things like Southern slavery. He argues: "the hypothesis of a God who provides moral knowledge is falsified by the observable fact that many of the moral teachings found in the scripture that are supposed revelations are not obeyed by even the most pious faithful." (p. 173). And "the very fact that humans have a common moral conscience can be taken as evidence against the existence of God." (p. 210).

Lastly Stenger argues that the amount and intensity of evil in this world is evidence against the existence of God. He concludes the book by arguing that religion has a negative impact upon society.

This is a very good book, scientifically speaking, as far as I understand the science that forms the background to his argument as a whole. He's best when it comes to science, having authored a number of books on science. It should be read and discussed by everyone who is interested in the God question.

I find him lacking, as I do most scientifically minded people, when it comes to the areas of philosophy and theology though. His arguments with regard to failed prophecies and the problem of evil are too brief, and too simple. There are several objections Christian believers can make against these arguments that he doesn't show awareness of, or deal with, although, in the end I agree with his analysis. Stenger does provide further references for further reading which does what he doesn't do, in many cases. Christians can claim there is historical evidence which shows Jesus arose from the dead, which may lead them to believe, despite the other problems Stenger finds with their belief. How does science dispute this claim of theirs? Christians can also argue God isn't hidden in that the Holy Spirit reveals himself inwardly to everyone, even though I find these arguments unpersuasive.

This biggest problem I have with the book is that it isn't just science that shows God probably doesn't exist. It's always the sciences taken together with philosophy that confirms or denies anything we believe. Without the philosophy, science can't show much in the area of the existence of God. But in taking them both together this book presents a powerful case against the existence of God. I highly recommend it.[7]

Now I think differently as you will see. First off, reasoning is not equivalent to philosophy, otherwise everyone does it. If everyone does it then philosophy becomes equivalent to reasoning. No one thinks science doesn't entail reasoning. Science is reasoning about objective evidence, but the point of science is that there is objective evidence to reason about. Second, I see no reason why Stenger needed to respond to obfuscationist theology, precisely because it is obfuscationist theology that seeks to hide from us the fact there isn't any good evidence for theology. Honest readers who are truly interested in the evidence could see the evidence speaks for itself. Third, Stenger's additional philosophical arguments come after he has shown science destroys Christianity. In other words, he threw them in for good measure, and they highlight some good problems Christians should consider, even if they don't convince believing pseudo-intellectuals. These philosophical arguments are good ones, no doubt, if done in the right context, as I'll explain in chapter 6.

My Education and the Value of Philosophy of Religion

I earned a bachelor's degree from Great Lakes Christian College, two master's degrees from Lincoln Christian University, and a Master of Theology degree at Trinity Evangelical Divinity School. In addition, I spent a year and a half in a PhD program at Marquette University in Theology and Ethics. Many people who have spent less time in school than me have PhDs.

I took classes titled "Religious Epistemology" (with Stuart Hackett), "Analytic Philosophy" (with Paul Feinberg), "Religion and Science" (with William Lane Craig focusing on the philosophy of science), "Plantinga's Thought" (yep, under Dr. Craig in the year 1984), "Calvin" (under the late Kenneth Kantzer, known as the dean of evangelicalism, where we went through Calvin's Institutes), "Philosophy of Knowledge" (with Marc F. Greisbach, who had been the president of the American Catholic Philosophical Association), "Theological Ethics" (with Catholic ethicist Daniel McGuire), and "Protestant Christian Ethics" (with Ron Feenstra, now the director of doctoral studies at Calvin Theological Seminary). I took a whole host of others like "Philosophers of Religion: Descartes," "The Concept of God," "God as Creator/Redeemer," "Making of the Contemporary Mind" (with James Strauss, who really enlightened me), "19th Century Theology," "Seminar: Word of God," "Philosophy of Language," "Apologetics: Discovering the Christian Mind," "Theology and Hermeneutics," "20th Century Theology," "Historiography of Theories of History," "Advanced Introduction to the New Testament," "Historiography of Physical Sciences," "Major Philosophical Thinkers/ Systems," "Historiography of Theories of Mind," "Atheism and Theism," and many others that were biblical and/or practical for ministry and teaching in the apologetical field. I learned Greek and Hebrew and could study the Bible in these original languages.

I have taught apologetics, hermeneutics, Christian theology, Christian ethics, and Bible classes for Lincoln Christian University and/or Great Lakes Christian College. I have also taught introduction to philosophy, philosophy of religion, introduction to ethics, critical thinking, and world literature classes for the College of Lake County, Kellogg Community College, and/or Trine University. I did this as an adjunct instructor, mostly while I was in the ministry for fourteen years in Christian churches in Illinois, Michigan, and Indiana as an associate minister, minister, and senior minister. I was the president of the ministerial association in Angola, Indiana, when I was a minister there. As an atheist I have read a paper for a regional meeting of the Evangelical Philosophical Society, and one for the Annual Meeting of the Society of Biblical Literature.

People question whether I'm really a scholar or a philosopher or one who has pretty much the equivalent of a PhD. Okay. Who cares? This is all in the mind of the beholder at my level anyway, so have at it. One thing is for sure. I have the attention of scholars on both sides of our debates. Both sides are recommending my works while atheist scholars are writing for me, for which I am very grateful.

More than once I have been told I should get a PhD to gain more credibility. At this point in my life, given where I live and work and the money and time needed to do so, this isn't a live option for me. Besides, given what I'm going to say about philosophy later in this post, why would I bother? The philosophy of religion is a dead end leading nowhere. And I'd rather be dragged through the mud than get a PhD in biblical studies. What a waste for me at this point!

I'm already doing what I think is important anyway, so why not keep on doing what's working? My goal, like German philosopher Friedrich Nietzsche, is to "philosophize with a hammer." Like Karl Marx, I say, "The philosophers have only interpreted the world . . . the point is to change it." I think I am helping to change the religious landscape as it is. I'm already doing what most PhD students wish they could do—make an impact.

Which brings me to the value of philosophy. Over the last decade I have found that one bastion for Christian apologists has been philosophy, especially the philosophy of religion. The scholars have honed their definitional apologetics in such a fine-tuned manner that when engaging them in this discipline, it's like trying to catch a greased pig. Or, to switch metaphors, trying to chase them down the rabbit's hole in an endless and ultimately fruitless quest for definitions. What's an extraordinary claim? What constitutes evidence? What's the definition of supernatural? What's the scientific method? What's a miracle? What's a basic belief? What's a veridical religious experience? What's evil? They do this just like others have done over questions like, "What is the definition of pornography?" And then they gerrymander around the plain simple facts of experience. I would rather deal in concrete examples like a virgin who supposedly had a baby and a man who supposedly was raised from the dead.

As a Christian myself I could read philosophical atheists and not be fazed at all. I read the appropriate journals along with large sections of J. L. Mackie's book, *The Miracle of Theism*, Michael Martin's *Atheism: A Philosophical Justification*, Bertrand Russell's debate with Frederick C. Copleston, Russell's *Why I Am Not a Christian*, and books and articles by Antony Flew, especially his "Parable of the Invisible Gardener" and the logical positivist debate that ensued from his parable. I could read that literature all day long and never be fazed in my delusional Christian beliefs. After all, none of them ever proved God didn't exist, a standard I had that was utterly unrealistic. Who in their right mind would ask that the opposition must show that it's impossible for God to exist? And these atheists either never argued against the reliability of the Bible or the resurrection of Jesus from the dead, or, if they did, they did not argue against them very well at all. These things were the linchpins of why I believed.

Even though I could do so, I don't much argue philosophically against the existence of God for three reasons. First, my own experience shows that while philosophy is important, it doesn't change the mind of the believer. Second, I have been soured by the way Christians can use philosophy to defend their faith. I was shocked when I saw Richard Swinburne's book, *The Resurrection of God Incarnate*, where he argued that if God exists then it's a 97 percent probability that Jesus was raised from the dead. This is one of the brightest Christian philosophers, mind you, who argued for an utterly ignorant conclusion. What? If philosophy can be twisted this badly then it can't be very useful in our debates. Third, better minds than mine have already made the philosophical case against God's existence—at this point there isn't much left to say.

Don't get me wrong. I value philosophy itself. In fact, I use it, and it has certainty helped me to think critically. It's just that what really caused me to doubt my Christian beliefs was reading the biblical scholars, initially James Barr, Conrad Hyers, Claus Westermann, and others. Of course, now I've read a host of them since that time. I've learned there is no basis for thinking philosophy of religion can substitute for biblical studies or for science. It cannot help save Christianity, not the biblical kind anyway. The philosopher's god is nothing like the biblical god. Just ask philosophers of religion what they would believe if there was no basis for the Bible being in any meaningful sense the word of God, and you'll see exactly what I mean.

Having at one time embraced the value of the philosophy of religion and now calling for it to end, what happened to me? Given what I have just shared, you really cannot claim I'm ignorant. I studied the issues deeply enough to know what I'm talking about, agreed? Claiming otherwise is not a position you can seriously entertain. I might be wrong, but I'm not ignorant.

So what exactly changed my mind about the value of the philosophy of religion to the point where I'm calling for that discipline to end in secular universities? It was the perspectives of three towering intellectuals, Drs. David Eller, Peter Boghossian, and Hector Avalos.

So What Happened to Me? David Eller!

As a professor of cultural anthropology David Eller has challenged me to think outside my cultural box.[8] Rather than think exclusively in terms of Westernized notions of faith, religion, and culture, he has forced me to adopt a global perspective. This global perspective has been a game changer for me. I used to think exclusively in terms of the Judeo-Christian god. And while I don't have a very deep knowledge of other religious cultures and their gods, my consciousness has been raised to consider these other religious cultures more than ever. When that happens you will see the problem of religious diversity for what it really is.

From Eller I was forced to acknowledge it is not the case that Westernized notions of religion have any superiority to them. That was a shocker to me, but then at that time I was still in my own dogmatic slumber. Again, when we adopt a truly global perspective on religion, none of them have anything more going for them than the others. This means for me as an atheist that when I choose to argue exclusively against one deity over the others, then by that very choice I'm acting as if one particular deity has more going for it than the others. That assumption is false. The reason it's false is because all religions are cultural. Our inherited religion is just a different cultural expression of the same kinds of hopes and fears over the problems we face with life and death, morals, and society itself.[9]

Since the dawn of human history religionists have been arguing over competing and even mutually exclusive religious faith claims. These claims on behalf of gods, goddesses, and other superhuman beings, along with their commands, prophecies, and promises, cannot all be true. If we try to strip religious claims down to an agreed-upon commonly shared bare minimum, what we might have left is the belief in a superhuman being, or beings, and/or superhuman force, or forces. That bare minimum does not represent a universally shared belief though. Religionist beliefs differ over the existence of one superhuman being (i.e., one God) or in many superhuman beings (i.e., gods, goddesses, angels, spirits, ghosts, demons), or in one superhuman force (i.e., panentheism, deism) or many superhuman forces (i.e., karma, fate, reincarnation, prayers, incantations, spells, omens, voodoo dolls), or some sort of combination of them all. Religionists who agree with one another on these beliefs also disagree over who these beings and/or forces are, how they operate, and for whom they operate.

Eller tells us, "there are many religions in the world, and they are different from each other in multiple and profound ways. Not all religions refer to gods. . . . No religion is 'normal' or 'typical' of all religions; the truth is in the diversity."[10] When it comes to belief in god(s),

> Many or most religions have functioned quite well without any notions of god(s) at all, and others have mixed god(s) with other beliefs such that god-beliefs are not the critical parts of the religion. . . . Some religions that refer to or focus on gods believe them to be all-powerful, but others do not. Some consider them to be moral agents, and some do not; more than a few gods are downright immoral. Some think they are remote, while others think they are close (or both simultaneously). Some believe that the gods are immortal and eternal, but others include stories of gods dying and being born . . . not all gods are creators, nor is creation a central feature or concern of all religions. . . . Finally, there is not even always a firm boundary between humans and gods; humans can become gods, and the gods may be former humans.[11]

Robert McKim tells us the stark reality, when he wrote,

> There is not a single claim that is distinctive of any religious group that is not rejected by other such groups, with the exception of vague claims to the effect that there is something important and worthwhile about religion, or to the effect that there is a religious dimension to reality and that however the sciences proceed certain matters will be beyond their scope.[12]

So if I were to use one word to describe what we know about religions, that word would be *diversity*. When dealing with such a diverse phenomenon where no religion has an advantage over others, we must treat all religions the same, privileging none (a rare number of religions are not based on faith, but rather on ignorance). Failing to do this is to be derelict in our intellectual duties as adult thinkers and investigators of religious phenomena in search of religious truth, if there is any.

So What Happened to Me? Peter Boghossian!

David Eller's works primed the pump for me, so to speak. He convinced me of the cultural and relativistic nature of religion. If it wasn't for him, I probably would've scoffed at Peter Boghossian's goading later, just as many philosophers of religion and amateurs have done without merit. Boghossian was the person most instrumental in changing my mind about the philosophy of religion. Although I was trained in that discipline and taught it at the college level, I now see clearly its irrelevance and inadequacy. But for my mind to change when it did, I had to be ready for it, and Eller did that. If atheist philosophers and amateurs want to truly understand my call for the end of philosophy of religion, then they must read Eller's works.

Boghossian first got my attention a year before I read his provocatively titled book, *A Manual for Creating Atheists*. I first heard of him when a talk he gave titled "Faith Based Belief Processes Are Unreliable" hit the web in April 2012. He began by critically examining several paranormal beliefs where faith was shown to be unreliable for gaining knowledge. After arguing in this way, at the 26:00 mark, he said, "We are forced to conclude that a tremendous number of people are delusional. There is no other conclusion one can draw." At the 38:30 mark, he said, "The most charitable thing we can say about faith is that it's likely to be false."[13] He had a way of putting things that resonated with me. Faith itself is the problem.

Faith is an utterly unreliable way to gain objective knowledge about matters of fact, like the nature, workings, and origins of the universe. It should be rejected if we want to gain any objective knowledge at all, including which religion is true, if there is one. The reason religious faith is false is because of faith itself, and as such, faith cannot settle which religion is the true one, if there is one. Boghossian furthered my thinking by putting all paranormal claims and religious faiths on an equal footing with each other. Religious faiths were now fully recognized to be a subset of paranormal claims in general.

But a significant turn took place for me—a tipping point—when Boghossian, who often wears the mantle of provocateur on social media, penned a single tweet. On June 15, 2014, he tweeted: "Being published in the philosophy of religion should disqualify one from sitting at the adult table." Keep in mind Boghossian had argued in his book that the adult table is where reasonable people sit to discuss important issues, a place for those who think exclusively in terms of the probabilities by proportioning their beliefs according to the evidence (*à la* David Hume). By contrast the children's table is for people of childish thinking, which allows faith to inform one's conclusions. This stuck me hard, for he was indicting not only theist philosophers of religion but also atheist philosophers of religion. How could non-faith-based responses to faith arguments be more or less on an equal footing with faith arguments, I pondered?

After reading Boghossian's tweet, Dr. James A. Lindsay interpreted it along these lines:

> To publish in the philosophy of religion requires taking theism seriously. He doesn't think people should take theism seriously. Neither do I.
>
> If I want to give a charitable take on Boghossian's tweet, it goes like this: Anyone that has continued to publish in the philosophy of religion after the zeitgeist has shifted, which I'd say happened right around when *The God Delusion* stopped being super-controversial, is taking theism too seriously for anyone's good.
>
> I don't think churning out counterarguments to more and more and more theological nonsense (because it will definitely always just keep coming) is all that valuable, but worse than that, many atheists in the philosophy of religion are so bent on "engaging the best apologetic/theological arguments" that they help make them for them![14]

Lindsay later fleshed out this position in a provocatively titled book, *Everybody Is Wrong About God*.[15]

Retired professor in evolutionary genetics at the University of Chicago, Jerry Coyne, also chimed in on the debate, saying:

> I have to agree with Peter Boghossian that the bulk of work in that field (indeed, nearly all of it) is worthless. I am a fan of philosophy as a

whole, or at least branches of it (especially the philosophy of science and ethical philosophy), and don't think it's worthless by any means, but I have no use for the philosophy of religion. . . . It's like a field called "the philosophy of fairies."[16]

Soon after thinking about this discussion, I came up with an analogical tweet. "Being published in the philosophy of Russell's teapot (or the Flying Spaghetti Monster or the Invisible Pink Unicorn, or Elves, Trolls or Fairies) should disqualify one from sitting at the adult table." What was the difference, I asked myself? Remember, Eller and Boghossian convinced me all cultural religious claims and paranormal claims were all equally unwarranted.

The only reason philosophy of religion exists is because there are people who believe without sufficient evidence and who seek to defend with logic what doesn't have sufficient evidence for it, which is obfuscationist in intent. For if no one accepted anything based on insufficient evidence, this discipline wouldn't even exist.

At the very least we should agree that scientifically uninformed philosophy of religion must end. But look at what this agreement ends up doing. Any scientifically informed philosophers of religion who are worthy of the title are atheists. So philosophers who philosophize about religion without good evidence should be disqualified to sit at the proverbial adult table. And again, if this were to take place, the discipline would not exist. What we would have instead is neurology, physics, astronomy, psychology, etc.

So What Happened to Me? Hector Avalos!

Harvard-trained biblical scholar Hector Avalos has effectively argued that biblical studies must end, a call I have enthusiastically supported. After Eller and Boghossian it dawned on me his arguments can equally apply to ending the philosophy of religion. I asked myself, why not issue the same call with regard to philosophy of religion? All I needed was to connect the dots. I don't expect many philosophers or amateurs to agree, but then my guess is they haven't been forced to consider the impacting arguments of David Eller and Peter Boghossian either.

Let me connect those dots here, by sharing Avalos's call to end biblical studies as we know them. In his book *The End of Biblical Studies*, Avalos shows us what biblical scholars have done with biblical studies:

Modern biblical scholarship has demonstrated that the Bible is the product of cultures whose values and beliefs about the origin, nature, and purpose of our world are no longer held to be relevant, even by most Christians and Jews.[17]

Even biblical scholars themselves have done this to their discipline:

Paradoxically, despite the recognition of such irrelevance, the profession of academic biblical studies still centers on maintaining the illusion of relevance by:

A. A variety of scholarly disciplines whose methods and conclusions are often philosophically flawed (e.g., translation, textual criticism, archaeology, history, and biblical theology).

B. An infrastructure that supports biblical studies (e.g., universities, a media-publishing complex, churches, and professional organizations).[18]

This should end. Avalos calls for ending this undeserved relevance:

We should now treat the Bible as the alien document it is, with no more importance than the other works of literature we ignore every day. Biblical studies should be geared toward helping humanity wean itself off of the Bible and toward terminating its authority completely in the modern world. Focus then could shift to the still thousands of other ancient texts still untranslated and unread. One day, the Bible might even be viewed as one of the curiosities of a tragic bibliolatrous age, when dependence on a text brought untold misery and stood as an obstacle to human progress. We might then study the Bible as a lesson in why human beings should never again privilege any book to this extent.[19]

With regard to the biblical studies discipline in secular universities, Avalos offers three alternatives:

1. Eliminate biblical studies completely from the modern world

2. Retain biblical studies as is, but admit that it is a religionist enterprise

3. Retain biblical studies, but redefine its purpose so that it is tasked with eliminating completely the influence of the Bible in the modern world.[20]

Avalos doesn't advocate for the first option, "at least for the moment" he says, because "the Bible should be studied, if only as a lesson in why human beings should not privilege such books again." While I'm sure option #1 is the goal, Avalos instead opts for what I see as a practical goal, a stopgap measure, one that will eventually give way when biblical scholars get honest about their own discipline. Avalos doesn't advocate the second option either. It doesn't do anything about the problem other than merely admit what is going on. He advocates the third option: "The sole purpose of biblical studies . . . would be to help people move toward a postscriptural society," which is "also the most logical position, given the discovery of the Bible's alien character."[21]

In calling for the end of the philosophy of religion I'm helping move people toward a posttheistic and a postreligionist society too, which is the logical position, given the charade known as the philosophy of religion (as you shall see).

I've Changed My Mind Many Times, So?

I've changed my mind a lot of times. I should be so lucky to have gotten everything correct from the time I was a young adult. I wonder if it's even possible for people never to change their minds, especially if they have any longevity to their lives at all. So I don't think changing one's mind is any indicator of ignorance or instability or gullibility or anything like that. It just means this is what thinking people do, given time, education, further thought, and the experiences of life.

What have I changed my mind about? I've changed my opinions about lots of people as I've gotten to know them better, about various foods and drinks as I've tried them, about sports and teams as I've watched them, about music genres as I've listened to them, about artistic styles as I've learned more about them, about politics as I've become more aware about various issues, and about faith and religion as I've read, discussed, observed, and thought about them.

When it comes to religion I began as a Catholic. In my earlier years I went through a paradigm shift of sorts. At the age of seventeen I became a "born again" Pentecostal who was also taught to believe Dispensationalism and Calvinism. Then I started going to a Church of Christ and had to unlearn what I was converted to. I learned to reject Pentecostalism, Dispensationalism, and Calvinist theology. Then I was taught that adult baptism by immersion was necessary for the forgiveness of sins, and that Arminianism and amillennial eschatology were biblically correct. Friends, all of this religious change took place in just two or three years of my young adult life. Soon I was set in my ways and stayed that way for two decades on major issues, although with more and more education I changed my mind slowly and gradually on lots of minor ones.

From 1991 to 1998 I went through a second paradigm shift of sorts. I went from being a conservative to a moderate to a liberal to a deist to an agnostic. I stayed there for about six years, during which time I basically ignored religion altogether. Then in 2005 I finally became an atheist, a weak or agnostic atheist.

Recently of this writing, in the last three years, I've gone through a third paradigm shift of sorts. I am now a strong atheist who has come to the conclusion there is no need to take the obfuscations of Christian philosophers seriously because all philosophical apologetics is special pleading—all of it. Philosophy itself is used to obfuscate Christian theology, not to clarify it. Because if theology was truly clarified believers would clearly see the Christian emperor has no clothes. Clarifying Christian theology rather than obfuscating it would strip away the blinders from the eyes of believers. Then believers could see the evidence-based truth. They would see their faith is a delusion on a par with Mormonism, Hinduism, Orthodox Judaism, and even Scientology, as well as see they've been indoctrinated if not brainwashed to believe. We need real clarity not more obfuscationism.

I have changed my mind about faith. I should not believe anything. Belief isn't something any reasonable person should do when it comes to gaining knowledge about matters of fact like the nature of nature, its workings, and its origins, or which religion is true, if there is one. Faith adds nothing to the probabilities. It has no method and solves no problems. If faith is trust we should not trust faith. It's a cognitive bias keeping believers away from objectively understanding the truth.

I have also changed my mind about the courtier's reply. I now agree it's an appropriate and reasonable response to believers who claim to have evidence for their faith. I say this as someone trained in the philosophy of religion who has changed his mind about his own field of study. Furthermore, while I previously desired a respectful discussion with believers, I no longer think it's of the uppermost importance. I have embraced the need for and the value of ridicule.

I'll get attacked for my present views, even from some atheists who do not realize I have been where they are now. I just want them to know I was once where they are now. They may attack me, but they cannot claim I'm ignorant. Christians will attack me also not realizing I was once where they are now. I might be wrong. But again, I'm not ignorant. You should take the fact that I've changed my mind as evidence I'm open-minded enough to consider different views. I have a lot to teach my atheist critics, precisely because I've changed my views. My atheist critics are playing a pretend game when they take the obfuscations of Christian pseudo-philosophers seriously. They do so because they enjoy an intellectually challenging game, much like chess. While it may be fun and interesting to play the game called "Christian," by playing that game they grant intellectual respectability to that which is bizarre and absurd, even if they win.

Notes

1. It was later published in *Faith and Philosophy: Journal of the Society of Christian Philosophers* 1 (October 1984), http://www.faithandphilosophy.com/article_advice.php.

2. John W. Loftus, *Why I Became an Atheist*, revised ed. (Amherst, NY: Prometheus Books, 2012).

3. P. Z. Myers, "The Courtier's Reply," Pharyngula, ScienceBlogs, December 24, 2006, http://scienceblogs.com/pharyngula/2006/12/24/the-courtiers-reply/.

4. "The Meaning and Origin of the Expression: The Emperor's New Clothes," http://www.phrases.org.uk/meanings/the-emperors-new-clothes.html.

5. "Show Me the Sausages!" Answers in Genes, June 2, 2011, http://answersingenes.blogspot.com/2011/06/show-me-sausages.html.

6. I did so in two posts on my blog Debunking Christianity: "PZ Myers and the Courtier's Reply Again," June 3, 2011, http://debunkingchristianity.blogspot.

com/2011/06/pz-meyers-and-courtiers-reply-again.html, and "What's Wrong with the Courtier's Reply of PZ Myers and Richard Dawkins," May 28, 2011, http://debunkingchristianity.blogspot.com/2011/05/whats-wrong-with-courtiers-reply-of-pz.html.

7. Victor Stenger, *God: The Failed Hypothesis: How Science Shows That God Does Not Exist* (Amherst, NY: Prometheus Books, 2007).

8. David Eller has written several chapters for my anthologies that I naturally recommend very highly. His works include *Natural Atheism* (Cranford, NJ: American Atheist Press, 2004); *Atheism Advanced: Further Thoughts of a Freethinker* (Cranford, NJ: American Atheist Press, 2007); *Cultural Anthropology: Global Forces, Local Lives* (London: Routledge, 2009); *Introducing Anthropology of Religion: Culture to the Ultimate*, 2nd. ed. (London: Routledge, 2015); and *Cruel Creeds, Virtuous Violence: Religious Violence across Culture and History* (Amherst, NY: Prometheus Books, 2010).

9. If anyone disagrees then I strongly recommend my book, *The Outsider Test for Faith: How to Know Which Religion Is True* (Amherst, NY: Prometheus Books, 2013).

10. Eller, *Cultural Anthropology*, p. xiii.

11. Eller, *Atheism Advanced*, pp. 13–15.

12. Robert McKim, *Religious Ambiguity and Religious Diversity* (Oxford: Oxford University Press, 2001), p. 131.

13. Link to the talk available at "Peter Boghossian: Faith Based Belief Processes Are Unreliable," Debunking Christianity, April 11, 2012, http://debunkingchristianity.blogspot.com/2012/04/peter-boghossian-faith-based-belief.html.

14. See the featured comment on "In Defense of Peter Boghossian's Tweet About the Philosophy of Religion," Debunking Christianty, June 18, 2014, http://debunkingchristianity.blogspot.com/2014/06/in-defense-of-peter-boghossians-tweet.html#comment-1443239167.

15. James A. Lindsay, *Everybody Is Wrong About God* (Durham, NC: Pitchstone Publishing, 2015).

16. Jerry Coyne, "The Best Argument for God? Really?" Why Evolution Is True, June 27, 2014, https://whyevolutionistrue.wordpress.com/2014/06/27/the-best-argument-for-god-really/.

17. Hector Avalos, *The End of Biblical Studies* (Amherst, NY: Prometheus Books, 2007), p. 16.

18. Ibid., p. 16.

19. Ibid., p. 29.

20. Ibid., p. 341.

21. Ibid., p. 341.

2

ANSELM AND PHILOSOPHY OF RELIGION

In this chapter let's see how to do philosophy of religion correctly, shall we? To do this we'll take a good look at Anselm of Canterbury (c. 1033–1109 CE). If anyone knows how to do philosophy of religion correctly he does. Anselm holds a preeminent place among the best philosophers of religion the church ever produced. He was the most important Christian intellectual between two other early Doctors of the Church, Augustine of Hippo Regius and Thomas of Aquino. Among other reasons for this high recognition, Anselm is the originator of the satisfaction theory of atonement and the ontological argument for the existence of God.

There is a common theme among his work and the work of other obfuscationist theologians and philosophers that needs to be highlighted. It's called faith, another word for special pleading, which requires a great deal of puzzle-solving when encountering new problems. We see this in Anselm with regard to his new atonement theory and his ontological argument, which obscures the fact there's nothing to see here but faith seeking understanding.

Anselm therefore is exhibit "A" in defense of what atheist philosopher Stephen Law said: "Anything based on faith, no matter how ludicrous, can be made to be consistent with the available evidence, given a little patience and ingenuity."[1] If I could pick one sentence, one aphorism, one proverb that highlights the main reason philosophy of religion (PoR) must end, it's Law's. I'll call it *Law's law of faith*.

Anselm, Atonement, and the Lack of Agreement

Prior to Anselm the earliest attempt to conceptualize what Jesus did for the world on the cross was the *ransom theory*. Such a version of the atonement stood for roughly a thousand years as the generally accepted one. According to Origen, the fall of Adam and Eve in a paradisiacal garden placed human beings under the jurisdiction of Satan, or the Devil. Humans became his possessions. God's son Jesus came to die on the cross to pay Satan's ransom price so we could be released from his slavery and rule. Origen believed Satan accepted the offer because Satan believed he would subsequently have ownership of God's son, Jesus. But because Jesus was sinless, death could have no power over him. So God tricked Satan and raised Jesus from the dead. Satan therefore got nothing out of the deal. Now anyone who believes on Jesus is ransomed from Satan.

Philosopher of religion John Hick comments: "Ransom had a poignant meaning in the ancient world, when a considerable proportion of the population lived in the state of slavery. . . . Being ransomed, and thus made free, was accordingly a vivid and powerful metaphor whose force most of us can only partially recapture today."[2]

But times had changed for Anselm in the eleventh century. No longer were large numbers of people in slavery. So what to do? Anselm set forth his *satisfaction theory* of the atonement for the people of his day to save Christianity from being irrelevant. He did this in his book *Cur Deus Homo* (*Why the God Man*). Concerning the ransom theory, he denied that the Devil could ever have any valid legal rights over the infinite creator God to demand a ransom. Anselm argued instead that our sins are an insult to God and detract from his honor. Therefore God's honor must be restored and the insult must be undone, but only through the death of the innocent God-man can God's honor be restored and satisfaction be made, since the satisfaction must be in proportion to the amount of sin, and the amount of sin is infinite.

John Hick informs us that Anselm's theory "made sense within the culture of medieval Europe" in that it reflected "a strongly hierarchical and tightly knit society." The whole idea of satisfaction "had long operated in both church and society. . . . The idea of disobedience, whether to God or to one's feudal lord, was a slight upon his honour and dignity, and required for its cancellation an appropriate penance of gift in satisfaction. . . . . When one did something to undermine the dignity and authority of one's earthly overlord, one had either to be punished or to give sufficient satisfaction to appease the lord's injured dignity."[3]

The first lesson to note from Anselm is that theology evolves to keep up with the times. Anselm was someone who did it, and taught others how to do it by example. What should theologians do when Christianity has an outmoded concept? Just change it to meet up with the times. Reinterpret the Bible if you have to. Deny the major voices in the Bible. Find the minority voices. Find the canon within the canon of "scriptures" that support the new doctrinal views alien to the overall thrust of these "sacred" texts. Surely somewhere in the Bible someone uttered some statement that aligns with the newer, more palatable doctrine. They're out there. Just find them. Disregard the fact that any collected book of writings composed by many authors and editors representative of about 1,200 years (or so) will have many disagreements in them, which is what we find.[4] Move the goal posts so critics of Christianity always seem to miss kicking the field goal. Then, after moving the goal posts so many times that the resultant Christianity is alien to the earliest forms of it that fought for dominance,[5] boldly claim Christianity has survived the attacks of all its critics.

Although Anselm may have made the atonement palatable for his era to people who needed to believe, almost no one today accepts Anselm's theory. It makes little sense to present-day citizens of modern democracies. It presupposes a feudal society that we rejected a long time ago. New Testament evangelical scholar Leon Morris writes, "In the end Anselm makes God too much like a king whose dignity has been affronted. He overlooked the fact that a sovereign may be clement and forgiving without doing harm to his kingdom."[6] Atheist Michael Martin adds that "the very idea of God's pride being so wounded and demanding such satisfaction that the voluntary sacrifice of his innocent son is required, assumes a view of God's moral nature that many modern readers would reject."[7]

Even though Anselm's satisfaction theory held sway for more than four centuries, it didn't make sense to the sixteenth-century Reformers who rejected it. They introduced *penal substitutionary theory*, which still holds sway in conservative Christian churches. The Reformers argued God's sense of justice demanded a payment for the debt our sins incurred, and that Jesus paid that debt by substituting himself in our place on the cross. Upon believing that Jesus paid our debt we are now forgiven for our sins. And guess what? They found "scriptural" support for this view!

The real reason for the change in atonement theory, following Anselm's example, was that views about law had changed in the sixteenth century. So the Reformers had to make the atonement palatable in their day to keep up with changing views of law. A new theory was needed to save Christianity from becoming irrelevant. In Anselm's theory the law was the expression of a king. To disobey the king brought dishonor to the king, for which satisfaction by punishment was needed in order to restore the honor due to the king. John Hick tells us why Anselm's view became irrelevant:

> [T]he concept of an objective justice, set over ruled and ruler alike, had been developing in Europe since the Renaissance. Law was now thought to have its own eternal validity, requiring a punishment for wrongdoing which could not be set aside even by the ruler. It was this new principle that the Reformers applied and extended in their doctrine that Christ took our place in bearing the inexorable penalty for human sin—a powerful imagery that has long gripped the Christian imagination.[8]

However, the Reformer's penal substitutionary theory had a built-in fatal flaw. We don't punish innocent people, nor do we allow people to be punished on behalf of others, nor do we require revenge, restitution, or reparations before forgiveness is granted. After all, victims have forgiven criminals even though they were never punished, while other victims won't forgive a criminal even after he or she is severely punished. If we don't punish people before forgiveness is granted, then what can be the rationale for the second person of the trinity to become incarnated and die on the cross?[9]

And on it goes. There continues to be a spate of anthologies being produced about the atonement, like James Beilby and Paul R. Eddy's *The Nature of the Atonement: Four Views* (2006); Michael Rea's *Oxford Readings in Philosophical Theology, Volume 1: Trinity, Incarnation, and Atonement* (2009), and Oliver D. Crisp and Fred Sanders's *Locating Atonement: Explorations in Constructive Dogmatics* (2015). The history of atonement theories in Christianity shows us, more than most other doctrines, the true nature of philosophy of religion. Editors Crisp and Sanders themselves recognize the proliferation of books on the atonement in their anthology, saying, "In the last decade there has been a renewed interest in the doctrine of the atonement. Weighty tomes have rolled off the presses, and there appears to be no sign of this abating."[10]

What they take to be a renewed interest I take to be something quite the opposite. One way to see whether there is a crisis in theology is to count the number of books, articles, and conferences Christians have to discuss/debate a topic. You won't see many conferences, debates, or anthologies instigated by Christians on whether Jesus was born in Bethlehem (he wasn't, if he was an actual baby at all, and most scholars acknowledge this). Nor will you see many conferences, debates, or anthologies instigated by Christians on whether Jesus died on the cross (something Muslims reject). So the doctrine of the atonement is in a crisis, a deep one. The early church never issued a specific creed about it, which might have staved off these types of debates, because anyone who deviated from an earlier creed, like the doctrine of the divinity of Jesus, could just be declared a heretic, thus ending any further discussion.

What we see among philosophical theologians like Anselm and others is special pleading, which requires *puzzle-solving*. In fact, all theistic philosophy of religion is puzzle-solving based on special pleading. Since I don't think there is sufficient evidence for the key doctrines of Christianity, all they have left, when building their theological castles in the sky, is consistency. When doctrines seem to conflict, then sophisticated obfuscationist theologians—especially of the evangelical kind who claim there is a systematic theology to be found—must harmonize what they believe. So the many different and even contrary atonement theories down through the centuries, even to today's morass, are excellent examples of brilliant minds defending unbelievable things. Brilliant minds like Anselm, who are wrong even though brilliant. Thus *Law's law of faith*: "Anything based on faith, no matter how ludicrous, can be made to be consistent with the available evidence, given a little patience and ingenuity."[11] Brilliant Christian minds have adjusted their faith with the times. They have never recognized their faith was refuted by the times. Rather, they change what they believe then subsequently claim it's the same faith. They learned from Anselm. Christian pseudo-philosophers simply take for granted a set of inconsistent beliefs that no reasonable person should ever grant, much like the Mormons do, and then try to find ways to intellectually gerrymander around the different doctrines to make them all fit each other.

If nothing else these subsequent theories about the atonement are a fascinating study of the psychology of the mind of the believer. It's fascinating to see otherwise intelligent people solve problems, even if in the end there isn't sufficient evidence for what they believe. They'll even deny the need for such evidence it's that bad. When it comes to harmonizing what they believe with the available evidence, they utterly fail. They fail in trying to make consistent what they believe with the evidence. They do not proportion their belief to the evidence, as David Hume argued. No wonder they bask in the vice of an unreasonable faith that seeks understanding. And no wonder so many of us don't believe.

Perfect-Being Theology

Let's turn to Anselm's fascinating and provocative ontological argument to the existence of God. It is generally agreed that the ontological argument never converted anyone (even though Bertrand Russell once thought it was correct but soon afterward changed his mind). It is an amazing argument—a philosopher's delight! According to Robert Paul Wolff, this is the "most famous, the most mystifying, the most outrageous and irritating philosophical argument of all time. . . . It remains as one of the most controversial arguments in all of philosophy." Yet, "whenever I read the Ontological Argument, I have the same feeling that comes over me when I watch a really good magician. Nothing up this sleeve, nothing up the other sleeve; nothing in the hat; presto! A big fat rabbit. How can Anselm pull God out of an idea?"[12] Well it's an interesting puzzle to be solved, that's for sure. Philosophers want to show why it is wrong. The short answer to Wolff is that he can't. But just because something is interesting doesn't make it important or relevant for us today. It's simply used as a way to escape the need for objective evidence, which is what faith does to an otherwise brilliant mind.

Anselm argued in this manner:

1. On the assumption that that than which nothing greater can be conceived is only in a mind, something greater can be conceived, because

2. Something greater can be thought to exist in reality as well.

3. The assumption is therefore contradictory: either there is no such thing even in the intellect, or it exists also in reality;

4. But it does exist in the mind of the fool, or doubter;

5. Therefore that than which nothing greater can be conceived exists in reality as well as in the mind.

Why anyone in his or her right mind would think this establishes the existence of a god is really beyond me. When people are asked, they can try to conceive of a maximally great superhuman being of some kind, a god, goddess, or God. However, most if not all conceptions of such a superhuman being are probably internally inconsistent ones. Many conceptions are mutually inconsistent with other conceptions as well. We can imagine a greatest conceivable being that is evil, just as others conceive of a greatest conceivable being that is perfectly good. And even perfectly good god conceptions admit of big differences. Surely barbaric people of the past, along with militant Islamist groups like ISIS, al-Qaeda, and Boko Haram, all conceive of a perfectly good theistic God too. But their perfectly good God is morally reprehensible to all reasonable civilized people.

Many conceptions of the greatest conceivable being are therefore different and depend on one's age, IQ, maturity, gender, race, and religion. They depend on accidents of birth, most notably when and where people were born. Conceptions of God are therefore parochial and geographical specific. Westerners cannot conceive of anything different from the god they were raised to believe, nor can Easterners. Easterners may say the greatest conceivable being is beyond personhood, or truth, or knowledge, or beauty, or any number of rational dichotomous categories. Easterners may even say the greatest conceivable being cannot be conceived. If Westerners counterargue that the Eastern conceptions are self-contradictory, they need only take a good hard look at their own contradictory conceptions, beginning with the equivalent doctrine of divine simplicity.[13] I can imagine a greatest conceivable being who can do the logically impossible. After all, if this conjured-up being can create the laws of nature, then he/she/it can create the laws of logic. Otherwise, if he/she/it is limited to that which is logically possible, logic would end up being greater than a greatest conceivable being (think of the Euthyphro dilemma applied to logic).

So Anselm's ontological argument begins with different and even mutually exclusive conceptions of the greatest conceivable being that are potentially internally inconsistent. Since this is the case, Anselm's further argument, that it is greater to exist in reality than merely be conceived of, entails that these different and even mutually exclusive conceptions of the greatest conceivable being also exist. But that cannot be. Specific content must be supplied as to which greatest conceivable being is the greatest conceivable being prior to arguing that such a being exists. Short of doing this from the start, Anselm's argument fails before it gets out of the gate. For if two mutually inconsistent beings can be conjured up from the same argument then something is fatally wrong with that argument.

We won't let these inconvenient and devastating problems trouble our little minds any more though, as we must proceed.

Truth is, Anselm's argument is little more than an equivocation of words. The informal fallacy of equivocation is when someone gives a key word or phrase with two different meanings. Sometimes they are difficult to spot, other times they are easy. One example I found online is this:

The sign said "Fine for parking here."
Since it was fine, I parked there.

Anselm depends on there being two conceptions of a maximally great being (or God for our purposes). On the one hand, we have a god who exists only as a conception in the mind; while on the other hand, we have a conception of a god who exists in reality, which is a greater conception. But both conceptions of God are still nothing more than conceptions. Anselm just substitutes a different higher greater conception for the original conception. That's his equivocation.

So Anselm falsely derives the conclusion that (1) the initial god conception we had truly exists in reality, from (2) the initial god conception we had. For the god conception we originally had can be known to exist only if we can subsequently conceive of a greater god than our original conception. If we can know that God exists because of a conception in our mind, then this only means we can conceive of a god greater than the original conception in our mind. Or to see this more clearly, if our original conception of God does not include the additional conception that this God exists in reality, then Anselm argues this God exists in reality after all. There are two different god conceptions involved, so there is no contradiction.

If the same conception of god were employed throughout his argument, we would see the fallacious nature of it. To see this just ask what would become of Anselm's argument if, when asked to conceive of the greatest conceivable being, we started out conceiving of an existing maximally great God. How can Anselm proceed at that point? Well, he can't. For our original conception of God already included that it existed in reality. Anselm needs both steps, both conceptions, for his argument to have the appearance of working. He cannot get to the second step that leads to a contradiction and the subsequent false conclusion that that maximally great being actually exists unless we first start out with a conception of God that didn't exist.[14]

One can look at this argument differently. We can look at it historically. Hebrews could conceive of no greater superhuman being than Yahweh, the god of Israel, who emerged out of a polytheistic amalgamation of gods known in the ancient Near East in prebiblical times. In the ancient Near East, all pantheons were organized as families, and Yahweh was simply one of the members of that family. Some biblical authors consider Yahweh, the god of Israel—as one of many gods fathered by Elyon, whose wife was Asherah[15]—to whom was given the people and land of Israel to rule over (Deut. 32:8).[16] This God was responsible for doing both good and evil, sending evil spirits to do his will and commanding genocide.

In the hands of Greeks they could conceive of no greater superhuman being than Zeus, the sky god who ruled as king of all other the gods on Mount Olympus. Then came Anselm's eleventh-century conception of a superhuman being as the classical omni-god unrelated to anything we find in the Bible. In all of these historical cases, according to Anselm himself, these superhuman conceptions must exist in reality since to exist is greater than a mere conception, even if they are all different conceptions, right? Wrong!

There is one other historical view of the divine not always recognized by Westerners. Easterners have a much higher "conception" of the divine, in that they believe she/he/it cannot be conceived at all. Every attempt to conceive of the divine falls short because it's much much bigger than what they can possibly conceive. According to Anslem's argument that superhuman being must exist too, right? Wrong!

The point of this all too brief history lesson is that if Anselm's argument leads to the existence of mutually inconsistent conceptions of the divine then the argument does not work. For not all of these divine conceptions can exist. If, however, Anselm's argument can only work after conceptions of God are settled between believers then it is worthless, since conceptions of the divine have not been settled, nor is there any hint they can be settled.

The ontological argument simply does not work for these reasons and many others. Philosopher Graham Oppy notes:

> What seems right to me is this: that no ontological argument that has been thus far produced evades a three-pronged criticism: either it has plainly question-begging premises; or it is invalid; or it establishes the existence of something uncontroversial (that can reasonably be taken to have no religious significance, e.g., the physical universe).[17]

Regardless of the failure of Anselm's ontological argument, its most important function was to help define into existence the concept of God, something that was to hold sway over Christendom ever since. For out of Anselm's concept of the greatest conceivable being came *perfect being theology*. Philosopher of religion Thomas Morris characterized "the core of perfect being theology as the thesis that: God is a being with the greatest possible array of composite great making properties." By his lights this God can be conceived of as "a thoroughly benevolent conscious agent with unlimited knowledge and power, who is the creative source of all else."[18]

Most Christian theologians follow in the footsteps of Anselm, and Christians have struggled to exasperation in defending their conceptions of a perfect being from the charges of incoherence, inconsistency, and unintelligibility ever since. Those who don't adopt it are hamstrung by biblical depictions of Yahweh, the God of the Bible, the God of the Old Testament. Such a God is described by Richard Dawkins in this accurate manner:

> The God of the Old Testament is arguably the most unpleasant character in all fiction: jealous and proud of it; a petty, unjust, unforgiving control freak; a vindictive, bloodthirsty ethnic cleanser; a misogynistic, homophobic, racist, infanticidal, genocidal, filicidal, pestilential, megalomaniacal, sadomasochistic, capriciously malevolent bully.[19]

For anyone who thinks Dawkins was wrong to describe God in this way, Dan Barker, the co-president of the Freedom From Religion Foundation, draws on the Bible's own words to document each of these qualities in a book titled *GOD! The Most Unpleasant Character in All Fiction.*[20] I've written a lot about the moral critique of the God of the Bible myself and I completely agree with this assessment.[21]

What we actually find in the Bible is an extremely not-so-good, very bad God! Yahweh, the part of the Godhead in the Old Testament, is exactly as Dawkins described. He's an embarrassment to all decent God-concepts. He's a God of war, a condemning bloodthirsty God of wrath. Christians want to focus our attention on Jesus instead. Jesus, the part of the Godhead we find in the New Testament, is representative of love, compassion, and redemption they tell us. The truth is not as they describe though. For according to Christian theology Jesus is one with Yahweh. This is not a good cop, bad cap routine.

Yahweh is Jesus. Jesus is Yahweh, in mind, will, and purpose. What Yahweh said and did in the Old Testament, Jesus said and did. Jesus is not a kinder, gentler deity. He's a full-fledged member of the Godhead who shares responsibility for every word, every goal pursued, every action, and every decision of Yahweh in the Old Testament. If Yahweh, the first person of the trinity, is a moral monster, as the biblical evidence shows us, then so is Jesus, the second person of the trinity.

So it can equally be said that:

> Jesus is arguably the most unpleasant character in all fiction: jealous and proud of it; a petty, unjust, unforgiving control freak; a vindictive, bloodthirsty ethnic cleanser; a misogynistic, homophobic, racist, infanticidal, genocidal, filicidal, pestilential, megalomaniacal, sadomasochistic, capriciously malevolent bully.[22]

Of course there are additional problems that the philosophical theologian cannot solve. John Hick expressed it as follows:

> Neither the intense christological debates of the centuries leading up to the Council of Chalcedon, nor the renewed christological debates of the 19th and 20th Centuries, have succeeded in squaring the circle by making intelligible the claim that one who was genuinely and unambiguously a man was also genuinely and unambiguously God.[23]

New Testament scholar E. P. Sanders just honestly admits, "It lies beyond my meager abilities as an interpreter of dogmatic theology to explain how it is possible for one person to be 100 per cent human and 100 per cent divine, without either interfering with the other."[24]

Starting with the God of the Bible, Western conceptions of God grew until he became the greatest conceivable being than which none greater can be conceived. James A. Lindsay delightfully and humorously described this trajectory as representing a schoolyard argument among children: "My god is bigger than your god; no, my god is twice as big as your god; no, my god is ten times as big as your god; no, my god is infinitely bigger, better, and more influential than any god you can imagine; yeah, well my god is even better than that; mine's that than which nothing greater can be conceived!" Lindsay concludes, "these omnis grow through time to the point of sheer ridiculousness. By that point the unfortunate faithful are left to incredible mental gymnastics to defend physical and philosophical impossibilities in a deity that exemplifies everything people wish it could be and yet that it cannot."[25]

In any case, ever since the widespread acceptance of perfect-being theology, Christian defenders have doubly struggled to defend their faith. For they now have two nearly impossible tasks. They must first harmonize the bloodthirsty, malevolent biblical descriptions of the God of the Bible with a perfect being, and then they must also defend conceptions of the perfect being from the charge of incoherence, inconsistency, and unintelligibility. One task seems quite impossible on its own, but both are now required, thus doubling the problem.

Faith Seeking Understanding

Anselm's most enduring legacy just might be his statement, *credo ut intelligam* ("I believe in order that I may understand"), or in its most famous form, *Fides quaerens intellectum* ("faith seeking understanding").[26] While others have expressed this idea, the point is that people first believe then seek to understand. First they believe then they seek data. First they believe then they seek to confirm their beliefs. No one in the history of the confessional church probably said anything different, or if they did, faith was surreptitiously smuggled in the back door. No one ever said "understanding seeks faith," because the obvious sequitur is that if we achieve understanding we don't need faith. It reverses what reasonable people think in the modern world. In fact, it goes against science since science is based on trying to understand.

In 1987 a large-scale US antinarcotics campaign by Partnership for a Drug-Free America launched. It featured two televised public service announcements (PSAs) and a related poster campaign. The original thirty-second ad showed a man who held up an egg and said, "This is your brain." Then he showed a hot frying pan and said, "This is drugs." Then he cracked the egg and put it in the pan. It immediately began to cook. He brought the pan closer to the camera and said, "This is your brain on drugs." He ended the PSA by saying, "Any questions?" It was a very powerful commercial.

I want people to consider the drug metaphor for faith, taking our cue from Karl Marx, who described religious faith as the opiate of the people. When you think of the commercial you need to hear the actor say, "This is your brain on faith." That's what I think. Here then are five ways faith makes the brain stupid:

1. Faith causes the believer to denigrate or deny science.

2. Faith causes the believer to think objective evidence is not needed to believe.

3. Faith causes the believer to deny the need to think exclusively in terms of the probabilities.

4. Faith causes the believer to accept private subjective experiences over the objective evidence.

5. Faith causes the believer to think faith has an equal or better method for arriving at the truth than scientifically based reasoning.

Any questions?

Christian, before you mindlessly quote mine from the Bible or the theology based on it, consider what you think of other brains on faith, like those of Scientologists, Mormons, Muslims, Jews, pantheists, and so on. Clearly you think their brains are on the opiate of faith just as I do. Watch some videos about these other faiths. Study them. Talk to practitioners of them. Try to argue with the best representatives of them and see if you can penetrate their brains with reason and science. Can't do it? Why? Why do you think their faith makes them impervious to reason and your faith does not make you impervious to reason?

I had a discussion with a person of faith not long ago where she said there was nothing I could ever say to change her mind. I simply replied that no scientist would ever say such a thing. I went on to say she should think like a scientist and recommended that she read Guy Harrison's chapter in my anthology, *Christianity in the Light of Science*, titled, "How to Think Like a Scientist: Why Every Christian Can and Should Embrace Good Thinking." I recommended it because thinking like a scientist is the antithesis of thinking with the drug of faith on one's brain.

Scientifically minded people argue we should reason like a scientist, and we should. Believers in different faiths will demur, saying we cannot justify our own reasoning capabilities, since we accept the fact of evolution. I think my evolved brain can make reliable (though not perfect) judgments based on the evidence of course, and that should be good enough. But ignoring this for the moment, what if these believers are correct? Then what? It gets them nowhere as in no-where. They still cannot settle their differences because they are left with no method to do so. They will argue for faith over reason, which leaves them all back at the starting gate, with faith. They are special pleading and that's it, thinking that if they can deny reason in favor of their particular faith then it follows their particular faith ends up being the correct one. No, if they deny reason in favor of faith the result is there's no way to settle these disputes between people of different faiths. My claim is that religions debunk themselves and because this is clearly the case, the only alternative to know the truth about the world is through scientifically based reasoning.

The fact that I can say nothing to convince most of them of this is maddening. They are impervious to reason, almost all of them. This is what faith does to their brains.

Randal Rauser is an associate professor of historical theology at Taylor Seminary, Edmonton, Canada. He and I coauthored a debate-style book together titled *God or Godless?*[27] He is a Christian believer. I cowrote the book to reach any honest believers since I consider him impervious to reason. I could say it of any Christian pseudo-intellectual to some degree, depending on how close he or she is to the truth (liberals are closer than progressive evangelicals who are closer than fundamentalists). I admit Rauser reasons well in other areas of his life unrelated to his faith. He could even teach a critical thinking class. So he's rational, very much so. But like all believers his brain must basically shut down when it comes to faith. When it comes to faith his brain must disengage. It cannot connect the dots. It refuses to connect them. Faith stops the brain from working properly. Faith is a cognitive bias that causes believers to overestimate any confirming evidence and underestimate any disconfirming evidence. So his brain will not let reason penetrate it, given his faith bias. Some people have even described faith as a virus of the brain (or mind). It makes the brain sick. Maybe Marx said it best though. It's an opiate, a deadening drug.

Alvin Plantinga has argued that what's essential to have a "warranted belief" is "the proper functioning of one's cognitive faculties in the right kind of cognitive environment." I actually think he's right. But faith, like an opiate, causes the brain to stop functioning properly in matters related to faith. Christian apologetics is predicated on a host of logical fallacies. Take away the logical fallacies they use in defense of their faith and they wouldn't have any arguments left at all. They certainly don't have good objective sufficient evidence for what they believe. A critical thinker like Rauser, who thinks more rationally than most others in every area unrelated to his faith, cannot see this, but it is the case.

Now why can't Rauser see this? Why can't he come to the correct religious conclusions? Why can't he think rationally about his faith? Because his faith, like an opiate, will not let him. The opiate of faith deadens those areas in his brain that are related to his faith. Rauser surely sees this with regard to other believers in different religious faiths. He will say the same things about them that I say about him. But he refuses to see the same drug deadening his own brain. Once again, faith is a cognitive bias, a virus of the mind, an opiate. It prevents people of faith from connecting the dots.

Rauser admits that like everyone else he depends on "motivated reasoning" to some degree. Well then, why won't he apply the antidote, which is to require sufficient objective evidence for what he believes? That's the only way to overcome the cognitive bias of faith, the only way to kill that virus in his mind, the only way to nullify the opiate of faith, and the only way to stop being swayed by his own motivated reasoning. Yet he questions the need for sufficient *objective* evidence apart from a private subjective ineffable *feeling*. Who in their right mind would do this after admitting he depends on "motivated reasoning" to some degree? No reasonable person, that's who.

Subjective private ineffable religious *experiences* offer believers the most psychologically certain basis for believing in a particular divine being or religion. When believers have a religious *experience* it's really hard, if not psychologically impossible, to argue them away from their faith. How is it possible then for believers who claim to have had such experiences to look at those experiences as an outsider might? We can point out the mind often deceives us and provide many examples of this phenomenon (brainwashing, wish-fulfillment, cognitive dissonance). But believers will maintain their particular religious experience is real because it was experienced, despite the odds their brain is deceiving them. We can point out that countless others of different faiths all claim to have the same type of religious experiences, whether they are Mormon, Muslim, Catholic, or Jew, but believers will still say their experiences are true ones (or veridical), despite the odds that what others believe as a result of their experiences makes it seem obvious they could be wrong too (and vice versa).

Sometimes in the face of such an experiential argument I simply say to the believer, "If I had that same experience I might believe too. But I haven't. So why not? Why doesn't your God give me that same religious experience?" At this point the believer must blame me and every living person on the planet for not being open to such a sect-specific religious experience. Depending on the religious sect in question that might include most every person, 7.4 billion of us and counting. But even this realization doesn't affect believers who claim to have had such religious experiences. Calvinists among them will simply say, "God doesn't want various people to have a saving religious experience." It never dawns on any of these believers what this means about the God they worship, that only a mean-spirited barbaric God would send people to an eternal punishment because that same God did not allow them a certain type of religious experience.

Believers will always argue in such a fashion in order to stay as believers. No matter what we say they always seem to have an answer. What they never produce is any cold hard objective evidence, convincing evidence, for their faith claims. Ever. They are not only impervious to reason. They are also impervious to the evidence. They even see evidence where it doesn't exist because they take the lack of evidence as evidence for their faith. When it comes to prayer they count the hits and discount the misses.

There is only so much a person can take when dealing with people who have lost touch with reality. Must we always maintain a patient attitude when we already know their arguments? Must we always respond in a dispassionate manner to people who are persuaded against reason to believe something delusional? We know this about them based on everything we know (i.e., our background knowledge). They are pretending to know that which they don't know when they pretend to know with some degree of certainty their faith is true. If it's faith, how then can something be known with any degree of probability at all, much less certainty? Faith by definition always concerns itself with that which is unsure. Something unsure involves lower probabilities. So faith is always about that which has lower probabilities to it. So again, how can something based on faith be known with any degree of certainty? It can't, and only deluded minds think otherwise, minds that are impervious to reason and evidence. We can only hope they can function in life. It can be quite surprising they can.

Concluding Thoughts

Anselm of Canterbury's key theological contributions in philosophy of religion highlight what reasonable people see as the need for philosophy of religion to end. He holds a preeminent place among the best philosophical theologians the Church ever produced. And yet, as we've seen, even among the best of the best there's nothing here but rhetoric without substance based on his faith and the social climate of his day. His best contributions didn't solve anything. Almost no one accepts his atonement theory today. His idiosyncratic perfect-being conception was based on nothing more than special pleading on behalf of his parochial Western concept of god. His ontological argument does not work either. Further, we've found that when Anselm's perfect being is compared to the biblical god Yahweh and his supposed son, it doesn't make any sense nor can it be reconciled. So the only reason to study Anselm seems to be one of historical curiosity. Anselm's key contributions did not advance anything since we are no closer at getting to objective knowledge about anything than we would be if he never wrote a thing. When it comes to the history of philosophy he made no contributions that furthered understanding, the very thing he sought to do.

It does no good to say we've learned from Anselm what is false and cannot be defended, as if by learning what isn't the case he advanced our understanding. He sidetracked our understanding for a millennium. He was doing obfuscationist puzzle-solving theology unrelated to the honest desire to understand. If we proportioned our intellectual assent to the probabilities based on sufficient evidence (per Hume), we would know all we need to know to know that Anselm and many other unevidenced beliefs are false and cannot be defended.

Karl Barth, considered one of the greatest theologians of the last century, who rejected natural theology with a big fat "Nein," argued Anselm's ontological argument was an example of his faith seeking understanding, rather than an argument proving God exists. Anselm did not seek to "prove" the truth of the Christian faith, Barth argued, but to understand it.[28] Anselm's ontological argument in chapter 2 of the *Proslogion* comes after asking God for help to understand his faith in chapter 1. There he prays, "I do not seek to understand that I may believe, but I believe in order to understand. For this also I believe, — that unless I believed, I should not understand." Then just before developing the argument in chapter 2, Anselm prays, "Lord, do you, who do give understanding to faith, give me, so far as you know it to be profitable, to understand that you are as we believe; and that you are that which we believe." So while there is disagreement about what he was doing, Anselm at least *tacitly* acknowledges his argument comes *from* faith rather than leading *to* faith. And that's exactly what we find. The ontological argument depends on his Christian faith, which subsequently seeks to understand what he already believes about his parochial god. There's a recognized informal fallacy here I've mentioned a time or two. It's called special pleading.

Philosophers of religion who have dealt with Anselm's argument and developed their own versions of it, such as Charles Hartshorne, Norman Malcolm, and Alvin Plantinga, should take note. They don't know their own theology. Or, perhaps more correctly and importantly, *they fail to realize they're doing the same thing Anselm honestly admitted doing, special pleading.*

What we're led to conclude is that the problem of philosophy of religion stems from faith. If faith is trust then there is no reason to trust faith. Anything based on faith has lower probabilities to it by definition. Christian pseudo-philosophers do no more than build intellectual castles in the sky without any solid grounding to them. There doesn't seem to be any good principled reason for not getting fed up with the pretend game of faith with its ever-receding theology.

Notes

1.   Stephen Law, *Believing Bullshit: How Not to Get Sucked into an Intellectual Black Hole* (Amherst, NJ: Prometheus Books, 2011) p. 75.

2.   John Hick, *The Metaphor of God Incarnate* (Louisville, KY: Westminster Press, 1993), p. 114.

3.   Hick, *The Metaphor of God Incarnate*, p. 117.

4.   A few of my favorite books on this are as follows: Thom Stark, *The Human Faces of God* (Eugene, OR: Wipf & Stock, 2011); Randel McCraw Helms, *The Bible Against Itself* (Altadena, CA: Millennium Press, 2006); Bart D. Ehrman, *Jesus Interrupted* (HarperOne, 2009); Paul Tobin, *The Rejection of Pascal's Wager: A Skeptic's Guide to the Bible and the Historical Jesus* (Authors Online, 2009).

5.   See Bart D. Ehrman's two books, *Lost Christianities* and *Lost Scriptures*, both published by Oxford University Press in 2003.

6.   Walter A. Elwell, ed., *Evangelical Dictionary of Theology* (Grand Rapids, MI: Baker Book House, 1984), s.v. "Atonement," p. 101.

7.   Michael Martin, *The Case Against Christianity* (Philadelphia, PA: Temple University Press, 1991), p. 256.

8.   Hick, *The Metaphor of God Incarnate*, pp. 118–19.

9.   I devote a whole chapter to critically examining atonement theories and find no justification for any of them in *Why I Became an Atheist* (Amherst, NJ: Prometheus Books, 2012), chapter 20, "The Passion of the Christ: Why Did Jesus Suffer?" pp. 399–409. See also Ken Pulliam's chapter "The Absurdity of the Atonement" in my anthology *The End of Christianity* (Amherst, NJ: Prometheus Books, 2011), pp. 181–194. Pulliam focuses on the penal substitutionary theory.

10.   Oliver D. Crisp and Fred Sanders, ed., *Locating Atonement: Explorations in Constructive Dogmatics* (Grand Rapids: Zondervan, 2015), p. 13.

11.   Law, *Believing Bullshit*, p. 75.

12.   Robert Paul Wolff, *About Philosophy*, 7th ed. (Upper Saddle River, NJ: Prentice-Hall, 1998), pp. 284ff.

13.   On this see Graham Oppy's *Describing Gods: An Investigation of Divine Attributes* (Cambridge: Cambridge University Press, 2014), along with Michael

Martin and Riki Monnier's anthology, *The Impossibility of God* (Amherst NY: Prometheus Books, 2003), parts 4 & 5, pp. 181–421.

14. This is my argument but I also found that Skeptico made the same type of argument in a post titled, "The Ontological Argument for God," August 17, 2009, http://skeptico.blogs.com/skeptico/2009/08/ontological-argument-for-god-rebuttal.html.

15. On this see William G. Dever, *Did God Have a Wife?* (Grand Rapids, MI: Eerdmans, 2005).

16. On this point see chapter 2 in the book I cowrote with Randal Rauser, *God or Godless? One Atheist. One Christian. Twenty Controversial Questions* (Grand Rapids, MI: Baker Books, 2013), pp. 21–35; chapter 5 in Thom Stark's book, *The Human Faces of God,* especially pp. 70–74; and Hector Avalos, *The End of Biblical Studies* (Amherst, NY: Prometheus Books, 2007), pp. 44–47.

17. Graham Oppy, *Arguing About Gods* (Cambridge: Cambridge University Press, 2006), p. 57.

18. Thomas V. Morris, *Our Idea of God* (Vancouver: Regent College Publishing, 1997)p. 40.

19. Richard Dawkins, *The God Delusion* (Boston: Houghton Mifflin Company, 2006), p. 31.

20. Dan Barker, *GOD! The Most Unpleasant Character in All Fiction* (New York: Sterling, 2016).

21. See especially chapter 5 in *Why I Became an Atheist*; my cowritten book with Rauser, *God or Godless?*; and also my anthology *Christianity Is Not Great* (Amherst, NY: Prometheus Books, 2014).

22. Robert M. Price made this type of argument very forcefully in his book *Blaming Jesus for Jehovah: Rethinking the Righteousness of Christianity* (Valley, WA: Tellectual Press, 2016).

23. As quoted in chapter 3 of N. F. Gier, *God, Reason, and the Evangelicals* (Lanham, MD: University Press of America, 1987).

24. E. P. Sanders, *The Historical Figure of Jesus* (London: Penguin, 1993), p. 134.

25. James A. Lindsay, *God Doesn't; We Do: Only Humans Can Solve Human Challenges* (CreateSpace, 2012), p. 89.

26. From the preface to Ian Logan, *Reading Anselm's Proslogion* (Burlington, VT: Ashgate, 2009), p. 24.

27. Grand Rapids, MI: Baker Books, 2013.

28. Karl Barth, *Faith Seeking Understanding: An Introduction to Christian Theology* (Grand Rapids: Wm. B. Eerdmans, 1991), p.14.

3

CASE STUDIES IN THEISTIC PHILOSOPHY OF RELIGION

In this chapter let's continue to see how to do philosophy of religion correctly, shall we? In the last chapter we critically examined one of the best philosophers of religion in the Western world and found his arguments to be nothing more than puzzle-solving based on special pleading. They are irrelevant and uninteresting for people in today's world except as a historical curiosity that could be better spent learning other things.

Let's turn in this chapter to the contemporary philosophy of religion scene. In order to see it for what it really is, we need to look at how contemporary practitioners do it, which will include Christian theists in this chapter, and atheists in the next one. We will draw some examples out into the light for all to see. Again we should see enacted before our eyes *Law's law of faith*: "Anything based on faith, no matter how ludicrous, can be made to be consistent with the available evidence, given a little patience and ingenuity."[1]

Christianity and Philosophy

Many Christians have taken an unenthusiastic view of philosophy because there are dangers in it for their faith. According to Paul in Colossians 2:8,

"See no one takes you captive through hollow and deceptive philosophy." Jesus purportedly said, "I praise you, Father, Lord of heaven and earth, because you have hidden these things from the wise and learned, and revealed them to little children. Yes, Father, for this was your good pleasure" (Luke 10:21). Paul wrote, "The message of the cross is foolishness to those who are perishing, but to us who are being saved it is the power of God. For it is written: 'I will destroy the wisdom of the wise; the intelligence of the intelligent I will frustrate.' Where is the wise man? Where is the scholar? Where is the philosopher of this age? Has not God made foolish the wisdom of the world? . . . For the foolishness of God is wiser than man's wisdom" (1 Cor. 1:18–25).

Tertullian (160–220 CE) asked: "What has Athens to do with Jerusalem?" In words reminiscent of Søren Kierkegaard, Tertullian wrote of the incarnation of Jesus by saying, "Just because it is absurd, it is to be believed . . . it is certain because it is impossible." Martin Luther called reason "the Devil's greatest whore." As such, reason "can do nothing but slander and harm all that God says and does." Luther argued against the magisterial use of reason, in which reason judges the gospel, and approved of the ministerial use of reason, in which reason submits and serves the gospel. William Lane Craig agrees with Luther. He argues that "reason is a tool to help us better understand our faith. Should faith and reason conflict, it is reason that must submit to faith, not vice versa."[2] I'll argue in this chapter that this kind of faith-based reasoning is unreasonable because it's nothing short of special pleading. There is something wrong with any belief system that needs to disparage reason like this.

Alvin Plantinga's Faith-Based Philosophical Apologetics

In my book *How to Defend the Christian Faith: Advice from an Atheist*, I wrote a chapter titled, "Accept Nothing Less Than Sufficient Objective Evidence." It's a unique chapter. I personally haven't seen anything like it anywhere else. In it I critically examined the various apologetical strategies Christian defenders use to show their faith is true. Unlike the misleading taxonomies Christians themselves use, I classified the strategies correctly according to their primary apologetical method for defending Christianity. I divided them into five groups:

1. Apologetics Based on Sufficient Objective Evidence
2. Apologetics Based on Special Pleading
3. Apologetics Based on Assuming What Needs to Be Proved
4. Apologetics Based on Private Subjective Experiences
5. Eclectic Pragmatic Apologetics Based on Prior Conclusions[3]

I argued the only method that has any merit at all is the first one, usually called evidentialism by its proponents. It's the one that proponents of subsequent methods reject or degrade to second-class status at best. Christians should find this troublesome. After all, we're talking about apologetics, defending the truth of Christianity. And it cannot be done without sufficient objective evidence. What else is there? What else is there by comparison? In fact, I went on to argue that the very existence of other methods to defend the Christian faith is proof, all by itself, that Christian apologists themselves don't think there is sufficient evidence to believe. For if they did, they never would have come up with any other apologetical method to defend the faith. There can never be enough evidence for something. The more the better. The very fact that most Christian apologists reject the need for and/or existence of sufficient objective evidence is telling. It's because it does not exist. The problem, as I pointed out, is that deists were first and foremost evidentialists, but look where evidentialism led them. It caused them to reject Christianity. They came to the mere belief that there was a creator God, which in turn couldn't be sustained after Darwin.

I cited Alvin Plantinga as representing a prime example of apologetical method number 3—Apologetics Based on Assuming What Needs to Be Proved—with regard to his *Reformed epistemology*. Plantinga seeks to show that Christians can be entirely rational in having a "full-blooded Christian belief"[4] in "the great truths of the gospel"[5] without sufficient objective evidence. Now even if I could go against reason to think it might be rational to believe in a Supreme Being without evidence, a belief in a particular triune God who created the universe from nothing, who tested Adam and Eve in the Garden, who rescued the Israelites from Egyptian slavery, who sent an incarnation of himself to Earth who was born of a virgin in Bethlehem, who did and said the things we read about in the canonical Gospels, who was crucified as a substitutionary sacrifice for our sins, who bodily arose from the dead, and who ascended into the sky with the promise of coming again to judge the world, is simply not a god-belief that is rational to hold without evidence! There's just way too much belief going on there.

Plantinga says the great truths of the gospel found in a self-authenticating scripture are evident in themselves:

> [W]e don't require argument from, for example, historically established premises about the authorship and reliability of the bit of Scripture in question to the conclusion that the bit in question is in fact true; for belief in the great things of the gospel to be justified, rational, and warranted, no historical evidence and argument for the teaching in question, or for the veracity or reliability or divine character of Scripture are necessary.[6]

Pay close attention to what Plantinga said earlier: "Faith involves an explicitly cognitive element; it is, says Calvin, knowledge. . . . and it is revealed to our minds. To have faith, therefore, is to know and hence believe something or other." And Christian beliefs come "by way of the work of the Holy Spirit, who gets us to accept, causes us to believe, these great truths of the gospel. These beliefs don't come just by way of the normal operation of our natural faculties, they are a supernatural gift."[7]

I said other things in criticism of Reformed epistemology. But in the midst of it I quoted Plantinga as saying something every Christian apologist and philosopher should heed: "I don't know of an argument for Christian belief that seems very likely to convince one who doesn't already accept its conclusion."[8] Isn't that interesting, coming from someone who's revered among evangelicals?

I had posted this particular quote of his on my Facebook wall and received some harsh criticism from someone who was able to quote Plantinga—book, chapter, and verse. He argued I took his words out of context. The reason Plantinga admitted this wasn't because he didn't think there were good arguments for God, I was told. In fact, Plantinga came up with a modal version of the ontological argument, and upon being pressed by others came up with two dozen (or so) theistic arguments, which I knew.[9] The reason Plantinga admitted this was because he thinks human beings are fallen creatures, I was informed. Due to sin we cannot be convinced God exists because we don't want to believe in him, so the arguments can't break through to us.

I offered three responses I think are instructive. The first is that Plantinga is a very thorough philosopher who has written three large works defending Reformed epistemology: *Warrant: The Current Debate* (1993), *Warrant and Proper Function* (1993), and *Warranted Christian Belief* (2000), all published by Oxford University Press. What Plantinga has done is attempt to come up with an answer to every known objection. In those cases where he doesn't provide a direct answer to an objection himself, he at least acknowledges the objection and points readers in the right direction for study, as he sees it. So anything I might say in criticism of Plantinga has already been considered by him for the most part. That's why he's a good thinker, no doubt. But the fact that he acknowledges the objections and offers answers to them *does not mean he offers good answers to them*.

For instance, at the end of *Warranted Christian Belief* he acknowledges he still has not shown Christian belief to be true. This "really important question" of truth, he says, must "pass beyond the competence of philosophy, whose main competence, in this area, is to clear away certain objections, impedances, and obstacles to Christian belief."[10] Christian philosopher of religion Richard Swinburne says this makes his work out to be "of little use." For Swinburne says,

> Plantinga works up to the conclusion that "if Christian belief is true, it very likely does have warrant." But this conditional is of little use to anyone without some information about the truth of the antecedent (whether Christian belief is true); and on that, Plantinga explicitly acknowledges in his final paragraph, he cannot help us. For he writes there that on the really important question of "is Christian belief true," "we pass beyond the competence of philosophy."[11]

My second response was to admit that when Plantinga says an argument to the existence of God won't "convince one who doesn't already accept its conclusion," he does indeed think it's due to our fallen sinful human nature. For he believes sin distorts our capacity for responding positively to the arguments to God's existence.[12] But think about how Plantinga first came to the conclusion, along with so many others, that the consequences of sin keep sinners from apprehending the truth? Sure there is the Bible, but not everyone sees it that way. There is a debate between Calvinists and Arminians on this issue.[13] So I'm sure the main reason many Christian theologians believe that sin seriously impairs our capability to have a sense of divinity (or *sensus divinitatis*) isn't the Bible. The reason they believe this about the effects of sin on our incapacity to accept the arguments to God's existence is because so many people are nonbelievers in their sect-specific faith. They must account for this fact. Surely it isn't due to the lack of sufficient evidence that so many of us don't believe. Oh no! And surely God wouldn't allow any invisible demons to keep people from believing. So it must be self-imposed freely or federally imposed by the original human beings who chose to sin on our behalf. It must be due to the consequences of our sin. It could never be due to God or the lack of evidence. But the inconvenient truth is they have come to this conclusion because so many nonbelievers exist.

One way to see this is to suppose 90 percent of the world's population were Christians. Could they continue to believe in the disastrous effects of sin for reasoning to God? Just think what happened when Darwin found the objective evidence for evolution. Since then Christians have reinterpreted their Bible to come up with different, better views of the Creation accounts in Genesis. In the same way, if millions and even billions more people were believers, then Christians would not believe the effects of sin were that serious for reasoning to God. They would find ways to reinterpret some of the passages in the Bible by favoring those passages that stress we can reason to God, like the greatest commandment of Jesus, to "Love the Lord your God with all your heart and with all your soul and with all your *mind* and with all your strength" (Mark 12:30). From my perspective Christians lack an imagination at what could have resulted if things had turned out differently. So they miss points like this one.

So when Plantinga says an argument to the existence of God won't "convince one who doesn't already accept its conclusion," it means he does not think these arguments can convince reasonable outsiders, nonbelievers. It means Plantinga's God did not produce the evidence to reasonably convince someone on the other side of the planet. Sinners, nonbelievers, can only be saved directly by God, or by believing against the evidence, or in spite of it, or by ignoring it, or by simply being ignorant of it. Plantinga ends up embracing an apologetics whereby one must assume what needs to be proved, since there is nothing left, and that is pathetic for an apologist to admit.

"Fundamentalism on Stilts"

My third response was to simply quote the context of what Plantinga wrote. Plantinga explains why he offers no argument for why Christian belief is true. The context is italicized by me in what follows:

> I don't know of an argument for Christian belief that seems very likely to convince one who doesn't already accept its conclusion. *That is nothing against Christian belief, however, and indeed I shall argue that if Christian beliefs are true, then the standard and most satisfactory way to hold them will not be as the conclusions of argument.*[14]

We've already seen that Plantinga isn't interested in arguing for the truth of his faith, and that his work is "of little use" according to Richard Swinburne. Again, if there were sound arguments based on sufficient evidence then Plantinga wouldn't have to ingeniously yet disingenuously find other ways to believe apart from those arguments. He lacks an imagination at what could have resulted if things had turned out differently. What he doesn't tell us is why things didn't turn out differently.

Let's return then to what Plantinga said at the end of *Warranted Christian Belief*, where he acknowledges he still has not shown Christian belief to be true. This "really important question" of truth, he says, must "pass beyond the competence of philosophy, whose main competence, in this area, is to clear away certain objections, impedances, and obstacles to Christian belief."[15] Plantinga has done nothing of the sort. There is, however, a real sense at which I think he's right that the best philosophy of religion can do is to examine objections and obstacles to belief, or analyze ideas for consistency and meaning. Philosophy is not the same as evidence though. On that I am sure. A good argument is based on something. What else can it be based on but evidence, solid objective evidence? The more the better. And where does this evidence come from? One must appeal to scientific evidence, but there is still historical evidence that comes from studying the Bible, looking at archeological findings and sources contemporary with the Bible in its various stages of development, and so forth.

Jaco Gericke is an Old Testament scholar and philosopher of religion. He has written what can be considered a refutation of Plantinga's Reformed epistemology. "The trouble with Craig and Plantinga," he told me, "is that their philosophy of religion conveniently ignores the problems posed for their views by the history of Israelite religion. They might as well try to prove Zeus exists. People sometimes forget 'God' used to be Yahweh and it is possible to prove from textual evidence that 'there ain't no such animal.'"

Gericke writes: "Not so long ago I was so irritated by a book of Alvin Plantinga's that I wrote a rebuttal from the perspective of a biblical scholar who happens to know what goes on in the philosophy of religion. It concerns the foundations of Plantinga's views and can be applied to William Lane Craig as well. Their philosophy may sound complex and formidable but if you know both the philosophy of religion and also the history of religion their smarts ain't nothing but Fundamentalism on Stilts."[16] Below I share important highlights from his rebuttal, with permission.

> It is my conviction that while the philosophy of religion can and should be applied to biblical thought (something I do myself), it is hermeneutically problematic when one does this while at the same time failing to take seriously the philosophical implications of the history of (Israelite) religion.
>
> However, up to now no Old Testament scholar that I am aware of has bothered to respond to the charges of [Reformed epistemology], to the effect that their views are still considered intellectually respectable in many philosophical circles (in biblical scholarship the movement is mostly unknown). So, out of a concern to expose the fallacies of the sort of philosophy of religion one might call "fundamentalism on stilts" (i.e. making outdated biblical-theological conceptions seem respectable with the aid of philosophical jargon) I have decided to accept the invitation of Stump (1985) and others and to devote this article to a discussion of why I believe some of [Reformed epistemology's] philosophy of religion is seriously damaged by a failure to appreciate the problems of Old Testament theology. . . . I have no pains with the concept of a "Reformed" epistemology per se but I do believe that in the writings of some philosophers of religion it really involves little more than a disguised attempt to sneak fundamentalist theology back into the academia.
>
> What is relevant to the present discussion is the fact that past critiques of Plantinga have tended to focus almost exclusively on problems in the philosophical "superstructure" of [Reformed epistemology] with little real attention being paid to the biblical-theological "base structure" of his arguments. And yet it cannot be disputed that the latter is ultimately foundational to the former—its raison d'être, if you will. But if this is indeed the case, it means that whatever the merits of Plantinga's

sophisticated philosophical rhetoric, if it can be shown that his biblical foundations are both mistaken and/or nothing of the sort, the entire modus operandi of [Reformed epistemology] will have been fatally compromised.

Like most Protestant fundamentalists accusing the rest of the world of not being "biblical" enough and constantly calling everyone to return [sic] to a "biblical" view on just about every particular theological subject, Plantinga is neither as "biblical" nor as "Reformed" as he thinks. His philosophical arguments aimed at discrediting the work of biblical scholars engaging in historical-critical analysis are riddled with a number of glaring fallacies, stereotypically encountered in the writing of all fundamentalist philosophers of religion.

First of all, Plantinga claims that belief in God is properly basic and that the God with reference to whom belief is such is, conveniently for him, the God of the Bible (Plantinga 2000c:384). Yet Plantinga's view of YHWH [Yahweh or God] is radically anachronistic and conforms more to the proverbial "God of the Philosophers" (Aquinas in particular) than to any version of YHWH as depicted in ancient Israelite religion. This means that the pre-philosophical "biblical" conceptions of YHWH, the belief in whom is supposed to be properly basic, is not even believed by Plantinga himself. His lofty notions of God in terms of "Divine Simplicity," "Maximal Greatness," and "Perfect-Being Theology" are utterly alien with reference to many of the characterizations of YHWH in biblical narrative (e.g. Gen. 18).

The second problem follows from the first: What kind of God is it with reference to which Plantinga asserts belief to be properly basic? It is useless to say belief in God is properly basic unless one can specify what the contents of the beliefs about God are supposed to be. But in this Plantinga's philosophy is radically undermined by his failure to take cognizance of the fact that he is committing the fallacy of essentialism. Like all fundamentalists he seems to know nothing (and want to know nothing) of the philosophical problems posed by conceptual pluralism in Old Testament theology or the diachronic variation in the beliefs about YHWH in the history of Israelite religion. In short, he seems blissfully unaware that there is no such thing as the "biblical" perspective on God.

A third problem concerns another way in which Plantinga's philosophy of religion brackets the history of religion . . . the fact is that it is wrong to assume, as Plantinga does, that the Old Testament is anti-evidentialist. On the contrary, there is ample reason to believe that a "soft" evidentialism is in fact the default epistemology taken for granted in ancient Israelite religion given the nature of many of the pre-philosophical epistemological assumptions in the biblical narratives. The whole idea of miracles (signs) and revelation via theophany, audition, dreams, divination and history can be said to presuppose an evidentialist epistemology (see the oft-repeated formula "so that they may know . . ."). After all, of all the religious epistemologies that come to mind, it is difficult to imagine that the prophet Elijah in the narrative where he takes on the Baal Prophets on Carmel was endorsing anything remotely similar to "Reformed epistemology" (see 1 Ki 18). If that is not an instance of evidentialism in the Old Testament, what is?

A fourth biblical-theological shortcoming concerns Plantinga's naïve-realist hermeneutics. . . . Plantinga imagines himself to be loyal to and fighting for the Bible as such when in fact he is not so much defending the Bible for its own sake but struggling to place his own Reformed Fundamentalist view of the Bible beyond the possibility of critique.

The fifth problem—and this point follows from the previous one – Plantinga argues along typical fundamentalist apologetic lines that one either assumes beforehand that the Bible is the Word of God or merely fallible human superstition. . . . Plantinga's own presuppositionalist hermeneutics show that he is more interested in safeguarding his own fundamentalist assumptions than allowing them to be modified should the nature of the biblical data require it. In wanting to prejudge the issue on inspiration, Plantinga conveniently forgets that the question of meaning precedes the question of truth (as analytic philosophy has taught us), and that without this insight no corrective from the Bible on dogmas are possible to begin with.

The sixth problem is that Plantinga claims that his own readings of the Bible follow a "traditional" approach. However, not only is any appeal to tradition in itself a potential logical fallacy in the justification of truth claims in the philosophy of religion, but the problem is also that the concept of a singular "traditional" reading is meaningless, for there never was a single way of reading the text anywhere in the history of interpretation.

A seventh and final matter for discussion concerns the non-sequitur involved in the ultimate objectives of [Reformed epistemology] in the context of the discussion with biblical scholars and the critique of biblical criticism. Plantinga thinks that if he can discredit historical criticism and evolutionary theory, then his own fundamentalist and creationist hermeneutics win by default and can be taken seriously again (2000c:398). In this he seems to forget that proving historical criticism wrong is not the same as proving historical/grammatical hermeneutics correct – that is another task on its own. The same is the case with regard to his raging against evolution—even if Plantinga could somehow demonstrate a fatal problem in the theory, this does not vindicate creationism. The latter still needs to be justified as part of a separate project and imagining that it gets a second chance if evolution is someday left behind is as naïve as thinking that astrology gets another shot at it if a contemporary astronomical theory is discredited. It does not work that way—one has to go forwards, not backwards, and creationism and fundamentalism have had their day.

In the end . . . it eventually becomes readily apparent that Plantinga's entire case is in fact little more than a huge demonstration of special pleading. Time and again it is implied that the main reason Plantinga cannot and will not accept a critical approach to the text is not because he really understood what biblical criticism is all about, but rather because of what he takes to be its implication—that he would have to take leave of his own cherished personal "properly basic" dogmas about the text. This is why Plantinga will not be taken seriously by mainstream biblical theologians.

Plantinga has mistaken the philosophy of religion for fundamentalist Christian apologetics. In doing so, he turns out to be neither biblical nor Reformed (or even really "philosophical") in his arguments. It hardly matters how sophisticated, coherent, interesting, orthodox, complex or convincing the philosophical and specifically epistemological arguments in justifying [Reformed epistemology] in its current format might be or become. As long as the assumptions underlying the philosophical jargon are riddled with such biblical-theological fallacies as demonstrated above, Plantinga's version of [Reformed epistemology] will be considered by many to be no more than fundamentalism on stilts.

William Lane Craig's Faith-Based Philosophical Apologetics

William Lane Craig gets in line behind Plantinga and defends what he says. On his website Reasonable Faith he answers readers' questions. Question #237 was whether Plantinga's Reformed epistemology is question begging.[17] What you will see when you read Craig's answer, ladies and gentlemen, is something to behold. Get out your extra dollar and step right up to see this strange oddity. Christians repeatedly are forced into arguing that their faith claims are possible and demand that we show their claims are nearly impossible before they will consider them to be improbable, which is an utterly unreasonable epistemological standard. Here we see it in plain sight.

Craig thinks Alvin Plantinga's argument is significant, in that "Christian belief can be shown to be unjustified, irrational, or unwarranted only if it is shown that Christian beliefs are false." Craig says:

> On behalf of his model Plantinga claims, not that it [Christianity] is true, but that:
>
> (i) it is epistemically possible, that is to say, for all we know, it may be true;
>
> (ii) if Christianity is true, there are no philosophical objections to the model;
>
> (iii) if Christianity is true, then something like the model is very likely to be true.
>
> None of this begs the question, I hope you can see. For the key claims are conditional. Neither of them assumes that Christianity actually is true.

Wow, such a conclusion just takes our breath away, doesn't it, even if we grant it. Guess what folks, Christianity is possibly true, and if so then something like Plantinga's model is very likely to be the case! Sheesh. It takes Plantinga three massive books to make that point. That's what's on display for your viewing pleasure folks. Plantinga's argument could equally be used by a Muslim, Mormon, Moonie, Marcionist, Mithraist, Mandaeist, Manichaeist, Mazdakist, Mohist, Macumbaist, Masaist, Mayanist, Meher Babaist, and so forth. Which means folks that, to use another conditional statement, even if Plantinga's argument succeeds it says nothing at all about whether Christianity is true. Which is the same point Richard Swinburne made against Plantinga. The issue is whether it's probable that Christianity is true. Mere possibility does not count.[18] If it did, then all other religions could claim the same thing with their own sect-specific version of Reformed epistemology, by claiming their religion is not unjustified, irrational, or unwarranted until it is shown to be false. As to others claiming the same thing goes, Craig simply denies others have it, saying, "Of course, the Muslim can say the same thing, and so we have a standoff. But . . . he does not in fact have a genuine witness of the Holy

Spirit to the truth of Islam . . . his experience was either non-veridical or misinterpreted." Nah nah na boo boo, he says, I have one and you don't, so take that. And Craig thinks this response is not question-begging? What does he think it means to beg the question? We can only shake our heads. In his signature book, *Reasonable Faith*, Craig wrote on this topic. We find him saying things like, "We know Christianity to be true by the self-authenticating witness of God's Holy Spirit." What does he mean by this? He says, "I mean that the witness, or testimony, of the Holy Spirit is its own proof; it is unmistakable; it does not need other proofs to back it up; it is self-evident and attests to its own truth." And that, "the testimony of the Holy Spirit trumps all other evidence."[19]

Craig claims he *knows* Christianity is true irrespective of all the arguments and evidence to the contrary. He's saying that the inner witness of the Holy Spirit gives him all the evidence anyone needs to believe, even if he cannot show this evidence leads to God, even if he cannot sufficiently defend the whole concept of the inner witness of the Holy Spirit. Craig doesn't ignore other evidence but claims it is "secondary." The primary evidence is his inner witness of the Holy Spirit. When it comes to this other evidence, believers do not need it to believe, period. Christians do not need supporting evidence to believe, not him . . . not anyone. That's his position.

When seeking to *show* his faith is true over others, Craig offers arguments of course. But as I've argued elsewhere he fails to propose any objective method at all to get at the truth.[20] Craig needs to tell us all what method he proposes to establish the probability of his particular brand of Christianity. If believers all can say the same thing as he does, then how does he propose to solve the problem of religious diversity? Religious faith produces more and more diverse and even mutually exclusive religions with no method to settle differences among them. By contrast I've proposed a consistent, single standard for testing all religious faith claims, as outlined in my book, *The Outsider Test for Faith*. What alternative does he propose? He and Plantinga argue against other faiths by showing there are *de facto* defeaters to them, in that they show other religions are false. These defeaters could be based in philosophical argumentation, internal and external inconsistencies, and/or the lack of sufficient evidence. What neither he nor Plantinga realize, though, is that when arguing for these defeaters they do so with the reasonable assumption these other religions have the burden of proof. However, when it comes to testing their own faith they reject shouldering the same burden of proof with a sleight of hand Houdini would be proud of, based in this so-called private subjective inner witness of the spirit. So this whole enterprise keeps them from being honest about their own faith and allows them to disingenuously adopt a big fat double standard.

It doesn't matter how you dress it up philosophically. A delusion is a delusion is a delusion. I'm arguing Craig is deluded to claim such a thing. Listen up, God spoke privately to Moses and privately to Paul, and likewise to Joseph Smith, and to Muhammad, and to many Pentecostals, and to David Koresh, and to many of the prophets we read about in the Old Testament. Why does God always speak to people privately? Why do most people claim to know God in a private way? A private subjective experience of a god or religion has no more evidence for it than none at all. Given that most people are delusional when they make such claims it's extremely probable Craig is too. The ONLY reason evangelicals buy into this is because they need to believe. They would never entertain Craig's faith if they were a Mormon, or Muslim, or Catholic, or Jew.[21]

For more on this I've placed Robert M. Price's debate rebuttal against William Lane Craig in the Appendix, with his permission.

Paul Moser's Faith-Based Philosophical Apologetics

Paul Moser is an expert in epistemology by all accounts. So he was chosen to write a fresh chapter in one of the most comprehensive philosophy of religion textbooks today, *The Routledge Companion to Philosophy of Religion* (2nd ed., 2013). Edited by evangelicals Chad Meister and Paul Copan, it contains over eight hundred pages! Professor Meister personally gave me a copy for which I am thankful.

In Part 1 of this textbook, there are seven contributed essays, with one each on Hinduism, Buddhism, African religions, Chinese religions, Judaism, Christianity, and Islam. If instructors are to teach the philosophy of religion at all, then the table of contents for Part 1 shows us how to do it right. It privileges no religion over the others. It borders on what we might find in anthropology of religion classes or comparative religion classes, which I will argue is the best way to look at religions. So I turned the pages and began reading and learning of the various issues and divergent opinions within each of these religious traditions. All of them stressed the wide diversity of thought within these faith traditions.

All but one, as I found out when I read Paul Moser's essay on Christianity. You may be stunned with what I'm about to write. Even I was very surprised at what I found from this supposed expert in epistemology. Moser did not play well with the others in Part 1. He would not do what the others did. We don't have a clue from reading his chapter that there are any divisions within the Good Ship Christendom. In fact, about 85–90 percent of his chapter is something an intelligent and educated Bible thumper could have written, since Moser merely refers to the Bible without also saying there are Christians who disagree with his interpretations. We know nothing of his particular branch of Christianity out of all the other sects either, and he never locates his faith on the Christian spectrum, running from fundamentalist to moderate to liberal to radical to secular Christianity. We just don't know. If we were ignorant it would seem all Christians believe what he's writing. Here is a very brief sample:

> We need to look for the right kind of evidence of God as supplied by God himself. So, we must set aside our misleading preconceptions of such evidence.
>
> The evidence of the good news is supplied and ratified by God's Holy Spirit, whom Paul identifies the Spirit of Christ (Rom. 8:9–11). In John's Gospel, Jesus identifies the cognitive and moral role of God's Spirit [Moser quotes John 16:8, 13–14]. God's Spirit has the cognitive role of making things known regarding Jesus. Jesus is God's unique revealer (Matt. 11:25–7). He calls us (a) to receive God's Spirit of redemption through trust (that is, faith) in God and (b) thereby to live as God's dependent children. This theme emerges at various places in the New Testament, including 1 Cor. 2:11–12 and Rom. 8:14–16; cf. Matt. 16:16–17. It has important, widely neglected cognitive implications.
>
> God's Spirit seeks to "lead" people to Jesus and his Father as their Lord and their God. This experience of "being led" is cognitively significant. It includes the authoritive call to relinquish our selfish willfulness for God's unselfish will exemplified in Jesus . . . [Blah Blah Blah].[22]

Moser continues his sermon by preaching that the "evidence from the presence of God's Holy Spirit" does not depend on "an argument for God's reality." "God can have his Spirit call people to turn to himself without his providing them with an argument for God's existence." "God provides his own means for humans to know him: the good news of Jesus coupled with the ratifying testimony of God's own Spirit." Amen brother, amen, the pew sitters must respond. After all, he quoted the Bible!

Forget for the moment that the other religious traditions represented in Part 1 would all scoff at what he says. By his lights they would be skeptics. In fact, every believer who does not accept his particular sect or the exact point on the spectrum he is at would be skeptics, for the evidence of the Spirit should be evidence on behalf of something, some kind of specific faith that has content to it. Surely Moser wouldn't want to say the Spirit provides evidence for what a different kind of Christian believes, say, one who is a racist, sexist, child-beating, young earth creationist, King James inerrant Bible thumping right-wing Republican who claims his politics are God's politics. If the Spirit provides evidence of something then what exactly is the Spirit providing evidence on behalf of? What about evangelicals in Africa who burn accused witches and beat homosexuals? Would the Spirit confirm their beliefs in this manner? Why can't they accept what Moser defends and say the Spirit provides evidence for what they believe? Is Moser's God happy with them for committing such acts? If not, is Moser's God happy with him for not committing such acts?

Even though Moser is writing a chapter in a textbook that is philosophical in nature, purporting to rationally discuss his religious faith, he says his faith is not philosophical. His strategy reveals a deep crisis about Christian apologetics from which I don't think apologists can escape. If there was sufficient evidence for Christianity then Moser would not have to argue this way. The very fact that apologists like Moser are forced into arguing in this fashion is a good reason, all by itself, to walk away from this delusion.

Moser's essay, if true, undermines the very philosophy of religion textbook for which he's writing. He's doing theology not philosophy, since philosophy is by its very nature an abstract discipline. He's writing as a religionist, even a preacher, who doesn't care that the other authors in Part 1 of the book would flatly disagree with him. He's claiming to have private subjective evidence that no one else but a certain sect of Christians on a certain point on the Christian spectrum have, one that others are willfully ignorant about. The apologists in other religious traditions represented in Part 1 could stoop that low too, and say the same thing Moser does. To their credit they don't do so, which should say something important about their intellectual honesty relative to his intellectual honesty.

So I put it to you. If Moser is correct the philosophy of religion should end. Keep in mind Meister and Copan chose Moser out of the many other Christian pseudo-intellectuals to write that chapter. So they think he best represents Christianity. And they also approved what he wrote and placed it in their textbook. Thus Moser's chapter all by itself shows this anthology is not an objective one purporting to look objectively at arguments. It isn't what it appears to be. It is a veiled Christian apologist's book to be used in philosophy of religion classes. It is a prime example of what highly accomplished philosopher of religion Dr. Nick Trakakis alluded to when he announced he was leaving Christianity for an unspecified religious faith. He said, "I have come to regard religious commitment as incompatible with philosophy."[23]

There is no use discussing philosophical questions with Christians like Moser. I've tried. I have been told by Moser I know little about epistemology, which he seems to be a pseudo-expert in. Okay, got it. He knows more than I do on how to justify ridiculous beliefs. In my view he's an expert in obfuscation. The goal of all sophisticated theology/philosophy of religion is to obfuscate the fact it's being done to defend the indefensible. Moser, like many others, is throwing up as much smoke as he can to keep us from seeing what he's really up to.

It's quite the strange phenomenon that Christians all make the same arguments for the truth of their faith, yet have different individual beliefs, as Matt Dillahunty noted in a lecture of his I once watched online. If anything this observation falsifies Moser's (and Plantinga's and Craig's) arguments and their supposed private subjective experiences. Let me explain with regard to just one doctrine, the virgin birth of Jesus.

Evangelicals like Plantinga and Craig, who argue for the same things with regard to epistemology that Moser does, believe a virgin gave birth to the second person of a Trinitarian Godhead in an ancient superstitious world before investigative journalists and cell phones, and before the rise of the modern science of genetics. Does it change anything to inform them other ancient people were also believed to have been *sired* by gods (like Plato, Alexander the Great, Hercules, Pythagoras, Augustus Caesar, Apollonius of Tyana, and others).[24] No, of course not. That information is irrelevant to their claims of a private subjective experience. You see, it says

God provides such experiences in that there evangelical Bible, and lo and behold—surprise!—they believe it despite reason.[25]

Without showing any signs of embarrassment at all, Plantinga and Craig believe this incarnate God-baby (yes, baby!) birthed by a virgin was 100 percent divine and 100 percent human with every essential divine characteristic included without excluding any essential human characteristic. Does that logical inconsistency cause them to doubt their private subjective experiences? No, of course not!

Does it change anything to inform them Paul Moser disagrees with them? He does. The Catholic Moser does not believe in the virgin birth of Jesus. Following Emil Brunner, he told me he doesn't think the apostle Paul believed in it so he doesn't either. There are plenty of Christian clergy who agree with Moser. Journalist Bob Unruh reports:

> According to a 1998 poll of 7,441 Protestant clergy in the U.S., the following ministers said they didn't believe in the virgin birth:
>
> American Lutherans, 19 percent
> American Baptists, 34 percent
> Episcopalians, 44 percent
> Presbyterians, 49 percent
> Methodists, 60 percent

Unruh also reports that another poll surveying 103 Roman Catholic priests, Anglican priests, and Protestant ministers in the United Kingdom "found 25 percent didn't believe in the virgin birth," while a "2004 survey of ministers in the Church of Scotland found 37 percent don't accept the virgin account.[26]

Does this poll data cause Plantinga and Craig to doubt? No, of course not. That others disagree is irrelevant to their claims of having a private subjective experience of a "full-blooded gospel," they would assert. You see, it says God provides veridical experiences in that there evangelical Bible. But think for just a second, think! Many of the clergy who disagree on the virgin birth question would agree they too have private subjective religious veridical experiences showing what they believe is true! So there are Christians like Moser and the clergy represented in the poll data who adopt Plantinga/Craig/Moser epistemological mumbo-jumbo of a self-authenticating inner witness of a spirit and/or full warrant in the proper basicality of their own full-blooded faith, who would disagree with the content of the one true faith. Something must give. Either they are all wrong to take seriously any wish-fulfilling inner private subjective experience of a purported god, or a god is not the originator of these private subjective experiences and doesn't give a damn what Christians believe. What seems more likely? That's the choice. I'm sure as sure can be Plantinga/Craig/ Moser will fail to answer correctly.

Just consider what Moser would say to Plantinga and Craig to convince them he's correct on the virgin birth issue. How would he go about it? If he did as we read in his aforementioned chapter, he would merely assert he experienced the evidence for his faith by virtue of a private subjective experience, which in turn validated his faith, and with it the content of his faith, which is self-authenticating (for surely to have a faith is to believe something). That then would end the discussion. What if Plantinga and Craig responded to Moser in the same way for the same reasons? Then they would be at an impasse at the O.K. Corral. I know they would respond to me in unison that this isn't how Christians discuss and arrive at theology. But my question is why not? Their faith is either self-authenticating by nook, crook, or cranny, or not? Their actual practice betrays they don't actually believe it is. More than this, since they all agree they can know the truth through private subjective experiences yet hold to different doctrines of faith, this is a sure sign they don't have real veridical experiences sent from heaven above. They are simply making shit up to believe and to justify why they believe. They are doing nothing more than listening to the voices in their heads playing tricks on them. The believing brain desires to believe so badly it will self-deceive its very own host for the sake of believing.[27] The choice is between self-authenticating experiences or self-deceiving ones. We already know with the highest degree of assurance the believing brain will deceive its host, so the rational choice is a no-brainer.[28]

The upshot of this is that no amount of expertise in epistemology can lead Moser or Plantinga or Craig to believe what they do based on subjective private experiences. A private subjective experience is only evidence of a private subjective experience. How does being an expert in epistemology help when it comes to examining other Christian beliefs, like a talking snake and donkey, or an axe head that floated, or a worldwide flood, or the parting of the Red Sea, or a man born blind who was healed, or Jesus ascending into the sky? Moser's epistemology does not help anyone examine these questions, especially because Christians themselves disagree. He's using his expertise in epistemology as a Klingon cloaking device to hide the fact he's escaping his true epistemic responsibilities, which includes examining the historical evidence on its own merits. Who knows but if Moser did this and changed his mind then the Holy Spirit would change his mind too, and send him different religious experiences!

Pseudo-intellectuals like Moser have lost touch with reality. But it's worse than that. Moser has lost touch with reality *and he's proud of it!* I recently heard a contemporary Christian song by Mercy Me titled "Crazy" in which a believer proudly proclaims he's "losing touch with reality" for choosing God's call over worldly wisdom. "Call me crazy" we hear over and over. I'm sure Moser would sing it, and embrace it, seriously!

Okay, I'll call Moser and Plantinga and Craig crazy then. Let them embrace it as a badge of honor if their delusional minds can be that twisted. They have lost touch with reality. People who believe as they do should not be at the adult table. They should stay at the children's table. They must grow up before we should listen to them. They are disqualified from teaching us. People like them should not be teaching in any secular university. They are all faith peddlers. Faith is an unreliable way to gain knowledge.

Let this be a litmus test for anyone who wants to teach the philosophy of religion. Ask them what they think of Plantinga, Craig, and Moser, and if they blindly embrace the same theological ideas they peddle, then do not hire them. Anyone who teaches and argues like this should not be teaching our youth, just as creationists should not be teaching in our universities. If they are in your department get them fired. I'm serious. They are crazy people who should not be teaching our students. Unfortunately (or fortunately) for the rest of us, it's not obvious to see them as crazy since they function in life quite well I suppose. But they have abandoned reasonable ways of knowing despite their utterly unreasonable and unfounded clucking.

Notes

1. Stephen Law, *Believing Bullshit: How Not to Get Sucked into an Intellectual Black Hole* (Amherst, NY: Prometheus Books, 2011), p. 75.

2. William Lane Craig, *Apologetics: An Introduction* (Chicago: Moody Press, 1984), p. 21. This quote is left out of the third edition of the book, titled *Reasonable Faith: Christian Truth and Apologetics* (Wheaton, IL: Crossway Books, 2008).

3. John W. Loftus, *How to Defend the Christian Faith: Advice from an Atheist* (Durham, NC: Pitchstone Publishing, 2015), pp. 86–87.

4. Alvin Plantinga, *Warranted Christian Belief* (New York: Oxford University Press, 2000), p. 200.

5. Ibid., pp. 245, 262.

6. Plantinga, *Warranted Christian Belief*, p. 262.

7. Ibid., pp. 245.

8. Plantinga, *Warranted Christian Belief*, p. 201.

9. "Two Dozen (or so) Theistic Arguments: Lecture Notes by Alvin Plantinga," https://www.calvin.edu/academic/philosophy/virtual_library/articles/plantinga_alvin/two_dozen_or_so_theistic_arguments.pdf.

10. Plantinga, *Warranted Christian Belief*, p. 499.

11. Richard Swinburne, *Faith and Reason*, 2nd ed. (Oxford: Oxford University Press, 2005), pp. 74–75.

12. Alvin Plantinga, *Warranted Christian Belief*, chapter 7, pp. 199–240.

13. See for instance Jerry L. Walls and Joseph R. Dongell, *Why I Am Not a Calvinist* (Downers Grove, IL: IVP Books, 2004), and Robert A. Peterson and Michael D. Williams, *Why I Am Not an Arminian* (Downers Grove, IL: IVP Books, 2004).

14. Plantinga, *Warranted Christian Belief*, p. 201.

15. Plantinga, *Warranted Christian Belief*, p. 499.

16. Jaco Gericke, "Fundamentalism on Stilts," http://www.up.ac.za/dspace/bitstream/2263/12356/1/Gericke_Fundamentalism%282009%29.pdf. See also his chapter "Can God Exist If Yahweh Doesn't?" in *The End of Christianity*, ed. John W. Loftus (Amherst, NY: Prometheus Books, 2011), pp. 131–154. For another great response see Graham Oppy's essay "Natural Theology," in *Alvin Plantinga*, ed. Deane-Peter Baker (Cambridge, Cambridge University Press, 2007).

17. Q & A #237, "Is Appeal to the Witness of the Holy Spirit Question-Begging?" http://www.reasonablefaith.org/is-appeal-to-the-witness-of-the-holy-spirit-question-begging. See also Q & A #68, "The Witness of the Holy Spirit," http://www.reasonablefaith.org/the-witness-of-the-holy-spirit.

18.   I wrote a whole chapter on this titled "You Must Punt to Possibilities" in my book *How to Defend the Christian Faith*, pp. 137–148.

19.   William Lane Craig, *Reasonable Faith: Christian Truth and Apologetics*, 3rd ed. (Wheaton Books: Crossway Books, 2008), pp. 43–50.

20.   See chapter 5 in *How to Defend the Christian Faith*, pp. 84–103.

21.   On this whole topic I've written a great deal. See "Private Subjective Experience Is No Evidence at All: Against William Lane Craig's Inner Witness of the Spirit," Debunking Christianity, February 14, 2012, http://debunkingchristianity.blogspot.com/2012/02/private-subjective-evidence-is-no.html.

22.   Chad Meister and Paul Copan, eds., *The Routledge Companion to Philosophy of Religion*, 2nd ed. (New York: Routledge, 2013), pp. 73–74.

23.   N. N. Trakakis, "Why I Am Not Orthodox," ABC Religion & Ethics (Australia), December 7, 2015, http://www.abc.net.au/religion/articles/2015/12/07/4367489.htm.

24.   The best book on this is by Jesus Seminar fellow Robert J. Miller, *Born Divine: The Births of Jesus & Other Sons of God* (Santa Rosa, CA: Polebridge Press, 2003).

25.   See Miller, *Born Divine*.

26.   Bob Unrah, "'Fairy Tale': Many Pastors Don't Believe Jesus Born of Virgin," WND.com, December 23, 2015, http://www.wnd.com/2015/12/christian-preacher-nativity-story-just-fairy-tale/#xE65b9VQDaZy1hAo.99.

27.   Michael Shermer, *The Believing Brain: From Ghosts and Gods to Politics and Conspiracies—How We Construct Beliefs and Reinforce Them as Truths* (New York: Times Books, 2011).

28.   I made this case in my book *How to Defend the Christian Faith: Advice from an Atheist*, chapter 3, "Become an Honest Life-Long Seeker of the Truth," pp. 52–67.

4

CASE STUDIES IN ATHEISTIC PHILOSOPHY OF RELIGION

On September 1, 2010, Keith Parsons, an atheist and professor of philosophy at University of Houston, Clear-Lake, announced he was no longer going to teach in the area of the philosophy of religion (PoR). He wrote:

> Over the past ten years I have published, in one venue or another, about twenty things on the philosophy of religion. I have a book on the subject, *God and Burden of Proof*, and another criticizing Christian apologetics, *Why I am not a Christian*. During my academic career I have debated William Lane Craig twice and creationists twice. I have written one master's thesis and one doctoral dissertation in the philosophy of religion, and I have taught courses on the subject numerous times. But no more. I've had it.
>
> I now regard "the case for theism" as a fraud and I can no longer take it seriously enough to present it to a class as a respectable philosophical position—no more than I could present intelligent design as a legitimate biological theory. BTW, in saying that I now consider the case for theism to be a fraud, I do not mean to charge that the people making that case are frauds who aim to fool us with claims they know to be empty. No, theistic

philosophers and apologists are almost painfully earnest and honest; I don't think there is a Bernie Madoff in the bunch. I just cannot take their arguments seriously any more, and if you cannot take something seriously, you should not try to devote serious academic attention to it. I've turned the philosophy of religion courses over to a colleague.[1]

This was big news and his announcement went viral. I even began my chapter in *The End of Christianity* with what he said. Finally an atheist with balls did the only respectable thing to be done with PoR. End it decisively, by example. Not going to play that pretend game no more! Good on him, I thought.

Peter Boghossian Enters the House

A couple of years later Peter Boghossian gained the attention he deserves. After having heard Boghossian's arguments against faith-based reasoning in all of its forms, I challenged Parsons to reconsider. You see, Boghossian had written an article titled "Should We Challenge Student Beliefs?"[2] In it he challenged the so-called *received model* of teaching. The received model, the one I used in teaching philosophy, is that as instructors the main goal is to help students learn to think critically. The class could be on ethics or philosophy or the philosophy of religion, but for the most part these classes are little more than extensions of an introduction to critical thinking class. The subject matter is important, since there is specific factual content to teach the students for each class, like Aristotle's view on ethics for an ethics class, or Plato's theory of forms for an introduction to philosophy class, and Anselm's ontological argument for a philosophy of religion class. But the main goal is the same, to teach students to think critically, no matter what the subject matter is before them. In general, the philosophy instructor is not to "spoon feed" students the "answers" but let them hash it out themselves. If the class leans in one direction the instructor leans in the other, and vice versa, just to make the students think critically. The goal of this model of teaching is to let students come to their own conclusions for the most part. It's not that the professor's conclusions don't come through at times. It's just that the professor is not to argue for them much at all.

Boghossian argued that professors should have a primary goal of changing students' beliefs if those beliefs are false, and to help students replace those beliefs with true ones:

I believe our role as educators should be to teach students not just factual data, but the importance of critically examining beliefs by exposing them to facts, and then revising cherished notions when confronted with reliable but discomforting evidence. . . . The primary goal of every academic should be to bring students' beliefs into lawful alignment with reality.

Boghossian challenged the received model, and I endorse his words. I think atheist philosophers should teach philosophy in this way, challenging theistic beliefs to a much greater extent whenever possible without completely alienating their students (which can still be a difficult balancing act depending on the students). I mean, come on, the facts are in: there is no positive empirical evidence for the existence of God, much less any so-called revealed religion. There is overwhelming disconfirming evidence for God's existence, and all of the philosophical arguments to the existence of God have huge holes in them. Thus, philosophers of religion who argue to God's existence must utilize a number of informal fallacies to do so. If they want to teach students to think critically then they must show students what believers must do in arguing their case.

In his book *A Manual for Creating Atheists*, Boghossian calls teachers to action: "We need to train educators not just to teach students how to think critically, but also how to nudge attitudes about faith on their downward spiral."[3] Teaching students to be critical thinkers is very important but teaching them to have a skeptical disposition is more important. "Anyone can develop a critical thinking skill set," he says, even people who are pretending to know things they don't know.[4] Case in point, consider Alvin Plantinga or William Lane Craig, who are brilliant at defending the indefensible. I taught critical thinking classes as a believer so teaching critical thinking is not enough. Instructors must teach them how to think skeptically.

Educators have given faith-based claims preferential treatment, Boghossian argues. "It is taken for granted that faith-based claims are invulnerable to criticism and immune from further questioning" in the so-called "soft sciences" like sociology, philosophy, anthropology, etc. "This intellectual rigor mortis is not allowed to occur across all disciplines." In the hard sciences like mathematics, chemistry, and biology, "challenging claims and questioning reasoning processes are 'intrinsic to what it means to teach students to reason effectively.'" So Boghossian says, "This needs to end."[5] Educators in all disciplines of learning should grant faith-based conclusions "no countenance. Do not take faith claims seriously. Let the utterer know that faith is not an acceptable basis from which to draw a conclusion that can be relied upon."[6]

If educators began doing this across the board it could revolutionize our institutions of higher learning. I welcome this revolution in the philosophical discipline, especially the philosophy of religion. This is very much needed. Let's call on professors to accept this challenge, which risks offending students, parents, and administrators. We desperately need them to do so across the board in every discipline of learning if we want to change the religious landscape. Boghossian argues that if we're just too afraid to offend our students or others then "we silence ourselves."[7]

With only the received model at his disposal it was frustrating for Parsons to give equal time to theistic arguments in his philosophy of religion classes. I understand that, definitely. I had hoped Parsons would change his mind and teach these classes again. I think by adopting Boghossian's teaching model it would keep more atheist PoR instructors teaching and doing more good for their students. There was another live option for Parsons, which he had not considered before. If Parsons had accepted it he would never have quit teaching PoR classes, and he would've been able to have a positive impact on those students and thus the world. The reason I'm sure he didn't consider this is because of how he responded to my challenge to continue teaching PoR classes.

Boghossian 1, Parsons 0

Parsons' initial response starts out by misunderstanding what he read, I'm sorry to report. When something is misunderstood it can be because the idea is completely foreign to a person. He wrote of the received model of education:

> Boghossian challenges what John calls the "received" view of pedagogy. The received view can be summed up by the slogan that the instructor's job is to teach students how to think, not what to think. The motivation behind the received view is the insight that education is something very different from indoctrination. Indoctrination is the inculcation

of an ideology or worldview, with the aim of insulating dogmas from doubt and creeds from questioning. Indoctrination aims at making True Believers. Totalitarian states and the Christian Church have been the major practitioners of indoctrination. ("Give us a boy of seven," the Jesuits used to say, "and he will be ours for life.") Education, on the other hand, aims to create Free Inquirers rather than True Believers. Hence, the received view has rightly emphasized the nurturing of students' critical thinking abilities and not the imposition of doctrine.[8]

Continuing, Parsons wrote:

Should we go further and teach, as John reports of Boghossian, that ". . . faith is a cognitive malaise and should be given no credence in the classroom"? At what point is a professor no longer presenting facts but exploiting his position to browbeat students from a bully pulpit? I really do not think that this is a very hard question. Consider two assertions:

1) Evolution occurred.

2) Faith is a malaise.

(1) is an established scientific fact. (2) is Professor Boghossian's opinion. It may be an informed opinion, but it is an opinion. For the sake of argument, let's suppose that (2) is true in whatever sense Prof. Boghossian intends. Still, if Prof. Boghossian presents (2) to his classes as an established fact on par with (1), then he is doing a disservice to reason. That one regards an assertion as true, or even its actual truth, is insufficient justification for presenting it to a class as established fact.

In the comments section to Parsons' response, Peter Boghossian commented as follows:

This article, however, makes one egregious error: It confuses metaphysics with epistemology—conclusions with processes of reasoning. What matters are the processes one uses, because this makes it more likely that one will come to conclusions upon which one can rely. Faith is an unreliable process. Faith will decrease the likelihood that one will align one's beliefs with reality.

Parsons in turn responded:

Thanks for the clarification. I certainly agree that the exercise of faith does not constitute nor is it an essential part of a reliable belief-forming process. Still, I would be uncomfortable presenting that conviction to a class as an established fact on par with the best supported scientific theories. The reason is that some thinkers of note have taken the opposite view. Anselm, for instance, said *credo ut intelligam*, "I believe in order to understand" . . . for Anselm, faith is an essential aspect of a reliable belief forming process in which subjection of the will to revelation opens the mind to truth imparted by grace.

Now I certainly disagree with Anselm, but I do not consider his view to be fatuous or obviously wrong or merely contrary to established facts. In other words, I think that one could espouse Anselm's view of faith without committing epistemic sins of the order of those committed by proponents of YEC. Hence, I would not present the negation of Anselm's claims as an established fact, i.e. on par with the best science.

Of course, if one interprets "faith" to mean only "wishful thinking" then certainly it is an unreliable belief-forming process. However, I think we need to be clear that in attacking "faith" we are attacking it only in this rather trivialized sense, and not in a more sophisticated or nuanced sense.

Boghossian commented further:

Two points. First, you wrote: "Still, I would be uncomfortable presenting that conviction to a class as an established fact on par with the best supported scientific theories."

Let's see if we can rephrase this without bringing metaphysics into the conversation. Let's substitute "scientific method" for "best supported scientific theories". The sentence becomes, "Still, I would be uncomfortable presenting that conviction to a class as an established fact on par with the scientific method."

Now we're talking about epistemology and processes of reasoning. It's not about conclusions (scientific theories, evolution) it's about processes (scientific method, flipping coins, faith, goat sacrifice, etc.). Are you comfortable definitively asserting to your students that flipping coins is not a reliable process to ascertain what type of material one should use in bridge construction? If a surgeon wants to make an incision, would you be comfortable if she decided how deep to cut based upon the position of the stars that morning?

Certain processes are inherently unreliable. If students use these processes it is the professor's duty to say so—unapologetically. Why should our saying so suddenly change if the unreliable process is faith, as opposed to goat sacrifice?

Second, the histories of philosophy and theology are replete with people trying to define faith. Anselm's definition is floral mumbo-jumbo.

There's simply no way around these facts: Faith claims are knowledge claims; different faith traditions make contradictory knowledge claims; these cannot all be true (but they can all be false). Definitions like Anselm's obscure these facts.

One can talk about "a more sophisticated or nuanced sense" of the word "faith," but this does not change the fact that faith claims are knowledge claims. It also does not change the fact that certain processes of reasoning are unreliable. Faith is not a reliable process of reasoning. If the professor does not point this out, he's not doing his job.

Parsons then conceded to Boghossian:

When the claims are epistemological rather than scientific, which ones are so beyond a reasonable doubt? Shamelessly oversimplifying, consider these two:

1) Scientific method is a reliable belief-forming process.

2) Faith is not a reliable belief-forming process.

Now, I certainly agree that scientific method constitutes (or encompasses) reliable belief-forming processes and that (pace postmodernists, social constructivists, epistemological relativists, etc.) there is no reasonable doubt that these cognitive processes are indeed reliable means to knowledge of objective, external, non-socially-constructed reality. I would have no hesitation at all about presenting (1) to a class as simply so . . .

What about (2)? Should I present it to a class with the same degree of aplomb? First, of course, I have to consider practical matters. I teach in Texas, and if an instructor is perceived as too truculently anti-religious, the students just clam up and you can practically see the mental doors slamming. In that case, your chances of effecting any sort of enlightenment are nil. Still, even Texas students (maybe especially Texas students!) need to have their assumptions challenged, so what do we do? I would assert (2) to a class but I would be very careful to say just what I meant by "faith." I would make it abundantly clear that what I was attacking was something like "faith" in the sense defined by Ambrose Bierce: "Belief without evidence in what is told by one who speaks without knowledge, of things without parallel." "Faith" is a vague term, and to attack it without proper and careful qualification would be perceived as an attack on religious belief per se and—at least in these here parts—would certainly be wholly counterproductive.

In his last comment Parsons admits he just could not teach Boghossian-style because the students wouldn't like it. Now I understand this, I do, but then this means Parsons doesn't offer a principled objection to what Boghossian argued. He merely offers a pragmatic objection. And while he does clarify the kind of faith he stands against, he fails to understand that faith is always about that which lacks sufficient evidence or even no evidence at all. I consider faith to be an unrecognized-as-yet cognitive bias that gives believers permission to pretend what they believe is true, even if there is no objective evidence at all, as we saw in chapter 3. Does Parsons actually think faith has any epistemic warrant at all, any virtue? Shouldn't we rather think exclusively in terms of the probabilities? If we think exclusively in terms of the probabilities there is no need for faith as an explanation or justification for knowledge.

The dividing line in this debate is between academics who think faith has epistemic warrant and those who don't. I don't. Boghossian doesn't. Neither do Hector Avalos, Jerry Coyne, James Lindsay, and a growing number of others. Why should faith be granted any privilege at all in our secular universities when no other discipline of learning can appeal to faith in God, gods, goddesses, or supernatural forces as explanations or justifications for knowledge claims? I don't think it should, especially in a secular university. So in the end, after seeing what the real challenge was, Parsons just refused to offend his students, their parents, and his administrators. As Boghossian has said though, if he's just too afraid to offend others, then "we silence ourselves. This needs to end."[9] Every academic must at least consider this challenge and do whatever can be done.

More about this story can be read in Appendix A ("My Interview with Keith Parsons on Philosophy of Religion"). In 2016 Parsons began teaching PoR classes again without any fanfare or public notice. So I asked him a few questions about it that he graciously answered. Since he knew I was writing this book he was not overly friendly. He still does not appear to adopt the Boghossian-style model of teaching.

Give Me That Old-Time Atheism

Evangelicals seem to love Keith Parsons. And he likes it. When it comes to writing something in Christian anthologies he's the go-to guy. That slap on the back must feel good. Now he's a good guy I'll admit. But even the obnoxious Catholic apologist Edward Feser likes him. Something's gotta be wrong! ;-) They agree in that they both want to return to that old-time religion, er, atheism. I understand why Feser wants to live in the past, but Parsons?[10] That makes no sense.

For my part I am not interested in merely having a discussion. I'm interested in changing minds. Karl Marx spoke for me when he quipped, "The philosophers have only interpreted the world in various ways; the point, however, is to change it." At issue are the differences between old atheism and so-called new atheism. Parsons prefers the old atheism as does Feser. My view is they want to live in the past. One must accept the changes and move on into the future. There is no going back. Christianity is dying. Why in the world would Parsons want to return to the good old days when Christianity had a huge monopoly in American academia, and where it was considered a respectable faith? There is at the present time a massive exodus from Christianity by young people. In April 2016 it was reported that over half the people in Scotland are nonreligious.[11] Not long afterward another study was released showing England and Wales were predominantly nonreligious.[12]

As this continues to happen in Westernized countries we no longer need to respect faith-based reasoning. Rather, we can tell the whole truth and nothing but the truth about it. Since Parsons stands against the new atheism I have suggested it might be because he has not moved on with the times, the newest poll data, the failed theistic arguments, and especially the accumulating assured results of science. I've suggested in a tongue-in-cheek way it was because he was old, old in his thinking that is.

What are the unique differences between old and new atheism? The old existed before September 11, 2001. Afterward the new arose, where intellectuals got serious about the irrationality of faith. The old took the arguments of believers seriously in order to convince them they are wrong. In doing so they stayed strictly within their own disciplines. The new represents intellectuals who are so convinced religious faith is wrong from within their own disciplines that they will venture outside their disciplines, disregarding the fact that people like Feser and Parsons will call them ignorant for doing so. They are reaching out to others. They are not attempting to persuade people like Feser, since delusional intellectuals like him cannot be reached. No wonder he doesn't like it. What gives with Parsons? The old was respectful toward belief. The new can and will ridicule religious faith. Faith deserves little or no respect because of the woeful lack of evidence and the harms of faith.

We have passed the point of no return. Now is the time to ridicule Christian faith and other faiths in our world, just as we ridicule the dead religions and gods of the past. That doesn't preclude reasonably dissecting the beliefs of Christians, which I do daily, but ridicule is now acceptable. Science has progressed past the tepid passions of the old atheism. Science is now destroying faith, as it provides atheism with a newfound passion and bite.

Once again, for whatever reason except that these thoughts are just too foreign for Parsons to consider, he misunderstood my suggestions. So his response is one I merely wish to note:

> I do think that ridicule is sometimes justified when directed at the truly ridiculous—e.g. the Ken Hams of the world. . . . But how do you treat people who offer you rational arguments and demonstrate that they are willing to listen to your arguments? Do you shove a pie in their faces? I guess Loftus thinks that my supposition is absurd since no theist is capable of rational argument. In his book, they are all foaming fanatics, defending a fantasy so pernicious and absurd as to preclude patience or even politeness. People like me, Graham Oppy, the late, great Michael Martin, Herman Philipse, J.L. Schellenberg, Eric Wielenberg, Adolf Grunbaum, Robin Le Poidevin, Colin Howson, and others are just wasting our time trying to engage in rational critique of theism. You might as well try citing *The Groundwork of the Metaphysics of Morals* to a misbehaving two-year-old.
>
> My worry is that Loftus and the "new atheists" may get their way. There will be no rational discourse, and only a shouting match. The trouble is that my bet is that the religious people will be able to shout a lot louder.[13]

In a subsequent post titled "Doing It Right the Old Way," Keith Parsons clarified his views:

Do you need a Ph.D. in philosophy to be a legitimate and respectable participant in the theism/atheism debate or the science/religion debate? Of course not. But you do need to know what you are talking about. Those, however accomplished in other fields, who leap into the debate philosophically uninformed inevitably commit freshman mistakes that expose them to the scorn of sophisticated opponents. . . . So, who has done it right? Have I set up too high a standard by requiring those who debate philosophical or religious issues to inform themselves? Can any one person be a scientist and also have the expertise and skill needed to debate religious or philosophical issues? Sure. T.H. Huxley did. Thomas Henry Huxley (1825–1895) was one of the leading scientists and educators of his day. Known as "Darwin's bulldog" for his aggressive defense of Darwinism, he was also a public intellectual who carried on disputes on topics in philosophy and religion with learned opponents—and beat them at their own game. In all of his controversies, whether with theologians or prime ministers, he displayed an exemplary depth of knowledge and sophistication of argument.[14]

Despite what Parsons is attempting to do, what's really on display is his philosophical elitism. Parsons is claiming elitist privilege and uses Huxley to defend it. Huxley knew the philosophy of his day as well as the science of his day. No one denies that both disciplines have become more complex than in Huxley's day, and consequently much harder to gain a good grasp of them both. Those kinds of intellectuals are so rare Parsons had to stretch back into the nineteenth century to find one. (Actually Massimo Pigliucci, professor of philosophy at CUNY–City College, earned PhDs in both philosophy and botany.) This means only a rare person or two has the qualifications to do both philosophy and science. Any scientist who criticizes theistic pseudo-philosophy must still know enough to do so, according to Parsons. Nonphilosophers need not apply. This is the domain of Parsons and other highly trained philosophers of religion. Nonexperts need to wait on the philosophical experts to criticize another expert in philosophy. There is a downside to his position. It also means Parsons cannot criticize Mormonism or Islam or Hinduism or Orthodox Judaism or Scientology or polytheism since he's not an expert in any of them. He cannot utter any criticism of their faith-based claims either.

However, in the same post Parsons said of Huxley:

Because of his success as a controversialist, Huxley was, of course, furiously abused by those whom he had bested, and was accused of being a hater of Christianity who went out of his way to attack the Bible. Huxley strenuously denied both charges, accusations which, I imagine, today's "new" atheists would enthusiastically embrace.

Wait just a minute! Is Parsons saying believers accused Huxley of hating Christianity even though he properly understood it enough to criticize it? I assure readers of this book I understand many of the different Christianities very well, and I am met with that same exact response. I have also been accused of being ignorant so many times that if each time I received a dollar I might be a well-off man. So I'm as sure as sure can be it doesn't matter if one earns the right to criticize religion. Believers will treat any critics of faith in the same fashion they treated Huxley, which is the same fashion they treat Richard Dawkins and many others today. It makes no difference and says nothing specifically about whether the criticisms are well-founded. The difference between Huxley and new atheists like Dawkins is that Dawkins doesn't have to care what theists say. He can "embrace" their responses as delusional and laugh them off. Huxley not so much. After all, Huxley needed to be respected by faith-heads in those days when doubt had it a lot tougher. By contrast, Dawkins refers to books written against him as fleas.

The Arrogance and Ignorance of Old-Time Atheists

Although I have respected Keith Parsons as a good philosopher of religion, it is with great displeasure to say I no longer do so. He's both arrogant and ignorant, or his views are anyway. First, Parsons is arrogant to think only sophisticated atheist philosophers can adequately respond to sophisticated Christian philosophers, such that any nonphilosopher who tries is ignorant and shouldn't respond at all.

What does Parsons say to philosophically unsophisticated atheists who cannot adequately respond to sophisticated Christian philosophers? Should they wait until a sophisticated atheist philosopher like Parsons himself finally gets around to writing a response to the latest philosophically sophisticated Christian paper? Why is it that Parsons places himself and his discipline at the top of the heap, such that no one else but atheist philosophers can respond to Christian philosophers? I think I know. It's arrogance on the part of Parsons. Maybe he thinks as a philosopher he should rule as a king too? There are reasons people don't believe that don't require sophisticated philosophical argumentation. And scientists like Richard Dawkins know more than enough to argue sophisticated Christian philosophers are wrong.

Second, I consider Parsons to be ignorant not to realize that the real ignorance is the ignorance of faith. Even an educated child of ten years old has a better grasp of biology, botany, chemistry, cosmology, geography, geology, math, paleontology, physics, and morality than the omniscient God of the Bible whom Christians say inspired the Bible. The whole reason sophisticated Christian argumentation exists in the first place is because it takes sophistication to make the Christian faith palatable. The more the sophistication then the more the obfuscation, since the Christian faith can only be defended by confusing people. Defenses of Christianity are nothing but special pleading hiding underneath several layers of obfuscation with a sophistication to make it appear otherwise. It's nothing less than special pleading all the way down, and it doesn't take sophistication to see this or to call it out. Even a child can recognize what it is. Why can't Parsons?

Eric MacDonald, a former Anglican priest turned atheist, is another case.[15] He defended the views of Parsons, saying:

> The problem is precisely that the New Atheists think it appropriate to dismiss theology and philosophy of religion without understanding the first thing about it. Some New Atheists say, "I know enough about it. I was brought up as a Catholic or an Anglican or . . ." But that's not qualification enough. Arguing from this point of view, where you really do not know what your opponent is arguing, because you have made no attempt to find out, is a simple informal fallacy known as special pleading. And the New Atheism is full of it. That's where Keith Parsons is way ahead of the New Atheists. Be an unbeliever by all means. But don't say that you know that there is no God or that theology is all make believe until you have really tried to understand what theologians are saying. And when you have done so, you will, I think, qualify your dismissal.[16]

I think MacDonald's criticism of the new atheism fails to understand the very phenomenon being criticized. Let's just repurpose MacDonald's quote: "The problem is precisely that the New Atheists think it appropriate to dismiss Scientology, or Mormonism, or militant Islam, or Hindu theology, or Haitian Catholic voodoo without understanding the first thing about it . . ." Need I go on? If anyone is special pleading it is MacDonald, for it didn't enter his mind to consider the many other religious faiths out there he easily dismisses without knowing that much about them.

Reasonable people don't have to know a lot about religious faiths to reject them. We can dismiss these and other faiths precisely because they are faiths. The evidence is not there and even runs contrary to them. The moralities of these faiths also count against them. Do we need to know something about them to dismiss them? Sure, we should know something about them. In fact, to reject one of them we should at least hear about it. But even a rudimentary level of knowledge is enough for that, since faith is the problem. As outsiders we don't need to look into the many varieties of faith to know that the results of faith are not likely to be true. We can do this simply by generalizing from the many mutually inconsistent false faiths to the probability that any given particular faith is false, even before getting an in-depth knowledge about it.

In Defense of the New Atheists

My specialties are theology, philosophy of religion, and especially apologetics. I am an expert on these subjects even though it's very hard to have a good grasp of them all. Now it's one thing for theologically unsophisticated intellectuals like Dawkins, Harris, Hitchens, and Stenger to argue against religion. It's quite another thing for a theologically sophisticated intellectual like myself to defend them by saying they are within their epistemic rights to denounce religion from their perspectives. And I do. I can admit they lack the sophistication to understand and respond point for point to sophisticated theology. But it doesn't matter. The reason is because all sophisticated theology is based in faith: faith in the Bible—or Koran or Bhagavad Gita—as the word of God, and/or faith in the Nicene creed (or other creeds), and/or faith in a church, synagogue, or temple. No amount of sophistication changes this.

The reason there is sophisticated theology in the first place is because Christians are responding to their critics by reinventing their faith every decade. We atheists are trying to hit a moving target, and each time we hit it, it morphs into something different, as I have previously argued.[17]

I've read some unsophisticated responses to sophisticated theology. These responses lacked a particular distinction, or a precise definition of a term, or they failed to take into consideration a recent study that says X, Y, or Z. But I have found that by using the principle of charity their arguments are still good ones despite this lack. Take for example the main argument Richard Dawkins used in *The God Delusion* to demonstrate that there is almost certainly no God. He called it the *Ultimate Boeing 747 gambit.* If "properly deployed," he claims, it "comes close to proving that God does not exist." He argues, "However statistically improbable the entity you seek to explain by invoking a designer, the designer himself has got to be at least as improbable. God is the Ultimate Boeing 747."[18] Alvin Plantinga explained what Dawkins means in these words: "Dawkins says a designer must contain at least as much information as what it creates or designs, and information is inversely related to probability. Therefore, he thinks, God would have to be monumentally complex, hence astronomically improbable; thus it is almost certain that God does not exist."[19] Atheist philosopher of religion Dr. Erik Wielenberg, writing in an Evangelical Philosophical Society creationist journal called *Philosophia Christi*, produced a fuller account of this argument:

(1) If God exists, then God has these two properties: (i) He provides an intelligent-design explanation for all natural, complex phenomena in the universe and (ii) He has no explanation external to Himself.

(2) Anything that provides an intelligent-design explanation for the natural, complex phenomena in the universe is at least as complex as such phenomena.

(3) So, if God exists, then God has these two properties: (i) He is at least as complex as the natural, complex phenomena in the universe and (ii) He has no explanation external to Himself. (from 1 and 2)

(4) It is very improbable that there exists something that (i) is at least as complex as the natural, complex phenomena in the universe and (ii) has no explanation external to itself.

(5) Therefore, it is very improbable that God exists. (from 3 and 4)[20]

Richard Dawkins has been widely criticized for this gambit since he was supposedly ignorant of the fact that God is believed to be a metaphysically simple being, not a complex one.[21] Erik Wielenberg makes this point:

A central element of my critique is that Dawkins's Gambit provides no reason at all to doubt some of the most widely-held versions of the target of his attack, the God Hypothesis. I do not know exactly how much theology one needs to know to disprove the existence of God, but one needs to know at least enough theology to understand the various widely-held conceptions of God. In general, in order to argue effectively against a given hypothesis, one needs to know enough to characterize that hypothesis accurately. Furthermore, if one intends to *disprove* God's existence, it is hardly reasonable to dismiss criticisms of one's putative disproof on the grounds that God doesn't exist anyway. Thus, the central atheistic argument of *The God Delusion* is unconvincing.[22]

Dawkins did not respond to these types of criticisms for a decade until the 2016 Reason Rally held in Washington, DC. In a videotaped message to the assembled crowd, he said this:

Some of our best theologians, if indeed theology is a subject that can be good at all, if theology is a subject at all, some of our best theologians prophetically tried to argue that "far from being complex, god is simple." There is no limit to the explanatory purposes to which the simple god's infinite power is put. "Is science having a little difficulty explaining X, no problem. Don't give X another glance." God's infinite power is effortlessly wheeled in to explain X along with everything else. And it's always a simple explanation, because after all, there is only one god. What could be simpler than that?

The effrontery of it is beyond astounding. This supposedly simple god had to know how to set the nuclear force 1,039 times stronger than gravity. He had to calculate with similar exactitude the requisite values of half-a-dozen critical numbers—the fundamental constants of physics. Do you, with your prodigiously complex brain, understand quantum mechanics? I don't! Yet god, that paragon of ultimate pure simplicity, not only understands it, but invented it. Plus special and general relativity, plus the Higg's boson, and dark matter. Finally, the icing on the cake, on top of being the ultimate mathematics and physics genius; this "simple" god has enough bandwidth to listen to the prayers of billions of people simultaneously in all the world's languages. He hears their confessed sins and decides which should be forgiven. He weighs out which cancer patients shall recover, which earthquake victims shall be spared; even who shall win a tennis match or a parking space. God may be almighty, all-seeing, all-knowing, all-powerful, all-loving. But the one thing he cannot be, if he is even to minimally meet his job description, is all-simple. The statistical argument against the divine designer remains intact, and inescapably devastating.[23]

What Dawkins meant was not some statement about God's metaphysical being. He was asking about the mind of God, that is, how and where did God get all of his knowledge? It's utterly incomprehensible to the point of refutation to believe God has always held true and utterly comprehensive propositional knowledge about everything, even of himself. I still cannot understand how this God chose his nature, or how the trinity came to be joined at the hip. Imagining just one eternal being who knows everything that can be known is incomprehensible on its own, but now there are three such divine persons who have this knowledge and never disagreed within the Godhead. It's clear that obfuscationist philosophers are making shit up as they go to save their Christian faith from refutation, since the only basis for believing this crap are some ancient prescientific writings.

It's also clear there are some atheist philosophers of religion who refuse to extend the principle of charity to "unsophisticated" atheist critics like Dawkins. All Weilenberg would have had to do is criticize the notion of God's simplicity, or ask and drive home the sorts of questions Dawkins did. Atheist philosopher of religion Graham Oppy, for instance, argued he cannot make any sense of a God who doesn't have any properties, which is what divine simplicity entails.[24] Why didn't Weilenberg do that? Dawkins surely was on to something even if it wasn't sophisticated enough for Weilenberg writing in a creationist journal. One might even ask why he was writing for that journal in the first place? I suspect atheists who do that are jockeying for position. They want to get noticed by the opposition as honest philosophers and worthy of being listened to. Loyal opposition has its benefits. Atheists offer the fundamentalist opposition credibility. Fundamentalists provide these atheists a pat on the back, so both sides win. What is lost is truth, in my opinion.

When picking the opposition to be loyal to, atheists must choose wisely, for it means picking the most credible opposition. But how does one do that when dealing with faith-based reasoning? Keith Parsons kindly wrote a chapter for my anthology *The End of Christianity*. In that chapter Parsons chose to write against an easy target, the traditional view of eternal suffering in an eternal fire. He did so with an understanding of the sophistication of its defenders, I gladly admit. But more sophisticated theologians can say Parsons doesn't really understand the nuances of the Bible, or the creeds or their sophisticated theology. In fact, more sophisticated theologians can scoff at his chapter in the same way as he does to Dawkins, Harris, Hitchens, and Stenger. They can say he makes glaring mistakes if he thought he was actually dealing with the Bible, the creeds, and theology. That's the point. They do just that. That's what I've heard anyway. I knew they would say this too. But Parsons wasn't willing to listen to me on this, since he had already formulated a draft of the chapter before I saw it for comment—which is okay as far as that goes. More sophisticated theologians can deny his chapter has anything to do with their more sophisticated views of hell. The scorn of sophisticated opponents about his chapter on hell is real, something about which Parsons has warned the rest of us against. Their more sophisticated views deny the requirement for belief unto salvation, or hell as eternal, or hell as a punishment, or even the presence of any occupants in hell. The point is that even though Parsons writes as if he's dealing with sophisticated theology, he is not doing so. He's not taking on the so-called heavyweights like Edward Fudge, Clark Pinnock, Thomas Talbott, Karen Armstrong, John F. Haught, and others.

There is no end to sophisticated theology, none. That's why I call it obfuscationist theology. No matter what theology we criticize there are always others claiming to be more sophisticated who reject that view, who will heap scorn on any of us who dares to criticize it. There are even defenders of other theologies who don't claim to be sophisticated, who claim God's word is easy to understand and that sophistication is a vice to be shunned at all costs. In their view they have the higher ground since the simpler the theology is the more likely that theology is true, even invoking Ockham's razor if they know of it. In essence, they claim the higher ground and take umbrage against the sophisticates.

So when it comes to sophisticated theology what exactly is Parsons talking about? ***One's theological heavyweights are another's theological lightweights, and vice versa.*** So why should we really care if we bring scorn down upon ourselves as atheist critics? Just think of restaurant or movie critics. Do we care if the critics upset the businesses they write about? Why should we care as patrons? We want to know the truth about that which they write about. Only the critics would care, if they stand to gain something by skewing the results unfairly in favor of that which they are supposed to honestly criticize.

What we have left is philosophical elitism. Parsons is telling us which theologies to respond to if we don't want the scorn of other theologians heaped upon us. He's chosen them for the rest of us. He's their sophisticated counterpart and he's telling everyone which theologies we should respect more. Apparently in his chapter on hell he thinks we should respect the traditional view of hell over others, you see. Seriously? And if we follow his advice by keeping silent when he says we should, then he gains respect from the theologians who will continue asking him to write chapters for their books, since he's their good old boy, propping up their theology over others because, well, their theology has more going for it than others, right? Right?! Furthermore, by keeping silent in deference to Parsons and MacDonald, many of us would subsequently fail to tell others what we think, which in itself is important. Just consider for a moment if there were never any new atheists, or atheist movement? Then where would atheism in America be right now? The good old days were not so good except perhaps for people like Parsons.

Describing Gods

Atheist professor Graham Oppy's book, *Describing Gods: An Investigation of Divine Attributes*, is the most erudite, important, and poignant example of what I'm talking about. By all standards of measurement Oppy is an atheist heavyweight. The growing number of scholarly works he's put out and the meticulous way he tackles theistic religion is very impressive—and helpful. In *Describing Gods* Oppy treats the divine attributes in the thorough way we have come to expect of him. It's a feast for the appetites of intellectuals, theologians, and philosophers interested in divine characteristics, and sure to be the standard textbook for decades and more. If you want to read a detailed discussion on what it means to say god is infinite, or perfect, or necessary, or free, or incorporeal, and more, then this is your book.

But this particular book of Oppy's helps to clarify much of what I'm arguing about here, more so than others. There are definitely some lessons to learn from reading it, no doubt. It will be nice to quote what he says on occasion, whenever needed. One can also learn how to reason better by reading what Oppy writes, so it's a good book for someone who wishes to become a better critical thinker. In these ways Oppy's book is helpful, especially for those of us who are arguing believers out of their faith. So I'm not saying works like this should not be produced. That would be anti-intellectual. An artist needs no justification for doing art but the art itself. Neither does an author. Even if no one ever reads a book, writing one can be worth the effort.

How should we judge the worth or value of this work by Oppy? James Lindsay judged it as follows:

> This book, scholarly as it is, is very difficult to see as anything but a perfect example of how seriously human beings can entertain ideas that we shouldn't. Given the existence of such explorations, we are left wondering why philosophers don't also produce painstakingly detailed academic tomes upon the unique and special qualities of dragonfire, be damned if there exist dragons to produce it. Put another way, we need exactly zero books written on any level of academic expertise to tell us that Superman's superpowers aren't real.
>
> Divine attributes are properties applied to a mythological fiction called "God" so that "God" can be believed to satisfy psychosocial needs, largely including needs for attribution and control. Exploring the attributes to a deity completely misses the point—people need their needs met and will pretend if doing so seems to get the job done. "What are divine attributes?" and "Are they coherent philosophical objects?" are the wrong kinds of questions to be asking. The right questions are "What needs cause people to give the myth they call 'God' these attributes?" and "How can we help them meet those needs without relying upon the mythology of theism to do it?"[25]

Is Lindsay being too harsh? Not if we think in terms of what is more helpful as opposed to less helpful. In chapter six I'll share what is more helpful, and by those standards Oppy's work is not helpful much at all. The most helpful thing in Oppy's book is that he shows certain kinds of gods with certain kinds of attributes don't exist because those gods with those attributes don't make any sense. Does this advance the discussion? Yes, definitely. That being said, Oppy is retrogressing. The proper order to discuss the existence of Gods, or superhuman beings, is to discuss the evidence first, as Jerry Coyne correctly noted:

Before you can discuss the nature of God, however deep and nuanced your discussion, you have to provide rational arguments for the existence of a God. No theologian, however sophisticated, has done that to my satisfaction, and I've read a lot of them. Absent such convincing evidence, theology simply becomes academic speculation about the nature of an unevidenced being.[26]

For the sake of discussion Oppy is granting the existence of a divine being after arguing against the existence of gods in his previous book *Arguing About Gods*.[27] If his previous book is correct there is no need to write this sequel. It's also not that helpful, since he either thinks his first book did the job or he doesn't. If he does, there is no need to write the sequel. Once it's shown there isn't sufficient evidence to believe then what more is left to be said? When we consider the mammoth amount of time and effort Oppy put into *Describing Gods*, and compare that to other projects he could have been doing with his time and talent, my judgment is the same as Lindsay's.

Why take for granted anything such as the existence of a divine being? I'll come back to this question in chapter 6. Taking things for granted for the purpose of discussion is an exercise in persuasion, yes. It helps have a discussion with people who fail to see the fundamental point, that one's faith lacks sufficient objective evidence for it. But if believers fail to see the fundamental point, why would anyone think they can be persuaded by other considerations? I don't think they can, or at least, this is not the best way to approach believers if the goal is to help them reason to reality.

Lindsay brings up a great analogy, Superman. What if there were millions upon millions of people who believe Superman exists, just as there are believers who believe some sort of god exists? Shouldn't we pull out every tool in our toolbox, including the sledgehammer of Oppy's book, written by a sharply focused mind that dissects the attributes Superman is believed to have? Well, here again, I would say that would not be the most helpful way to approach believers if the goal was to help them reason to reality. The main reason is that Oppy is doing theology. This is what theologians do. But just as any characteristic attributed to Superman must pass the evidence test before it needs to pass the conceptual test, so also must any deity. I doubt anything but scientific evidence could show that Superman can hover in the air, or propel himself faster than a speeding bullet, or burn things up with his vision, or see through walls, or pull the planet Earth away from danger, or catch bullets or deflect bombs. Those are the attributes of myths, fairy tales, fables, and, of course, cartoons, where anything can happen. If the objective scientific evidence wouldn't help change the beliefs of Superman's followers I don't know of anything else that could do it. Doing anything but asking for the evidence and showing any purported evidence is faked, or not evidence at all, is what would need to be done. Anything else, any gamesmanship, or puzzle-solving for the sake of puzzle-solving, would help to give Superman's followers the credibility they so desperately seek.

If It's Worth Doing, It's Worth Doing Badly

My view is that if something is worth doing, it's worth doing badly. If we should wait to do things right, then a lot less will get done. I think it's good to do important things even if we can only do them imperfectly. I first read this view expressed by Christian apologist G. K. Chesterton. Doing something badly is at least doing something productive, if what you're doing is the right thing to do. It's better than not attempting anything. All of the most important things we learned to do we started out doing badly, like walking, talking, singing, dancing, and riding a bicycle. You improve as you go. You cannot improve until you start. You begin by starting out badly. When it comes to our common goal of ridding ourselves of the influence of the religion, take Chesterton's advice: "If something is worth doing, it's worth doing badly." We need all of our voices. Don't be afraid of being wrong. And I invite all secular people to do the same thing, both the scholar and the nonscholar. Share what you know. Together we are making a difference. Join those of us who are already doing it.

Look at just a very brief listing of historic famous American atheist authors who may not have qualified under Parsons' strictures to say or write anything critical of religious faith. Women like Elizabeth Cady Stanton and Madalyn Murray O'Hair. Men like Thomas Paine, Robert Ingersoll, and Mark Twain. Scientists like the prolific Isaac Asimov and Carl Sagan. If these authors were not philosophically qualified may there be many more of them! If they are qualified what makes it so? Surely believers at that time and today would say they didn't correctly understand theology enough to do so.

People like Parsons, MacDonald, Weilenberg, and Oppy need to tell us what there is about sophisticated arguments that make something truer than arguments lacking such sophistication. Let's say someone claims she was abducted by aliens. That's a simple claim, isn't it? Why would its truth be contingent upon making all kinds of complex definitions complete with obfuscating Bayesian math to support it? I don't get it. Faith-based reasoning without sufficient evidence is the only indicator we need for rejecting a claim. Without sufficient evidence a high level of sophistication doesn't change a thing. What it becomes is obfuscationist. Faith is faith is faith is faith. It has no method, solves nothing, and even gets in the way of knowledge. It should be rejected by all intellectuals. Not to reject it is to be an anti-intellectual in my opinion, for only by rejecting faith-based answers in favor of evidence-based answers are we on the road to knowledge in every discipline in the university. Let's be consistent across the board by rejecting the philosophy of religion discipline too.

Notes

1. "Dr. Keith Parsons Calls It Quits Regarding the Philosophy of Religion," Debunking Christianity, September 4, 2010, http://debunkingchristianity. blogspot.com/2010/09/dr-keith-parsons-calls-it-quits.html.

2. Peter Boghossian, "Should We Challenge Student Beliefs?" *Inside Higher Ed*, July 19, 2011, https://www.insidehighered.com/views/2011/07/192/boghossian.

3. Peter Boghossian, *A Manual for Creating Atheists* (Durham, NC: Pitchstone Publishing, 2013), p. 177. Peter has said the title was not his initial choice but one decided upon to gain attention. That's what titles do and this one did its job well.

4. Ibid., p. 220.

5. Ibid., p. 188.

6. Ibid., p. 189.

7. Ibid., p. 213. For links to two talks on this subject, see "Faith Based Belief Processes Are Unreliable," Debunking Christianity, April 11, 2012, http://debunkingchristianity.blogspot.com/2012/04/peter-boghossian-faith-based-belief.html, and "Faith Is Pretending to Know Things You Don't Know,"

Debunking Christianity, June 18, 2012, http://debunkingchristianity.blogspot.com/2012/06/peter-boghossian-faith-is-pretending-to.html.

8. See Keith Parsons, "How to Think or What to Think?" Secular Outpost, June 25, 2012, http://www.patheos.com/blogs/secularoutpost/2012/06/25/how-to-think-or-what-to-think/#sthash.5C6rdkLa.dpuf.

9. Boghossian, *A Manual for Creating Atheists*, p. 213.

10. See "Parsons and Feser on Coyne," Dangerous Idea, April 1, 2016, http://dangerousidea.blogspot.com/2016/04/parsons-and-feser-on-coyne.html.

11. Joseph Patrick McCormick, "Church of Scotland Numbers Suffer as over Half of Scots Are Now Non-religious," *Pink News*, April 3, 2016, http://www.pinknews.co.uk/2016/04/03/church-of-scotland-numbers-suffer-as-over-half-of-scots-are-now-non-religious/?utm_source=ET&utm_medium=ETFB&utm_campaign=portal&utm_content=inf_11_60_2&tse_id=INF_f79f434ad3d942af890d472aaa4fae4c.

12. Jerry Coyne, "England and Wales Are Now Predominantly Nonreligious," Why Evolution Is True, May 24, 2016, https://whyevolutionistrue.wordpress.com/2016/05/24/england-and-wales-are-now-predominantly-nonreligious/.

13. Keith Parsons, "In Defense of Old Atheism," Secular Outpost, April 8, 2016, http://www.patheos.com/blogs/secularoutpost/2016/04/08/in-defense-of-old-atheism/.

14. Keith Parsons, "Doing It Right the Old Way," Secular Outpost, April 13, 2016, http://www.patheos.com/blogs/secularoutpost/2016/04/13/doing-it-right-the-old-way/.

15. Eric MacDonald left "new atheism" publicly, as discussed by Jerry Coyne, "Eric Macdonald Leaves New Atheism," Why Evolution Is True, March 10, 2014, https://whyevolutionistrue.wordpress.com/2014/03/10/eric-macdonald-leaves-new-atheism/.

16. "Keith Parsons Is Just Old. That Explains Why He Favors the Old Atheism," Debunking Christianity, April 4, 2016, http://debunkingchristianity.blogspot.com/2016/04/keith-parsons-is-just-old-that-explains.html#comment-2629784152.

17. "The New Evangelical Orthodoxy, Relativism, and the Amnesia of It All," Debunking Christianity, December 5, 2012, http://debunkingchristianity.blogspot.com/2012/12/the-new-evangelical-orthodoxy.html.

18. Richard Dawkins, *The God Delusion* (Boston: Houghton Mifflin, 2006), pp. 113–14, 147.

19. Alvin Plantinga, "The Dawkins Confusion: Naturalism ad Absurdum," *Books and Culture* (March/April 2007), http://www.christianitytoday.com:80/bc/2007/002/1.21.html.

20. Erik Weilenberg, "Dawkins's Gambit, Hume's Aroma, and God's Simplicity," *Philosophia Christi* 11, no. 11 (2009), p. 115.

21. What it means for god to be simple is that God is not divisible into separate parts. The attributes of God are not parts that together make up who God is, for God has no parts. God does not have properties like goodness or truth. Rather, God is goodness and truth. In essence, God has no properties. He's pure being. For my discussion of divine simplicity, see *Why I Became an Atheist* (Amherst, NY: Prometheus, 2012), pp. 97–100.

22. Weilenberg, "Dawkins's Gambit, Hume's Aroma, and God's Simplicity," p. 127.

23. See "Richard Dawkins 2016 Reason Rally Speech," video, published on June 8, 2016, https://youtu.be/G8NGf3L7foM.

24. Graham Oppy, *Describing Gods* (Cambridge: Cambridge University Press, 2104), chapter 4, "Simplicity," pp. 87–104.

25. James A. Lindsay, *Everybody Is Wrong About God* (Durham, NC: Pitchstone Publishing, 2015), p. 54.

26. Coyne, "Eric MacDonald Leaves New Atheism."

27. Graham Oppy, *Arguing About Gods* (Cambridge: Cambridge University Press, 2006).

5

WHY PHILOSOPHY OF RELIGION MUST END

Let me state for the record what I'm not proposing. This will better clarify my position before I argue it, as sort of a preemptive strike against misguided caricatures of my position. First and most importantly, I'm not saying philosophy proper is stupid or dead or unnecessary or that there has been no progress in that discipline. Massimo Pigliucci addresses these questions in his book *The Nature of Philosophy*.[1] Richard Carrier discussed these issues in a cursory fashion in a lecture titled "Is Philosophy Stupid?"[2] In it Carrier addresses the question, "what is pseudo-philosophy?" He defines it as "philosophy that relies on fallacious arguments to a conclusion and/ or relies on factually false or undemonstrated premises. And isn't corrected when discovered." Based on this definition alone all supernaturalist philosophy is pseudo-philosophy. Religious philosophy is to philosophy what "creation science" is to science.

Additionally I'm not proposing that atheist philosophers, or any other atheist or agnostic who specializes in a particular religion, should dismiss religions out of hand or ridicule them. As I'll argue later, they can do so, but I see no reason why anyone who specializes in a particular religion would do that regularly. Perhaps surprisingly, I'm not even proposing that atheist philosophers should cease writing books on philosophy of religion (PoR) or that they should cease all lectures or classes on such topics in secular universities. I will, however, be showing atheist philosophers and intellectuals how to approach religion correctly from now on, if they wish to continue dealing with it. Keep in mind, however, if they do PoR correctly it will no longer be considered the philosophy of religion as defined today, but something else.

What I Am Proposing

In this chapter I'll make a specific argument concerning ending philosophy of religion in secular universities and beyond. It follows the same pattern as Hector Avalos's call to end biblical studies as we know it, something I mentioned in chapter 1. Avalos argues that religion professors and those teaching in biblical studies departments should tell their students the truth about the Bible even though it's considered sacred to many of them. Essentially his call is to debunk the Bible for the good of any future society we might have because there is no reason to think it has any authority over us.

It's also something Peter Boghossian proposed in his provocative book, *A Manual for Creating Atheists*, in a chapter titled "Faith and the Academy." There he spoke of the importance of colleges and universities in combating "faith, poor thinking, epistemological relativism, and bad reasoning."[3] He argued that "employing universities in the struggle against faith is a cornerstone in the larger strategy to combat faith, promote reason and rationality, and create skeptics."[4] Since having faith "will decrease the likelihood of coming to true conclusions," educators in "all academic disciplines" should "give faith-based justifications no countenance."[5] In fact, educators in the soft sciences "should adopt a pedagogical stance identical to the stance that's essential in the hard sciences: Do not take faith claims seriously. Let the utterer know that faith is not an acceptable basis from which to draw a conclusion that can be relied upon."[6]

This same sentiment seems to be echoed in a small but mighty book titled *How to Defeat Religion in 10 Easy Steps: A Toolkit for Secular Activists*, by Ryan T. Cragun, an associate professor of sociology at the University of Tampa. Referring to public grade-school education in America, he says the first step in defeating religion is to ensure "that children are well educated *outside* a religious context and without religious indoctrination."[7]

I am primarily calling for the end of PoR as a separate subdiscipline under philosophy in secular universities. Further, whenever there is a PoR class, it should be taught correctly, if it's to be done at all. Like all other subjects in secular universities, PoR classes must be taught in a secular way by treating all faith-based claims equally and privileging none, if they are taught at all. If PoR is successfully taught in this bold and honest manner, the instructors themselves will help end the PoR and religion along with it. Philosophers of religion should go about the task of putting themselves out of a job by telling their students the truth—that faith is an unreliable way to gain any objective knowledge about matters of fact such as the nature of nature, its workings, and its origins. It is also an unreliable way to decide which religion is true, if there is one.

Since PoR topics are usually parochial in nature and localized in time and place, instructors who highlight localized topics in a secular university class are effectively saying those topics have more legitimacy than topics of concern in other parts of the world, which may have their own parochial PoR classes. When it comes to religious faith and paranormal claims, we need a truly global and historical perspective on all religions, dead or alive, with their gods and goddesses, and all other paranormal beliefs. When these types of classes are taught, religious and paranormal claims should all be treated the same from the perspective of secularism, reason, and science, without privileging any of them. That's not too much to ask if we honestly want to know and teach the truth.

I am also going further with my call than just the university setting. It's not limited to merely ending the PoR discipline in secular universities, although that's one of my main goals. My call is to end the current state of PoR period. Whether it's in secular universities, or lectures, or books or anywhere else people discuss PoR issues, my call for ending the PoR is a call for ending most all PoR discussions as they're currently being done. Thus, every atheist can participate in the demise of PoR, not just philosophers in universities.

That's it. It should never be considered stupid to tell students the truth. Scientists tell their students the truth. So should philosophers. There is no longer any debate about what the truth is among intellectually honest individuals. Faith-based reasoning is not a virtue. Faith as a method is unreliable. It should never be tolerated as a justification for anything in secular universities. We can no longer take obfuscationist philosophy used in defense of the Christian delusion or any other religion seriously. Atheists who want to deal with obfuscationist philosophy correctly must seek to end its grip over our institutions of higher learning. They must seek to end its influence in our world. It's time to remove faith from philosophy. Gamesmanship will not do. Puzzle-solving will not do. Special pleading will not do. Dealing with questions that are interesting for the sake of an interesting discussion will not do. Atheists who are seeking affirmation from Christian pseudo-intellectuals will not do. A delusion is a delusion is a delusion. Two thousand years of Christianity are enough, as Keith Parsons once said. It's time to lay it to rest, to put it away from the university and beyond. The sooner the better.

PoR is a discipline that has traditionally concerned itself with the claims and arguments of religion. The primary goal of traditional PoR is not to merely understand religion or learn about some aspect of it. That's for university departments and classes in disciplines such as *religious studies* or *comparative religion* or *anthropology of religion* or *sociology of religion*, or even *psychology of religion*. Rather, PoR seeks to understand the claims of religion (if possible) and examine the arguments put forth both pro and con by the canons of reason and evidence. This is how PoR has historically been understood among Western philosophers, unlike Eastern philosophers, who don't typically consider religion as a separate branch of philosophy.

The traditional kind of PoR that should end is the religious kind. But, and this is very important, if we end the traditional kind of PoR then we end PoR itself. PoR is usually to be distinguished in principle from theology, philosophical theology, religious studies, and biblical studies, all of which are typically religious, creedal, and confessional ways of approaching religion. In practice, however, this is not the case. Philosophers of religion are dealing with religion in religious, creedal, and confessional ways, and this must end. Atheist philosophers who engage in PoR have typically become enablers, providing the support believers need by legitimizing one particular religion over others (mostly a branch of Christianity), and this must end too. They must learn how to treat religion and paranormal claims correctly. To date hardly any of them do so.

Some universities have different names for PoR, so students should take note. What they have instead are Departments of *Philosophy and Religion*, or *Philosophy and Religious Studies*, or *Religion and Philosophy*. Just because a university has a PoR department does not mean they're doing it as historically understood though. Columbia University offers a PhD in the philosophy of religion, but it's a subdiscipline of the Department of Religion, not the Department of Philosophy. Graduate courses there include those with somewhat odd-sounding titles like "Religion and Pragmatism"; "Media and Religion"; "Ideology and Masses"; "Genealogy, Pragmatism and the Study of Religion"; "Genealogy and Time in the Study of Religion"; "Event, Ethnography, History"; "Seminar in the History and Philosophy of Religion"; "Hegel and Nietzsche"; "Hegel & Derrida", and a few others. The description tag RELI rather than PHIL is placed before the course numbers of these classes, even though they are gaining a PhD in the *philosophy* of religion. My guess is that Columbia University is doing religion, not the philosophy of religion as historically understood. I welcome this so long as they are being taught correctly by treating all religious faith-based claims equally.

The Current Crisis: Zagzebski, Trakakis, Oppy, and Parsons

By rationally analyzing religious beliefs that were not originally intended to be rationally analyzed in the first place (i.e., especially superstitious myths, legends, fables, and especially in the ancient prescientific world), philosophers of religion who assume that the PoR is the only way to effectively deal with religion are making a big mistake. James Lindsay says this in a bolder manner (via email): "The philosophy of religion is largely a waste of time because it mistakenly treats articles of faith, doctrines, myths, and cultural narratives as philosophical objects, which they are not."

Philosopher of religion Linda Zagzebski tells us "religion is a complex human practice involving distinctive emotions, acts, and beliefs."[8] *Religious emotions*, she informs, are the feelings of reverence, awe, dread, guilt, and joy described by Rudolph Otto as the "mysterious tremendum." *Religious acts*, she goes on to say, are the rituals and traditions of a religious community. In this context Zagzebski tells us, "religion is a practice, not an academic field."[9] Comparative religion professors and cultural anthropologists would agree with her on this. David Eller insists "religion is not what you believe, it's what you do."[10] *Religious beliefs*, says Zagzebski, "typically appear when a person becomes reflectively aware of his or her emotion and trusts it, so beliefs are consequent to the emotion. If so, the emotion of reverence is a more basic feature of religion than belief. That may turn out to be important because philosophers usually focus attention almost exclusively on beliefs."[11] And she indicates they have wrongly assumed "beliefs are the foundation of religion."[12]

I agree with Professor Zagzebski, who is the Kingfisher College Chair of the Philosophy of Religion and Ethics at the University of Oklahoma. The upshot of what she wrote is that developing arguments in support of one's religious faith will come *after* the emotions. So dealing with the arguments on behalf of religion is not to deal with religion itself, for that requires an analysis of faith. And faith is a cognitive bias. It has no method. If faith is trust we should not trust it, for faith is the reason for the arguments, as I must repeat myself throughout this book to help get this point across about faith.

Nick Trakakis explored the meta-philosophy of religion by discussing the various assumptions and ways of doing it, especially those coming to the foreground in the twentieth century, in his book, *The End of Philosophy of Religion*. Without mentioning Zagzebski's earlier work Trakakis argues somewhat along the same lines as she did. There's a backstory we need to rush through to get his point. There is a difference between the analytical tradition in PoR, which is largely the type found in the United States, from the Continental tradition in PoR, which is largely the type found on the European continent. This difference in the West reveals that the PoR is parochial rather than global in perspective. In addition, neither tradition typically takes into account Eastern approaches. Without going into these differences right now, Trakakis highlights "the weaknesses of the analytic approach in philosophy, particularly when it is applied to religious and aesthetic experience."[13] The analytic tradition is too rationalistic and fails to deal adequately enough with transcendence and the mysterious nature of reality of religious practices, he argues. In its place Trakakis thinks the Continental tradition of philosophy offers a needed corrective since it's more open to the supernatural. Religious "experiences," you see, are not germane to rational explanations or objective evidences or warranted justifications. Trakakis, I have been told, no longer holds the views expressed in his book. Perhaps it's because of Timothy Knepper's response to the book in an article published in the *Journal of the American Academy of Religion*, where he argued quite effectively that "if a philosophy of religion is supposed to philosophize *about* religion, then neither continental nor analytic philosophy of religion is philosophy of religion. Rather they are, at best, philosophies of narrow subsets of religions; at worst, theological efforts at understanding and defending these subsets." It's so bad, he argues, "it might be better if they no longer call themselves *philosophy of religion*."[14] More from Knepper later.

Probably the premier atheist philosopher of religion today is Graham Oppy. In 2014 Oppy published a book titled *Reinventing Philosophy of Religion: An Opinionated Introduction*.[15] He did an online interview about his book, where he both defended PoR as a discipline and expressed a way to reinvent it.[16] Oppy rightly mentions that philosophy gave birth to the sciences. Philosophers discussed issues before there was any evidence for them, but once evidence was found then a new discipline was born. After all, the sciences we call physics, cosmology, and psychology were at one time considered the domain of philosophy. What Oppy doesn't talk about is whether this process can be reversed. What if philosophy spawned a discipline and, after a few centuries or decades, science subsequently showed that that discipline doesn't deserve to be a separate one? That's what I am claiming. The PoR does not deserve its own discipline and never did. The PoR should end and go back where it came from, into philosophy proper. In this vein, Oppy reminds us, "Philosophy of religion as a discipline, I would think, probably doesn't date much earlier than the second World War." This historical lesson is significant, I think, for we did without it for centuries and we can do without it again.

Later in the same interview Oppy offers one of his criticisms of the PoR, saying, "Most of the people who have done philosophy of religion have been theists." So it stands to reason "it has had an extremely narrow focus. . . . It hasn't really been the philosophy of religion but rather Christianity with a very great emphasis on theism," and even apologetics/ Christian theology. Keith Parsons, writing for the Secular Outpost, echoes Oppy, saying, "If proclaiming the 'death of PoR' only means the death of a certain way of doing it, then I would certainly applaud this. . . . I think that we have had enough of theistic apologetics. It's over." One other Secular Outpost author agreed: "[T]he philosophy of religion is not 'dead,' but it is in serious condition, if not on life support. This can be shown by counting the number of philosophy departments at secular colleges and universities which have faculty lines for philosophy of religion. (They are very rare.)"

This isn't all they said,[17] but atheists can all agree about this half of the problem.

As it stands today PoR is dominated by Christian theists who discuss and argue for concepts and arguments germane to Christianity. Given what Oppy said, PoR definitely needs to be reinvented if it is to survive. The unaddressed question is why we should have a discipline in any secular university where theism, or Christian theism, Christian theology, or Christian apologetics is privileged and considered to the exclusion of all other religions or apologetics? We shouldn't. If this is the state of affairs then the only reasonable response is to end the discipline now.

Oppy offers his solution to this malaise. He argues the discipline must be reinvented. To reinvent PoR, Oppy argues, "it must address questions that apply to the phenomena of religion in general." He argues the philosophy of religion should also discuss global religions like Islam, Hinduism, and Buddhism and other religious views. By extension, I think, he would not be opposed to discussing other faith-based paranormal claims, all of them, and doing so equally by privileging none. Why stick to just discussing religions? Why not all faith-based paranormal claims? Oppy's proposal should include all of the dead religions too. Why not? Why assume that a dead religion, or a dead god, is no longer worthy to be discussed? Why not discuss Zoroastrianism, or Canaanite religions? Does the death of a religion mean it must not be a true one? I see no reason to think so. It just may mean its adherents died or were annihilated by a conquering army.

I don't know if I should credit Keith Parsons or discredit him for this, but he has actually proposed studying ancient paganism! Keep in mind this proposal comes from an atheist philosopher of religion who abandoned teaching PoR because he could no longer stomach it:

> Recent discussions here at *Secular Outpost* have focused on the future of philosophy of religion (if any), and some have queried where the field might go if, to some extent, it moves away from its traditional theistic/Christian emphases. I have maintained that certain discussions have pretty much played out. . . . Neither side has gained a decisive advantage. As an atheist, I naturally feel that atheists have had the better of the debate. Theists obviously will feel otherwise. . . . Maybe it is time to let that issue lie and recognize that both theism and atheism are reasonable options that may be espoused by reasonable people.
>
> If we are looking for new directions for philosophical reflections on religion, what are the possibilities? . . . One possible direction for PoR is to investigate the implications of pre-Christian, indeed, pre-monotheistic forms of religiosity. Is a rational paganism or animism

possible today? At a deeper level would be the investigation of the nature of the sacred—how it is to be understood and what are its implications? . . . Is the category of the numinous simply disposable? . . . How should the theistic religions respond to the fact that the numinous seems to be a category too broad, too deep, and too ancient to be contained within a monotheistic context? . . . Must religious pluralism be recognized as the inescapable implication of an enlightened understanding of the vastly multifarious human attempts to approach the sacred?[18]

Yes, he's serious! He actually thinks philosophers of religion should pay attention to dead religions. My point is exactly the reverse. Philosophers shouldn't pay much attention to living religions for the same reason they don't pay much attention to dead ones.

Regardless, my question is which professors could teach PoR adequately, if it's to be done at all? Secular ones, that's who. After all, we're talking about secular universities, ones which do not take a stand on religion but try to teach subjects without reference to God, gods, supernatural forces, or beings as explanations. However, if secularists were in charge of the discipline, they should seek to end it. Atheist philosophers know this. Yet faith is the very basis of all religions and religious concepts. If taught properly that's what the PoR should be about, ending faith in the classroom. But in teaching it correctly philosophy professors would be undercutting the discipline just by doing it right.

The Current Crisis: Dawes & Draper

It's a fact that the PoR field is dominated by Christian philosophers. In 2009 David Chalmers of the Australian National University and David Bourget of the University of London surveyed professional philosophers and others about their philosophical views. The survey was taken by 3,226 respondents, including 1,803 philosophy faculty members and/or PhDs and 829 philosophy graduate students.[19] The question that interests us here is what philosophers think about God.

God: theism or atheism?
Accept or lean toward: atheism 678 / 931 (72.8%)
Accept or lean toward: theism 136 / 931 (14.6%)
Other 117 / 931 (12.5%)

If we add in the "other" category, which would include New Age beliefs, deism, and agnosticism, then more than 85 percent of those surveyed are not theists. Among those philosophers who are theists I dare say most of them are probably not card-carrying evangelicals, since this includes Catholics, Muslims, Jews, and those who merely accept the philosopher's god. So much for William Lane Craig's claim that there is at the present time a renaissance of Christian philosophy in today's world. *cough*

When it comes to PoR the poll results are nearly reversed. Based on the data from this same survey, Anthony Gottlieb reports that among specialists in the philosophy of religion, "only 19.1% accept or lean toward atheism, while 72.3% accept or lean toward theism."[20]

Atheist philosopher Gregory Dawes authored the excellent book *Theism and Explanation*.[21] Richard Marshall interviewed him about this interesting poll data and why the professors in a subdiscipline of philosophy are disregarded by the rest of the field. He answers:

> Christian philosopher William Lane Craig writes somewhere about what he calls the "ministerial" and the "magisterial" use of reason. (It's a traditional view—he's merely citing Martin Luther—and one that Craig endorses.) On this view, the task of reason is to find arguments in support of the faith and to counter any arguments against it. Reason is not, however, the basis of the Christian's faith. The basis of the Christian's faith is (what she takes to be) the "internal testimony of the Holy Spirit" in her heart. Nor can rational reflection be permitted to undermine that faith. The commitment of faith is irrevocable; to fall away from it is sinful, indeed the greatest of sins.
>
> It follows that while the arguments put forward by many Christian philosophers are serious arguments, there is something less than serious about the spirit in which they are being offered. There is a direction in which those arguments will not be permitted to go. Arguments that support the faith will be seriously entertained; those that apparently undermine the faith must be countered, at any cost. Philosophy, to use the traditional phrase, is merely a "handmaid" of theology.
>
> There is, to my mind, something frivolous about a philosophy of this sort. My feeling is that if we do philosophy, it ought to be because we take arguments seriously. This means following them wherever they lead. . . . So why does the philosophy of religion have such a marginal status within the philosophical community? It may be (as some Christians assert) because atheist philosophers "love darkness more than light," but I

suspect it's because many atheist philosophers not only find the arguments unconvincing but also regard this style of philosophy as distasteful.[22]

Given the crisis of PoR atheist philosopher Paul Draper offers four suggestions on how to best approach it in hopes of reforming it.[23] I want to examine his suggestions in a little detail. First, Draper suggests that philosophers of religion should "distance themselves in every way possible from apologetics, whether theistic or atheistic," since the goal of PoR should be "genuine inquiry." What Draper concedes in the first half of his suggestion is what Hector Avalos has called for with regard to biblical studies, that it should not have a religious orientation in the secular classroom. This alone goes a long way toward the same goal of mine regarding the PoR, even if religious apologists in the classroom won't accept it.

The part of Draper's suggestion I find objectionable is that he thinks there's such a thing as atheistic apologetics, which he seeks to silence by the same standard believing apologetics should be silenced in the interest if genuine inquiry. But why? He either thinks the evidence favors nonbelief as an atheist himself, or he thinks faith has epistemic warrant. Is he proposing that he will shut up if Christian apologists do? Why? Who is to monitor this compromise? Why should he accept it in the first place? The case against faith has been slammed shut. I see no reason why religious apologists in the classroom would accept such advice anyway. In their minds apologetics trumps such dictatorial pronouncements by Draper. So why should atheist philosophers acquiesce? The truth is, atheist philosophers in the classroom need to level the playing field in the secular universities. Christians have been doing apologetics in the universities for centuries. It's time to level the playing field by teaching the truth about faith. Doing so is teaching on the right side of history.

Besides, what is atheistic apologetics? A few ideas come to mind, like obnoxious proselytizing, presenting only one side to students to the exclusion of the other side, or teaching students what to think rather than how to think. What I'm advocating is that atheist philosophers merely teach their students how to think about faith-based reasoning in these classes. It's very clear how we should think about it. Peter Boghossian has challenged us to give faith-based claims no preferential treatment. I agree. So should all atheists. So should all reasonable people. There should be no reasonable dispute about this. Why not teach students the truth about faith?

Draper says the goal would be "genuine inquiry." But the honest truth is that genuine inquiry begins the day we reject faith-based answers to matter-of-fact questions like the nature of nature, its workings, and its origins, not before. Boghossian argues that faith is a cognitive malaise and should be given no credence in the classroom. I agree. I see no reason why any atheist philosopher would disagree. There is no genuine inquiring into this factual conclusion. For all we know there might be a superhuman or supernatural realm. If it exists and acts in our world the only way we can objectively know it exists is by empirical means.

Second, Draper argues philosophers of religion should "use argument construction, less often as a method for making cases for the positions they hold, and more often as a method of testing those positions. This would require, of course, making a serious effort to construct arguments against one's prior religious beliefs."

In other words, philosophy of religion professors should test their own faith-based hypotheses. If that's what he's saying then I agree. In the first place you don't test things with arguments. You test them with experiments. Nonetheless, the problem is that atheist professors don't have any faith-based answers to test, or they shouldn't anyway. We already know faith provides no objective justification for anything. What he needs to do is offer an objective way to test our conclusions. I have done so in my book *The Outsider Test for Faith*. I consider this test the *only* way to test one's religious faith (yes, you read that right, the only way, given the nature of religious faith). So far as I know Draper has not done so.

Third, Draper argues philosophers of religion should "make a conscious effort to allow, as J. L. Schellenberg puts it, 'the voice of authority to grow dim in our ears.' All too often, viable arguments and positions never occur to thinkers because dominant, traditional forms of religion overly influence those thinkers." This too is welcomed advice. What he needs to do is offer a way to test one's conclusions objectively. Again, I refer readers to my aforementioned book on the outsider test for faith, the result of which is that faith-based reasoning always fails this objective test, always. The reason is that faith is for insiders. Faith seeks confirmation. Only by testing one's faith as an outsider do believers have a chance to overcome confirmation bias, for outsiders don't have anything to confirm when examining a religion.

Fourth and lastly, Draper argues that philosophers of religion should

make every effort to accept genuine risk. True inquiry requires risk, which is why philosophical inquiry is aided by doubt. In experimental science, balanced inquiry is easier (though still far from easy) to achieve. Even if a scientist is sure of some cherished hypothesis, testing that hypothesis by experiment is (in many cases) inherently risky. Apologetics by comparison is very safe insofar as pursuing it is very unlikely to result in apologists rejecting any of the central doctrines of the religious communities they serve. Philosophy should be riskier—philosophers of religion must be prepared to abandon cherished beliefs. But with that risk comes greater opportunities for growth and discovery, and for freeing oneself from service to inflexible orthodoxy.

Nearly all apologists in the classroom already think they're open-minded, but that doesn't deter them from thinking their faith-based claims have merit anyway. They would also say atheist philosophers should take this advice when it comes to being open-minded that faith-based claims are justifiable. I'm sorry. We already know they aren't. *To be open-minded is to accept the results of science rather than deny them*, as believers do in at least some areas to maintain their faith, something I argue in the introduction to my anthology *Christianity in the Light of Science: Critically Examining the World's Largest Religion*.

Draper ends by pleading with Christian apologists in the classroom to consider his suggestions:

> I realize, of course, that some philosophers who are sectarian theists might be unwilling to accept my recommendations. They might regard accepting them as in some way disloyal to their religious community or to their God. Yet in some sense such an attitude evinces a lack of faith. If there really is a God and if such a God wants us to engage in inquiry concerning ultimate reality, then surely such a God would want that inquiry to be balanced. The results of balanced inquiry, however, are unpredictable. For this reason, it is arguable that a theistic philosopher who decides to follow my advice . . . must have greater faith, greater trust in God, than one who decides to pursue the paradoxical path of the apologist.

This is welcome advice when it comes to Christian apologists, of course. It uses their own language game of words against them. But again

Christian apologists in the classroom would throw the informal fallacy known as *tu quoque* (or "you too") back on atheist philosophers. They would say atheists wouldn't be disloyal to their atheist communities if they took seriously the goal of genuine open-minded inquiry, as if there can be genuine inquiry beginning with any faith-based viewpoint, which I deny. Faith always stifles inquiry and keeps otherwise intelligent people ignorant of the facts. For faith is always searching for data, seeking to understand, looking for explanations, and justifying one's original viewpoints.

Draper is trying to reform the discipline rather than revolutionize it. What he offers is a compromise that won't do much of anything to change the PoR, as it's currently taught, for one major reason: most Christian apologists teaching PoR classes will not take seriously points 1–4. They will skirt these points by saying they should equally apply to atheist philosophers, before proceeding to ignore them. I simply see no reason why Christian apologists who are worthy of this ignominious title and teaching in the university would attempt to follow Draper's rules. So we would be left in the same position we now are in, or worse. Draper is advocating for a degree of secularization in the PoR, which I think is a start. However, nothing but the complete secularization of PoR departments and academia in general is what we should work toward, since faith should not be advocated in any class taught in secular universities. This is the only consistent position to take. It's also best for the students to learn the truth.

Avalos calls on biblical scholars to completely secularize their biblical studies classes because (1) this is the right thing to do, given the mythical nature of these ancient prescientific documents, and (2) because any other proposal would be inconsistent with the facts. He goes on to argue that secular professors should disabuse their students of the view that the Bible is relevant in today's society or divinely inspired. Peter Boghossian calls on secular professors in the PoR to do the same thing with regard to faith. They are to disabuse their students of faith as a means for gaining knowledge or a virtue. And they are both doing exactly what they advocate in their classrooms.

Why then would Draper as an atheist not propose teaching the PoR in the right way, the honest way, the way consistent with the facts? I don't get it, especially since his four suggestions are paper tigers with no teeth to them. Compromise is helpful when there are people willing to compromise and a position both sides can agree to. I see no reason at all to think

Christian theistic believers will compromise, so why not just tell it like it is? I see no reason why atheist philosophers should compromise when it comes to such an important truth as the utter inability for faith to discover any truths, offer any reasonable explanations, solve any problems, or justify any conclusions. The bottom line is faith is unjustifiable. Draper should understand this. Why doesn't he just say so? Why doesn't he propose to eliminate faith from the PoR just as Avalos proposed eliminating apologetics from biblical studies? Hector argues for what he thinks, and also walks the talk. So does Boghossian.

Just consider what's wrong with Islam, Judaism, Mormonism, Jehovah's Witnesses, Christian Science, Haitian Voodoo, Animism, Hinduism, Sikhism, Scientology, Armstrong's Worldwide Church of God, the Unification Church, and the many tribal and folk religions? Faith. The adherents of these religions do not believe based on sufficient evidence, because faith is an irrational leap over the probabilities. If they thought exclusively in terms of the probabilities by proportioning their belief to the evidence (per David Hume), they would not believe at all. Now that we've got that straight, what's wrong with Christianity? Faith!

What obfuscationist believing philosophers have succeeded at doing is morphing a small ancient cult religion into something so foreign that even the original Christians would not recognize it. We know the origins of Christianity are a sham, as Jaco Gericke wrote in a chapter for my anthology *The End of Christianity*, provocatively titled "Can God Exist if Yahweh Doesn't?" If the source of the religion can be shown to have no reasonable basis in evidence then it's based on faith. To be quite frank, I have come to the conclusion that Christianity, especially evangelical or fundamentalist Christianity, is no more to be respected than Scientology.

The longer Scientology exists the more sophisticated their theologians will become too. Should we take their concepts and have a go-around with them without asking for the evidence for their claims too? I think not. Christians have had about two thousand years to hone their skills at defending the indefensible, that's all. And in the process what they have created looks nothing like the earliest cults of Christianities in the first through third centuries CE.

I wonder how many atheists who defend the PoR simply like to entertain and solve the intellectual puzzles put forth by the likes of Richard Swinburne, Alvin Plantinga, and William Lane Craig. Perhaps they suspect these arguments might be valid, but I think it's a game with them. Solving such puzzles is more fun than simply saying forthrightly that Christian pseudo-philosophy is bogus by reminding them of the actual biblical basis for Christianity. Doing so will end the fun, the gamesmanship, and the pats on the back for being a good sport. I suspect most of them just enjoy the intellectually challenging game because winning is a challenge.

The Current Crisis: Schilbrak and Knepper

There have been some other philosophers to weigh in on the current crisis.[24] One is Kevin Schilbrak, professor teaching in the department of Philosophy of Religion at Appalachian State University. He wrote a manifesto on the PoR titled *Philosophy and the Study of Religions*.[25] Schilbrak talks about "traditional" PoR and claims it has focused "on a relatively narrow topic: the rationality of belief in God" and the divine characteristics. "Even the philosophers of religion who are skeptics or atheists fit that description of the discipline." Some forms of PoR don't focus on those issues, most notably Continental philosophy, which focuses on "religious experience, on the phenomenology of overflow experiences, and on overcoming ontotheology." It primarily "reflects on the limits of reason and on faith as a response to revelation. It is primarily concerned with the nature and limits of God-talk rather than with warrant for truth claims."[26] However, he informs us that "Continental philosophers of religion predominantly share with analytic philosophers of religion the narrow focus on theism."[27] His critique of PoR is that "it operates with an inadequate understanding of the task of the discipline. To avoid narrowness, intellectualism, and insularity, philosophers of religion should understand their task as having three parts."[28]

The first task of the PoR is that "it should exclude no religions."[29] I would go on to say all faith-based claims and religious faiths should be treated equally. None should be privileged with any special credence over others, even dead religions, as I previously said. Since the history of Christianity stretching back into the Hebrews of the Old Testament is nothing but one successive dead religion being replaced by others, which in turn were replaced by still others, the Judaisms and Christianities of the past must be given equal weight—that is, until someone can provide a good reason to think modern Christianity, the kind that did not exist until modern times, should be given special preferential treatment merely due to the fact it exists in our era. In other words, if faith is the justification for a religion, then what is different with the faith of the ancients? If faith is reasonable on its own apart from reason or science, then who's to say that the Christianities of previous centuries were wrong? If, however, reason and science are what show modern Christianities to be truer than ancient ones that are false, then what does faith do but put a stamp of approval on what was learned by other means, and hence superfluous.

At this point Schilbrak struggles to find an adequate description of what he's proposing, even saying it's "a post-secular, post-colonial, cross-cultural, comparative, global philosophy of religions."[30] He ends up saying, "Philosophy of religion properly means the philosophical study of religions in all their diversity, in all their aspects, and as a contributing part of a family of approaches in the study of religions. Thus the best name for the approach to the discipline proposed in this book is simply to reclaim the name, philosophy of religion."[31] I suppose academicians can call what they do by any name they want. I acknowledge this, but given the track record of PoR and the name recognition it has earned, my suggestion is to abandon the name (especially if one is an atheist philosopher). Just think of a generation of students who might be a bit confused when, after applying to philosophy of religion departments, they find themselves being taught comparative religion. Nomenclature matters.

David Eller recommended Schilbrak's book for my consideration, commenting via email, "The problem is with how philosophy of religion is currently conducted. It is essentially an exegesis and defense of Christian concepts. If philosophy of religion did what philosophy is supposed to do, it would be legitimate—but it would sure not be what it currently is!" Then he said, "Perhaps I am biased, but I think that a proper philosophy of religion would turn it into anthropology!!" Good for him!

The second task of PoR, Schilbrak argues, is that "the proper object of philosophy of religion is all aspects of those religions. On this understanding, it is the task of philosophy of religion to investigate all religious phenomena from a philosophical perspective, and not to investigate solely the work of religious philosophers."[32] Here Schilbrak faults traditional PoR for focusing on "religious doctrines and arguments. Some have also focused on religious experiences, usually to answer the question whether religious experiences can justify the doctrines. Philosophers of religion have given relatively less attention to religious ethics, and much less to political and ritual practices."[33]

I see nothing wrong with this second task of his. The only caution I have is that I am still interested in whether or not religions are based in reality. We should not let the pendulum swing away from a rational critique of religious doctrines and arguments against God. We shouldn't neglect the need to look for the evidence to believe either. After all, if the evidence is not there then it isn't there. Honest believers who want to know the truth are rare, but it doesn't mean we should neglect those debates entirely.

Religion is more than doctrines and arguments. As Schilbrak rightly says, "religion is largely a set of practices in which people engage in order to make their lives better: participating in the three kinds of religious practices provides the participants with rituals that heal, with disciplines that train their children in morality, and with structures for their communal lives that reflect a higher law."[34] Traditional PoR ignores these crucial aspects of religion, which are the real reasons people believe. That's why traditional atheistic PoR has been utterly ineffective in getting believers to doubt or change their minds. It's because religious doctrines are not the reason adherents believe, nor is it due to the arguments. They believe for community reasons, for ritualistic reasons, and for ethical obligations that bring them into safe conformity with others. They were usually not reasoned into their faith in the first place so it stands to reason they cannot usually be reasoned out of it either.

Next Schilbrak claims traditional PoR has become

> a relatively insular discipline. By this I mean that, intellectually speaking, traditional philosophers of religion keep to themselves. When it comes to the other disciplines in the academic study of religions, philosophers do not 'play well with others.' Philosophers of religion do not generally read or write about pilgrimage, dietary rules, raising children, offering sacrifices, celebrating marriage, or speaking in tongues. They leave religious practice or lived religion for the anthropologists, historians, comparativists and other disciplines in the field of religious studies.[35]

To remedy this he offers up a third task of PoR, to build "bridges from philosophy to other disciplines involved in the study of religions."[36] Thus,

PoR, as he conceives of it, includes "reflection not only on the philosophies of the religions around the world [the first task] and the aspects of those religions as they are lived [the second task] but also on the philosophical questions involved in the study of religions [the third task]. . . . One could call this set of questions: philosophy of religious studies."[37] But if this is what he has left why not just call it anthropology of religion, since that's what he just described!

Schilbrak's three tasks for the PoR sound good overall but there are interesting issues left unaddressed. Schilbrak fails to go beyond merely arguing for these three tasks. He fails to argue for a skeptical disposition toward the claims of faith-based reasoning. Critical reflection is one thing. A skeptical disposition is another. Neither do we see Schilbrak adopting an objective method for critical reflection on the PoR, like the outsider test for faith. To know whether a given religious faith claim is based in reality and not a delusion means placing all faith-based claims on an equal playing field, privileging none. Consequently we should treat Scientology the same as we would treat Christianity. I just don't see him doing that.

So although Schilbrak disagrees with traditional PoR he's neglecting the crucial aspect of skepticism based in an objective method for knowing which religion is true, if there is one. He's not asking philosophers of religion to adopt a skeptical disposition with regard to the claims of faith-based reasoning and religions in general. It's the only disposition to adopt given the number of faith-based claims, most of them mutually exclusive to each other, which cannot all be correct.

Timothy Knepper, a professor of philosophy of religion at Drake University, also wants to reform the PoR. His critique of the current status of PoR is that it

> is significantly out of step with, and therefore has very little to offer to, one of its parent fields, religious studies. And this is largely due to the fact that the content of reflection in philosophy of religion is usually either a fictionalized and rarified theism or the latest critical notion of some continental philosopher, not the historical religions of the world in their localized complexity and comparative diversity. But it is also due to the fact that philosophy of religion can look more like philosophical theology—not a (relatively) religiously neutral examination of reason-giving in the religions of the world, but an overt apologetic for (or against) the reasonableness or value of some kind of religion.[38]

In its place Knepper offers five proposals: (1) "The object of inquiry in any philosophy of religion that has something to offer to the academic study of religion must be religiously diverse—not the religious reason-giving of some one religion or type of religion but the religious reason-giving of all religions insofar as this is possible"[39]; (2) "The subject that inquires in a philosophy of religion that has something to offer to the academic study of religion should strive to remain as ideologically critical and corrective as possible. . . . it is of critical importance that a diversity of biases be represented among the inquiring community"[40]; (3) "Any philosophy of religion that has something to offer to the academic study of religion must begin with, and linger for some time over, the thick description of religious reason-giving in the religions of the world" (for which see note)[41]; (4) Any philosophy of religion that has something to contribute to religious studies "must work cross-culturally" and "comparatively, undertaking formal acts of comparison that are critically aware of . . . the methods by which comparisons are made"[42]; (5) "A philosophy of religion that has something to contribute to religious studies can and should critically evaluate those instances and forms of religious reason-giving that it describes and compares."[43] He admits this suggestion "might not make some in the academic study of religion too happy," even though he calls this kind of evaluation "multi-dimensional."[44] "Evaluation should not come," he writes, "at the expenses of description and comparison; in fact, evaluation requires antecedent description and comparison." Then he adds something quite shocking, saying, "it is therefore the case that, given the current state of the philosophy of religion, evaluation ought to be largely suspended."[45]

In chapter 6 I'll offer several suggestions on how best to do his fifth proposed evaluation task. For our purposes I see nothing wrong with his proposals even though he mistakenly thinks they will keep his own discipline relevant. What are we to call that which he advocates? My view is that he's doing religion and that the subdiscipline of PoR he seeks to defend is not needed at all. Religious studies classes already do what he's proposing. So do anthropology of religion classes. There ought to be a real difference between two disciplines, otherwise we don't need one of them. We don't need the philosophy of religion. The evaluation component toward religion that's essential and sufficient is for academics to critically evaluate faith itself. It is not a virtue. It is a vice. It hinders sound logical reason-giving. It hinders truth seeking. It hinders science and reason itself.

And it doesn't need a whole separate discipline to get that point across. We need just one philosophy class to do so: Epistemology 101.

Why Philosophy of Religion Must End

Let me end by succinctly summarizing why PoR must end:

1. Because the PoR discipline is being disconfirmed at every juncture by science. In short, it is unnecessary, as Pierre Simon LaPlace once quipped to Napoleon when asked why he made no mention of God in his study of the solar system. To see a good example concerning Christianity read my anthology *Christianity in the Light of Science*.

2. Because PoR depends on accepting, for the purposes of discussion, ideas that should not be given serious academic attention in the modern world. Can you imagine university PoR classes that take seriously the Mormon conception of a god who has a body with a plethora of wives living on the planet Koleb? Can you imagine atheist philosophers of religion teaching such classes? I can't. Wouldn't doing so grant those beliefs legitimacy in their own right? Imagine also an Internet atheist who publishes the latest argument on behalf of this god, saying, "Here's a new argument for the Mormon god I just discovered." We couldn't take such things seriously, for good reason, just as we couldn't take seriously the arguments themselves. Why shouldn't we transfer this same line of thinking to the Abrahamic gods? or the Egyptian gods? or the Greco-Roman gods? or the Norse gods? or . . . ? I think we should, thus destroying the PoR discipline in the process.

   Most religious ideas are based in conflicting testimonies from ancient people who claimed to privately hear the voices of gods in their heads or offered prescientific explanations of dreams, death, and any natural phenomena not yet understood by science. Christianities, for instance, fail to realize that Jesus studies have ended Jesus just as biblical scholars have ended biblical studies. Robert Conner expresses this well:

   > That Jesus Studies is rife with flawed scholarship, special pleading, fideism, rank speculation, manufactured relevance, careerism, homophobia and the misogyny that homophobia implies, sectarian

allegiances, personal agendas, fraud and simple incompetence should come as no surprise to anyone conversant with the field. Indeed, whether Jesus Studies is even an academic discipline as usually understood is debatable, and that Jesus Studies has precious little to do with history is certain.[46]

3. Because the PoR discipline is parochial in nature, whether in American or Continental universities. The very issues discussed in these classes, whether taught by secular or believing philosophers, are not multiculturally or anthropologically oriented. The questions discussed in the United States are almost exclusively dominated by recent analytical conservative (or evangelical) Christian philosophers, such as Alvin Plantinga, Richard Swinburne, and William Lane Craig, to mention the unholy trinity. That's simply too narrow of a focus and not representative of the field itself. Discussing these issues legitimizes them to the exclusion of a global perspective. It presumes way too much. It's based in special pleading.

4. Because the PoR discipline is dominated by Christian theists, who argue for the claims of their faith in these classes, even though no other intellectual discipline in a secular university would tolerate faith, or the belief in superhuman beings or forces, as explanations for a phenomenon or justifications for knowledge claims. It seems clear that Christian philosophers are simply more interested in PoR so they gravitate toward teaching it. I think PoR is the last bastion of Christians who want to avoid questions about the lack of sufficient evidence for superhuman beings or forces as explanations. They focus on definitions by attempting to make their theologies seem reasonable with arguments based on little more than special pleading. Again, think about it, in no other intellectual discipline in a secular university would faith-based claims be tolerated. If they are, then those disciplines need to be secularized as well. For another way to understand my call to end PoR in university is to see it as a call to secularize our secular universities. That's really not too controversial when one thinks about it. In secular universities we must have secularized classes. Secular universities must be secularized.

5. Because the PoR discipline as taught in the Western world, especially in the United States, is not being taught correctly. To teach it correctly

the professor should tell the truth about the lack of epistemic status of faith. Faith has no intellectual merit. It is not a virtue. It has no method. It solves no problems. It is not worthy of thinking people.

6. Because the PoR discipline doesn't treat all religious faith claims the same. The only mature way to deal with religious faiths, as a subset of all paranormal faith-based reasoning, is to treat their claims all the same no matter how sophisticated their arguments. They must all be placed together on an equal playing field. Why single out conservative Christian PoR as meriting respect over the millions of animists out there, or pantheists, or still others, some of whose beliefs seem to be quite ridiculous from the perspective of an outsider? This isn't a reasonable way to approach religions. This is sheer ignorance and gullibility, characteristics not high on anyone's list of the best intellectual virtues.

7. Because the PoR discipline doesn't treat all paranormal claims the same. Why is it you don't see various paranormal claims discussed in the usual PoR departments? Why not discuss ghosts, trolls, leprechauns, and other fairies? Why not discuss extraterrestrials, UFO "sightings," and alien "abductions"? Why not discuss Big Foot and Loch Ness "sightings"? There are plenty of topics to discuss. Like psychics, healings, ESP, haunted houses, demonic possessions, telepathy, ancient astronauts, clairvoyance and prophecy, mediumship, astrology, witches, reincarnation, and so on and so forth. The reason PoR departments don't discuss these things much is because philosophers don't consider any of these claims to be credible ones. But if they discuss religions that have no credible basis then they should discuss these claims as well because all of them are faith-based and deserve to be placed on an equal playing field, privileging none.

8. Because the PoR discipline fails to understand that religions self-destruct. A wide diversity of theists such as found in the sects of Islam, Judaism, and Christianity all argue to the existence of God using the cosmological, teleological, and moral arguments. But these arguments are mistakenly taken by them all to support their particular gods. Believers will fallaciously use these arguments not only to support their own particular God hypothesis but also to claim that their own miracle claims are more probable than not because their

own particular God is in the world. So in this way Christians argue for a natural theology in the same way other theists do. But there is no reasonable way to tell in advance whether these arguments point to their own particular God. So believers cannot use them to establish their respective natural theologies either. For how do they know which God these arguments lead them to in advance of looking at the evidence for their particular religion? They simply cannot reasonably assume these arguments lead them to their particular God. Therefore they cannot approach their own miracle claims as having any more probability to them than other miracle claims, even granting that the arguments work.

In other words, these arguments to God's existence simply do not grant any believer any relevant background knowledge, or "priors," prior to examining their own particular religious faith. They must still look at the raw uninterpreted data to determine if a miracle took place without using a potentially false presumption that their God performed the particular miracle under investigation. Hence this line of reasoning destroys natural theology in one fell swoop. Even if there is a God of some kind, believers still have no reason to think their particular God did the miracle under investigation. That is, even a world with a God in it does not make their own miracle claims any more probable than not after all. For if Allah exists then Jesus was not raised from the dead, and we all know that the Jews rejected the Christian claim that Yahweh raised him from the dead. And so on.

To Christians who respond that the arguments to God's existence open up the possibility of miracles, I simply ask them if they would ever seriously consider the Christian miracles if they were Muslims or Orthodox Jews? Theism does not entail that your particular miracles have any more probability to them than others. I suspect Muslims and Orthodox Jews, even as theists themselves, are no more open to your miracle claims than I am as a nonbeliever, so you shouldn't be either!

When it comes to Christianity I agree with the Protestant criticisms of the Catholics as well as the Catholic criticisms of the Protestants. And I also agree with the fundamentalist criticisms of the liberals as well as the liberal criticisms of the fundamentalists. And I agree with the Hindu, Muslim, and Jewish criticisms of Christianity, as well as the Christian criticisms against their religions. When they criticize each other I think they're all right! What's left is the demise of religion and Christianity as a whole.

9. Because faith-based reasoning must end. If PoR is using reason to examine the claims of religion, and if religion is based on faith, then philosophy of religion must end. For faith has no justification, nor merit, nor warrant. A reasonable faith does not exist, nor can faith be a guide for reasoning to any objective conclusion.[47] The claims of religious faith via PoR cannot be reasonably defended. Doing so makes otherwise brilliant people look stupid, as I argued in a chapter for my anthology *The End of Christianity* with regard to Alvin Plantinga, William Lane Craig, and Richard Swinburne, and again as I argued in chapter 3 in this book.

Religion is indeed based on faith in supernatural forces or entities. Faith is indeed an unreliable way to gain objective knowledge about the world. And faith-based reasoning cannot justify any claim concerning matters of fact like the nature of nature and its workings. So philosophy of religion is reasoning about that which is unreasonable. It takes the utterly unwarranted conclusions of faith seriously. To reason about religion requires granting more than a philosopher worthy of the name should do, since the very first principle of religion is faith. There are some things philosophers should not take seriously to remain as serious intellectuals. A faith-based claim is one of them. There are other ways to deal with those types of claims. The proper discipline to determine if a claim is faith-based or not is to be found in the sciences.

10. Because there are plenty of other classes that address relevant topics better, such as various science classes, comparative religion classes, anthropology of religion and psychology of religion classes, and religion classes themselves. The larger discipline of philosophy already addresses PoR questions, such as through classes on critical thinking, epistemology, ethics, the history of PoR, individual philosophers, and so on.

To the important question of how best to treat religious faiths we turn next.

Notes

1. The book can be read at Plato's footnote, beginning here: https://platofootnote.wordpress.com/2016/04/01/the-nature-of-philosophy-preamble/.

2. Richard Carrier, "Is Philosophy Stupid?" video of his talk at Skepticon 6, uploaded November 29, 2013, https://www.youtube.com/watch?v=YLvWz9GQ3PQ.

3. Boghossian, *A Manual for Creating Atheists*, p. 177.

4. Ibid.

5. Ibid., p. 189.

6. Ibid.

7. Emphasis is his. Ryan T. Cragun, *How to Defeat Religion in 10 Easy Steps: A Toolkit for Secular Activists* (Durham, NC: Pitchstone Publishing, 2015), p. 26.

8. Linda Zagzebski, *The Philosophy of Religion: An Historical Introduction* (Malden, MA: Blackwell Publishing, 2007), p. 2.

9. Ibid., p. 9

10. See "Quote of the Day, By Anthropology Professor David Eller," Debunking Christianity, April 12, 2015, http://debunkingchristianity.blogspot.com/2015/04/quote-of-day-by-anthopology-professor.html.

11. Zagzebski, *The Philosophy of Religion*, p. 3.

12. Ibid., p. 30.

13. Nick Trakakis, *The End of Philosophy of Religion* (New York: Continuum, 2008), pp. 46–50.

14. Timothy D. Knepper, "The End of Philosophy of Religion?" *Journal of the American Academy of Religion* 82, no. 1 (March 2014): 144. I thank Hector Avalos for alerting me to this article.

15. Graham Oppy, *Reinventing Philosophy of Religion: An Opinionated Introduction* (Palgrave Pivot, 2014).

16. "Armchair Atheism, Ep. 2—Why Philosophy of Religion? with Graham Oppy," video, uploaded July 23, 2014, https://www.youtube.com/watch?v=Yv3DVvxgo5E.

17. Jeffery Jay Lowder, "The Evidential Argument from Moral Agency Revisited: A Reply to Jerry Coyne," Secular Outpost, July 3, 2014, http://www.patheos.com/blogs/secularoutpost/2014/07/03/the-evidential-argument-from-moral-agency-revisited-a-reply-to-jerry-coyne/.

18. Keith Parsons, "Towards a Rational Paganism," Secular Outpost, August 18, 2014, http://www.patheos.com/blogs/secularoutpost/2014/08/18/towards-a-rational-paganism/. For a fuller discussion see this book's Appendix.

19. David Bourget and David J. Chalmers, "What Do Philosophers Believe?" *Philosophical Studies* 170, no. 3 (2014): 465–500, http://philpapers.org/rec/BOUWDP.

20. Adriano Mannino, "Theism and Expert Knowledge," Crucial Considerations, January 28, 2015, http://crucialconsiderations.org/rationality/theism-and-expert-knowledge/.

21. Gregory W. Dawes, *Theism and Explanation* (New York: Routledge, 2009).

22. Gregory Dawes, in an interview with Richard Marshall, "On Theism and Explanation," *3:AM Magazine*, May 23, 2014, http://www.3ammagazine.com/3am/on-theism-and-explanation/. His thoughts echo mine in chapter 3.

23. Paul Draper, "What is Philosophy of Religion?" Philosophy of Religion, http://philosophyofreligion.org/?p=14582.

24, For instance, Thomas A. Lewis, *Why Philosophy Matters for the Study of Religion—and Vice Versa* (Oxford: Oxford University Press, 2016). Lewis is a professor of religious studies at Brown University who offers "an interdisciplinary study of religion." See also John Cottingham, *Philosophy of Religion: Towards a More Humane Approach* (Cambridge: Cambridge University Press, 2014). Cottingham is a professor emeritus of philosophy at the University of Reading in England. He offers that which I stand against, "a spiritually focused . . . approach to the philosophy of religion." Ugh!

25. Kevin Schilbrak, *Philosophy and the Study of Religions: A Manifesto* (Malden, MA: Wiley-Blackwell, 2014). David Eller pointed this book out to me.

26. Ibid., pp. 9–10.

27. Ibid., p. 10.

28. Ibid.

29. Ibid.

30. Ibid., p. 14.

31. Ibid.

32. Ibid., p. 18.

33. Ibid., p. 19.

34. Ibid., p. 19.

35. Ibid., p. 20.

36. Ibid., p. 19.

37. Ibid., p. 21.

38. Knepper, "The End of Philosophy of Religion?" p. 123.

39. Ibid., pp. 125–126.

40. Ibid., p. 130.

41. Ibid., p. 134. Thick descriptive reasoning should be construed "broadly" according to Knepper, involving formal, informal arguments, covering the grounds for and ends of reason-giving, the ideas and theories therein, the authors and audiences and the proponents and opponents in their cultural contexts and historical trajectories.

42. Ibid., p. 137.

43. Ibid., p. 140.

44. Ibid.

45. Ibid.

46. Robert Conner, "Faking Jesus," review of Richard Carrier's book *Proving History: Bayes Theorem and the Quest for the Historical Jesus*, https://www.scribd.com/doc/125993290/Faking-Jesus.

47. I argued against the reasonableness of faith in chapter 10 of my book, *The Outsider Test for Faith*, "Why Should Anyone Believe Anything at All?" pp. 207–228.

6

HOW TO EFFECTIVELY DEAL WITH FAITH-BASED CLAIMS

The philosophy of religion must end in all secular universities now! It didn't have its own discipline prior to the 1950s, so it can go back where it came from. If for centuries and beyond the PoR was not a discipline in the universities, we can do without it again. This is all the more important as we consider the rising devastating impact of secularism upon the beliefs of most philosophers of religion.

The Advance of Secularism and the Retreat of Faith

Secularism, as largely conceived, is a principle (or attitude) requiring that our viewpoints and actions, our laws and our politics, our institutions and our organizations are based on a secular point of view (as opposed to a sacred point of view) without any religious or spiritual basis. It's to adopt a naked public square rather than a sacred public square. It's not that this is the best alternative available to a society, as if there were others that can compare to it. Given the results of faith around the globe that stretch into the distant past, *there isn't any alternative!*

We've learned that to reasonably govern a society we should adopt secularism as our best way to do it. The number of hate-filled laws and actions committed by religious believers around the world today show us clearly that theocracy is morally bankrupt. There is no going back to the past. Secularism is a "necessity" in our world, as Ronald Lindsay argues.[1] When it comes to conservative Christianity in America, criminologist Elicka Peterson Sparks specifically indicts Christian theocratic nationalism for making the United States such a violent nation, filled with so much crime. It's due to the tremendous impact of the Bible and Christianity on the culture, institutions, and political life of the United States, with its hateful, xenophobic, war-mongering, gun-toting, misogynistic, child-abusing, gay-bashing, get-tough-on-crime, right-wing nuts.[2] Given the progress of secularism the religious viewpoint cannot help us into the future. Faith-headed enablers should take note.

Adopting secularism is also the best way for gaining knowledge about the world of nature and how it works. It's usually identified with methodological naturalism, which calls upon scientists to offer natural explanations for a given phenomenon. But it's secularism just the same. I shouldn't have to remind readers that religion halted science until its slow rise in the 1500s,[3] and it still erects obstacles to science in our day when it comes to everything from climate change to medicine.[4] Secularism has advanced knowledge. Faith has not. If we want to know the truth about something, anything, we should therefore adopt the principle of secularism. Period. Again, here as well, it's not that this is the best alternative available for gaining knowledge, as if there were others that can compare to it. Given the failure of religious faith to gain knowledge and solve problems, *there isn't any alternative!* So faith-based reasoning has no place in the secular university because of its miserable track record, especially when compared to the progress of secularism in every area of living, organizing, learning, and understanding.

In what other academic discipline of learning besides the PoR are students allowed to deny scientifically based reasoning? In what other academic discipline of learning besides PoR does the need for evidence not apply? In what other academic discipline of learning besides PoR can students get away with not being required to think exclusively in terms of probabilities? In what other academic discipline of learning besides PoR is the requirement for sufficient objective evidence nullified in favor of private subjective experiences? In what other academic discipline of learning besides PoR would someone be able to claim faith has an equal or better method than scientifically based reasoning at arriving at the truth? None. None should anyway. So these justifications for faith should be disallowed in the PoR discipline as well.

Hector Avalos has called for ending biblical studies based on the principle of secularism. Biblical scholars should not favor any given religious interpretation of the biblical texts, nor should they privilege these texts over the many other texts discovered from the ancient Near Eastern world. No privileging. No favoritism. No faith. The goal is to try to honestly understand them in their contexts. Only when they aim for this can they understand them. For then they will not force the selected texts into the Procrustean bed of a faith that seeks understanding.

New Testament scholar Rudolf Bultmann wrote a key essay in 1957 that asked and answered the question, "Is Exegesis without Presuppositions Possible?"[5] He first argued that biblical interpreters (or exegetes) should not prejudice their own *conclusions* when trying to understand the biblical texts, which is excellent advice! He then went on to argue forcefully that they cannot approach these texts without prior *presuppositions*, that is, with a blank slate of mind. Okay, fair enough so far. However, the biggest presupposition that modern scholars have, or should have anyway, is their modernity, that they live in the twenty-first century where secularism has proven its worth. If there is a God who wanted readers to view these ancient texts as divinely inspired words, then even by adopting the presupposition of secularism s/he could've brought us to that conclusion. But s/he didn't.[6]

Because biblical exegetes cannot approach the ancient biblical texts without prior presuppositions, they should adopt the presupposition of secularism. It's the only one to adopt when trying to understand biblical texts. It alone can truly help eliminate confirmation bias, something Michael Shermer called the "mother of all cognitive biases."[7] Secularism represents critical scholarship. It does not accept a confessional stance toward these biblical texts. Lacking a confessional stance, it is open to what the texts actually say rather than being forced to harmonize them with preconceived systematic theologies. Jon D. Levenson, a professor at Harvard Divinity School in the Department of Near Eastern Studies and Civilizations, offered a good definition of what critical scholars do when he said they "are prepared to interpret the text against their own preferences and traditions, in the interest of intellectual honesty."[8] Why shouldn't all biblical scholars be critical scholars? They should. Confessional scholarship is special pleading. Special pleading has no place among biblical scholars.

As I said, I'm advocating for the complete secularization of our secular universities in the same way that Avalos is advocating for the secularization of biblical studies, and in the same way separation of state from church activists are advocating for the secularization of our government. The reason for advocating this is that it's the only way to achieve both a good society and objective knowledge about the universe and life in it. If anyone disputes my claim he or she needs to show how religious faith can produce a good society and any objective knowledge about matters of fact like the nature of nature, its workings, and even its origins. From a secular perspective, faith explanations, solutions, and interpretations should have no countenance in a secular university. No one should punt to faith when trying to solve problems in any intellectual discipline for that matter.

Peter Boghossian agrees, telling us that in the classrooms of educators,

> It is taken for granted that faith-based claims are invulnerable to criticism and immune from further questioning. This intellectual rigor mortis is not allowed to occur across all disciplines. In the soft sciences, questioning a student's belief-forming mechanism is taboo, but in the hard sciences (mathematics, chemistry, biology, etc.) challenging claims and questioning reasoning processes are intrinsic to what it means to teach students to reason effectively. . . . This needs to end.[9]

If educators began doing this across the board it could revolutionize our institutions of higher learning. I welcome this revolution. It is very much needed. Let's call the professors who accept this challenge, who risk offending their students, their parents, and their administrators, "academic epistemologists" who seek to produce doubt in the minds of believers using the Socratic or dialectic method of dialogue. We need them desperately if we want to change the religious landscape.

How to Effectively Deal With Faith-Based Claims in the University

Here then are ten of the best ways to treat the faith-based claims of religionists in the secular university.

1. We can replace the PoR subdiscipline with more classes in science like geology, physics, astrophysics, astronomy, psychology, and neurology. Until Christians can come up with sufficient evidence to believe then we should no longer have to deal in-depth with their rationalizations, gerrymanderings, non sequiturs, and baseless assertions masquerading as a reasonable discussion in a pseudo-subdiscipline. Given that faith is intellectually bankrupt there isn't a single PoR class subject that could not be treated better in the many other classes taught in the secular university, especially science classes. Teaching science overwhelmingly disconfirms all faith-based claims of religionists to be unnecessary at best, if not factually false. Evolution, for instance, destroys most religions, and you don't even have to pay attention to a particular religion when teaching the fact of evolution to do this. So teach evolution and most religions die.[10]

2. We can replace the PoR subdiscipline with global, multicultural, anthropological, and comparative religion approaches to religion. The classes covered could be taught under the umbrella of the religion discipline itself (with no need for a subdivision of PoR), or in other departments like anthropology of religion, comparative religion, or psychology of religion. Of course some of these disciplines might need to be secularized themselves. If so, then let's do that as well. All disciplines in secular universities must be secularized.[11]

   Cultural anthropology professor David Eller wrote the book, *Atheism Advanced: Further Thoughts of a Freethinker*, which should be in every atheist's library. In it he argues why this particular global approach to religion should end religion itself, rather than any parochial version of it. It's because "awareness of other religions reduces the truth-probability of one's own."[12] Why is it that most debates in Western culture are debates on such topics as "Christianity vs. Atheism," "Christianity vs. Islam," and so on? Eller wants us to think in larger terms than that. Eller says the real debate should be set in terms of "Christianity vs. Itself," since there are so many branches of it, or "Christianity vs. All Other Religions," since that's the proper way to think about religion. Eller writes: "Nothing is more destructive to religion than other religions; it is like meeting one's own anti-matter twin."[13] That's because "other religions represent *alternatives* to one's own religion: other people believe in them just as fervently as we do, and they live their lives just as successfully as we do. Then, the diversity of religions forces us to see religion as a culturally relative phenomenon; different groups have different religions that appear adapted to their unique social and even environmental conditions. But if *their* religion is relative, then why is *ours* not?"[14] So, he argues, "the comparative study of religion throws doubt on the specific truth-claims that any particular religion makes."[15]

3. We can replace the PoR subdiscipline with more secular classes taught the way Hector Avalos has argued for and modeled in his biblical studies classes. Students should be forced to examine the origination and early history of particular religions against the backdrop of the times they came from. Examining the basis for a given faith is a much better way to examine the claims of particular religions. That means looking into their origins, influences, and early history as best as we can. Take for instance the messianic hopes we find in the New Testament[16] and the belief in an evil angelic devil[17] and an eternal punishment in hell,[18] which play prominent roles in the early Christian documents. They all originated in the intertestamental period between the "closing" of the Old Testament canon of Scripture and the writings in the New Testament. So in effect, the earliest Christian writings began by believing in things that have no guarantee of being inspired. For these intertestamental writings are not believed to be inspired.

Let me stress Avalos's work and method here. His goal with the Bible is "to persuade people to abandon reliance on this book. I see my goal as no different from physicians, whose goal of ending human illness would lead to their eventual unemployment."[19] He asks, "Why do we need an ancient book that endorses everything from genocide to slavery to be a prime authority of our public or private morality?[20]

This is the main theme of Avalos's work. It concerns the theological, ethical, and political irrelevance of the Bible for the modern world. His first book in English, *Fighting Words: The Origins of Religious Violence*, was a response to the violent attacks by militant Muslim extremists on 9/11 and came out in 2005, a year after Sam Harris started the so-called new atheism with his book, *The End of Faith*. Avalos argues that the origins of violence run deep in the Abrahamic religions, as evidenced in their own scriptures. The scholars of these religions try to maintain the value of their sacred books for the modern world, despite the evidence that they promote inhumane barbaric violence against others. In his second book, *The End of Biblical Studies*,[21] Avalos masterfully shows how biblical scholars are preoccupied with maintaining the relevance of the Bible for the modern world, even though their own research shows the opposite. In his third book, *Slavery, Abolitionism, and the Ethics of Biblical Scholarship* (2011), he expertly demonstrates how modern biblical scholars are still unjustifiably defending the indefensible ethics of biblical slavery.[22] In his most recent book, *The Bad Jesus: The Ethics of New Testament Ethics,* Avalos takes on the overall ethics of Jesus himself—*oh my*—as represented in the four canonical gospels (irrespective of whether Jesus existed or not, which he remains an agnostic about).[23] Avalos skillfully shows how the Jesus depicted in the New Testament has a bad side, a side permeated by a "religiocentric, ethnocentric and imperialistic orientation." He reveals the bad side of Jesus that modern biblical scholars try to hide from view, making the central figure in the New Testament irrelevant for modern life as well.

He passionately tells us what any activist would say: "What I seek is liberation from the very idea that any sacred text should be an authority for modern human existence. Abolishing human reliance on sacred texts is imperative when those sacred texts imperil the existence of human civilization as it is currently configured. The letter can kill. That is why the only mission of biblical studies should be to end biblical studies as we know it."[24] Avalos is an intelligent activist scholar, a one-man debunking machine. I wish there were many others like him in every discipline of learning.

4. A fourth way to best treat the faith-based claims of religionists in the secular university is to emphasize skepticism, doubt, and science in the philosophy classes already being taught, especially in critical thinking and epistemology classes. Johnnie Terry of Sierra College tells me he's using Jerry Coyne's 2009 book, *Why Evolution Is True,* along with Edward Humes' 2008 book, *Monkey Girl: Evolution, Education, Religion, and the Battle for America's Soul Girl,* for his critical thinking classes. That's what I'm talking about! He tells me they provide "excellent

support for scientific reasoning, verificationism, and falsificationism." Along these same lines I would recommend using Victor Stenger's book, *God and the Folly of Faith: The Incompatibility of Science and Religion* (2012), Jerry Coyne's book, *Faith vs. Fact: Why Science and Religion Are Incompatible* (2015), and Carl Sagan's classic, *The Demon-Haunted World: Science as a Candle in the Dark* (1996). Readers will have to forgive me for including my anthology, *Christianity in the Light of Science: Critically Examining the World's Largest Religion* (2016), which I think kills it. The Christian faith cannot survive if believers honestly consider its overall case.

Phil Torres, an affiliate scholar at the Institute for Ethics and Emerging Technologies, commented on ending the PoR subdiscipline (on my blog). While he thinks philosophy is important, especially the philosophy of science (and I agree), he said this: "As for philosophy of religion, I think such classes could be replaced by Epistemology 101, which would help establish that faith is a quite unacceptable excuse for accepting propositions about what the world is like and how it ought to be." Ha! *Epistemology 101?* Phil combines insight with ridicule brilliantly and forcefully. For it doesn't take much epistemology to see the errors of faith. If it requires an in-depth amount of epistemology to believe a virgin really had a baby in the ancient prescientific world then that kind of epistemology is obfuscationist epistemology, which should easily and reasonably be rejected by a first-year college student.

In teaching like this instructors should reject the difference between thinking critically and thinking skeptically, for to think critically is to think skeptically, and vice versa. Believers can and do think critically, in so far as they can connect the dots of logical premises. But they are not truly critical thinkers since they do not think skeptically by questioning the false assumptions built into their logical premises. Teaching students to be critical thinkers is very important but teaching them to have a skeptical disposition is equally important. Critical thinking should lead to this disposition if it's to be considered critical thinking. The problem is that faith is a critical thinking stopper. It builds up a wall that stops believers dead in their tracks. They dare not go beyond it to the proper conclusion when applying the standards of critical thinking. I taught critical thinking classes as a Christian believer. So I know exactly what they are doing. Norman Geisler, one of the leading Christian apologists who defends the indefensible, even cowrote a book with Ronald M. Brooks titled, *Come, Let Us Reason: An Introduction to Logical Thinking.*[25]

So what's the problem? Faith. Faith stunts one's critical thinking skills. It prohibits a person of faith from applying the set of critical thinking skills we all agree about. You can see this by how they argue. What believers do is to defend their faith rather than look critically at it, no matter what the intellectual cost. Repetition alert! Here comes *Law's law of faith* again: "Anything based on faith, no matter how ludicrous, can be made to be consistent with the available evidence, given a little patience and ingenuity."[26] If Christian apologists could think logically, without the perceived need to defend their religious sect's faith, they would see they are not thinking critically. So there is no distinction between critical thinking and thinking skeptically. They are one and the same. That's why faith is an irrational leap over the probabilities, a cognitive bias that blinds them to the truth. Believers operate by double standards. When we say the party of agnosticism and atheism is one of reason and science we mean it. We invite believers to the adult table, where an adult conversation can be had. Stop the pretense, the fantasy-land world of faith-based unthinking.

The faith "virus," as Peter Boghossian calls it, produces "doxastic closure," that is, belief closure. People of faith are less likely to have doxastic openness, that is, to be aware of their own ignorance and open to the idea that they are wrong. They are less likely to revise their faith-based conclusions. They feel certain about their conclusions because that's the nature of this virus. Faith, he argues, "taints or at worst removes our curiosity about the world, what we should value, and what type of life we should lead. Faith replaces wonder with epistemological arrogance disguised as false humility."[27] He rightly argues:

> When someone suffers from a doxastic pathology, they tend to not really listen to an argument, to not carefully think through alternatives, and to lead with their conclusions and work backward. The moment we're unshakably convinced we posses immutable truth, we become our own enemy. . . . Few things are more dangerous than people who think they're in possession of absolute truth. Honest inquiry with sincere questions and an open mind rarely contribute

to the misery of the world. Passionate, doxastically closed believers contribute to human suffering and inhibit human well-being.[28]

Boghossian calls for the proper treatment for this virus of the mind. It's to do interventions with people as we meet them on the street. It's to *deprogram them* by creating doxastic openness within the believer through Socratic dialogue. He calls on a mass of evangelistic atheists to become *street epistemologists*, who seek to instill within people they meet "a self-consciousness of ignorance, a determination to challenge foundational beliefs, a relentless hunger for truth, and a desire to know. Wonder, curiosity, honest self-reflection, sincerity, and the desire to know are a solid basis for a life worth living. The Street Epistemologist seeks to help others reclaim their curiosity and their sense of wonder—both of which are robbed by faith."[29] Their goal "is to help people reclaim the desire to know—a sense of wonder. You'll help people destroy foundational beliefs, flimsy assumptions, faulty epistemologies, and ultimately faith."[30] "The tools of faith—certainty, prejudice, pretending, confirmation bias, irrationality, and superstition—all come into question though self-awareness of ignorance."[31]

To administer the proper vaccination to the faith virus the street epistemologist should not attempt to change the particular beliefs of the host, but rather change the way they form their beliefs. For the problem is the faith virus itself, "not the conclusions people hold."[32] "To demolish a building," he says, "start with the base. Take out the support beam and the entire structure will fall. Faith is the base. Faith holds up the entire structure. Collapse faith and the entire edifice falls."[33] So to be effective we should not target religion, God, morality, politics, or the hosts of the virus themselves. We should stick to asking Socratic dialectical questions about how they know what they know. "By undermining faith one is able to undermine almost all religions simultaneously, and it may be easier to help someone to abandon their faith than it is to separate them from their religion."[34] "Belief in God(s) is not the problem. Belief without evidence is the problem. Warrantless, dogged confidence is the problem. Epistemological arrogance masquerading as humility is the problem. Faith is the problem."[35] (To counter Christian philosophers who argue we all have faith and have it equally, see Appendix C: "The Demon, Matrix, Material World, and Dream Possibilities.")

I see no reason why philosophers should not teach their classes like this and be "academic epistemologists" as I've mentioned. They should! They should seek to liberate the minds of students. Boghossian: "We need to train educators not just to teach students how to think critically, but also how to nudge attitudes about faith on their downward spiral."[36] "Anyone can develop a critical thinking skill set,"[37] he says, even people he describes as pretending to know things they don't know.

5. We can teach students a sound method for properly evaluating religious faith-based claims, without double standards, that helps eliminate confirmation bias when examining one's own religion. We can develop classes on it. To help students develop a skeptical disposition, which is the necessary part of being a critical thinker, I've developed and defended the best and only method for doing so, which I call the *outsider test for faith*.[38] Emeritus Professor Jerry Coyne, a scientist who specialized in evolutionary genetics at the University of Chicago, says "the wisdom of this . . . quasi-scientific approach" is "unquestionable."[39] It asks believers to rationally test one's culturally adopted religious faith from the perspective of an outsider, a nonbeliever, with the same level of reasonable skepticism believers already use when examining the other religious faiths they reject.

One of the best authors to utilize the outsider perspective is Guy Harrison. In his book *50 Reasons People Give for Believing in a God*, he uses this perspective every time it's called for, about 75–80 percent of the time. He doesn't neglect other arguments when answering these fifty "reasons" though, so it's not a one-note song he's singing. When it comes to fearing hell as a reason to believe, Harrison reminds Christians that Muslims don't fear their hell, just as Christians don't fear Allah's hell:

> Each group of believers dismisses the threat of the other because they don't see any evidence or hear any compelling arguments to suggest that these alternative hells are real. They don't lose a wink of sleep over it because they know those claims are totally unsubstantiated. Meanwhile atheists don't fear anybody's hell because none of them are backed by any evidence.[40]

When it comes to proving God by answered petitionary prayers, Harrison reminds believers there are many other religionists who claim answered prayers prove their gods as well: "The fact that followers of so many contradictory belief systems claim that their prayers achieve positive results is a bad sign for prayer proponents."[41] When it comes to healings as proof of God, Harrison informs believers that, "If stories of faith healings prove that a particular god is real, then it means many other gods must be real too because numerous gods have been credited with miraculous healings since the beginnings of civilization."[42]

Harrison correctly tells us the specific problem believers have. Their problem is a basic ignorance of the diverse number of religions in the world and the arguments used to justify their faiths:

> One result of this widespread religious ignorance is that few believers are aware of just how similar their justifications for religious belief are to the justifications cited by people who follow different religions. They probably also do not know that almost all religions follow a nearly identical pattern. Most religions rely on authority figures, very old stories, early instruction to children, and faith in the absence of evidence. Discovering how similar religions are in the way they operate and survive can be surprising for many believers who have been misled to think that their justifications for belief are unique and superior.[43]

6. When teaching critical thinking and epistemology classes, we should place religious beliefs where they rightfully belong, as a subcategory of paranormal beliefs in general. When it comes to critical thinking and epistemology classes there are two books that should be required reading. The first one is a college textbook written by Theodore Schick Jr. and Lewis Vaughn, titled *How to Think About Weird Things: Critical Thinking for a New Age*, now in its seventh edition.[44] While I have an earlier edition this book puts faith-based claims on an equal playing field, privileging none of them. The authors treat religious faiths as a subset of paranormal claims, as we should. The other book is written by David. J. Hand, an emeritus professor of mathematics and former president of the Royal Statistical Society, titled, *The Improbability Principle: Why Coincidences, Miracles, and Rare Events Happen Every Day*.[45] I can do no better than to quote the summary on the dust jacket:

Hand argues that extraordinarily rare events are anything but. In fact, they're commonplace. Not only that, we should all expect to experience a miracle roughly once every month. But Hand is no believer in superstitions, prophecies, or the paranormal. His definition of "miracle" is thoroughly rational. No mystical or supernatural explanation is necessary to understand why someone is lucky enough to win the lottery twice, or is destined to be hit by lightning three times and still survive. All we need, Hand argues, is a firm grounding in a powerful set of laws: the laws of inevitability, of truly large numbers, of selection, of the probability lever, and of near enough.

To the question of whether miracles happen, Hand's reasoning is solid, that what we think is a purposeful event by a deity is best accounted for by chance events. As yet, not one religious apologist worthy the name has dealt with Hand's book. My claim is they cannot reasonably respond.

Along these same lines I would also recommend Guy P. Harrison's book *50 Popular Beliefs That People Think Are True* (2012) and two books by Michael Shermer, *Why People Believe Weird Things: Pseudoscience, Superstition, and Other Confusions of Our Time* (2002 edition) and *The Believing Brain: From Ghosts and Gods to Politics and Conspiracies—How We Construct Beliefs and Reinforce Them as Truths* (2011).

7. We can simply ignore faith-based claims in the secular university. By doing this academics would be teaching students that faith-based claims are undeserving of serious attention. Later I'll talk about the effective use of ridicule, mockery, and satire. Ignoring something that people take seriously is a form of ridicule. It's to treat it as a joke.

    If a PoR professor had a class on the evidence and arguments for a few "dead" religions like Zoroastrianism, Gnosticism, Mithraism, Norse theology, Paganism, etc., then doing so would be to take those religions seriously. Believers in Religion A no more take the religions they reject seriously than believers in Religions B, C, D, E, F, G . . . take Religion A seriously, and vice versa. Highlighting one religion for rational examination and discussion over others presupposes that it has more going for it. But if all religions are based in faith and if faith-type answers are no answers at all, and if atheist professors want to be honest about the PoR classes they teach, then paradoxically they should not even teach PoR classes. This proposal seems counterproductive and very impractical, I know, especially since most students in the Western world are *de facto* Christians and need to be forced to think skeptically through their faith, and also because PoR professors have a need to earn a living from their education. But I consider it a good option. By ignoring faith one can also ignore the controversy, if it's controversial to debunk faith where you live.

Just consider what universities might look like in the future in a largely atheist society? Universities would just educate students. They wouldn't have to pander to belief at all. Faith would be ignored. That's the goal, and to help facilitate this goal, ignoring faith is a good option. Don't let it into the discussion. It isn't relevant to anything serious. It discovers no knowledge. It doesn't help us justify any knowledge. It advances nothing at all. Faith should one day be labeled a cognitive bias. It keeps one's cognitive faculties from functioning properly. Faith is an irrational, unevidenced, or misplaced trust in something or someone.

8. Let's say you're an atheist philosopher teaching PoR classes and it dawns on you from reading this book you've been teaching your classes wrong. You could quit teaching and find another career, or you could attempt teaching in other areas, but I know that's asking too much. What to do? You should teach the truth not the controversy. We should not be afraid to debunk faith-based religious arguments in the classroom. Keep in mind, the focus is on faith, not the dogmas of faith. Faith is the problem, not any given specific item of belief. What you're aiming at is to produce doubt within your students.

Once every so often some Christian will email me with a supposed new philosophical argument for the existence of their God. Most often they are not new at all, but a hybrid of already debunked arguments. When they contact me I ask them the same thing. I'll thank them then say, "I'll take a serious look at this argument and try to show it's wrong if I can, but tell me, is this argument the reason you believe? Did it lead you to believe in the first place?" And so far to date they all answer me with a negative. We should deal with the real reasons why they came to believe in the first place. These arguments, new in every generation, come from faith. They never reason to faith. They always reason from faith. So then I proceed, like Socrates before me, to ask about the real reasons for their faith. "Why did you initially believe? That's the question I'm interested in most. Were you reasoned into your faith or was it taught on your mama's knees, so to speak?" This point is made very well by Guy Harrison:

> How do people choose a religion? They don't! The dirty little secret about religious belief is that it's imposed, not chosen, in almost every case. Very few believers voluntarily and consciously select their particular religion. The religion usually is introduced to a child by family members—without debate, questions, or consent—and then reinforced by the immediate social setting. This is clearly the case because we can look at the geography and family patterns of religious belief and see that the best predictors of a person's religious belief are what their parents believe and where they live. . . . What this shows is that very few of the world's people are doing much thinking, if any, when they first become tied to a religion. There is virtually no comparison going on when it comes to the adoption of religion throughout the global population. There is no weighing of evidence and assessing of arguments. There is no time given for fair hearings of alternative beliefs or counter explanations for religious claims. In almost every case religion is a family and social inheritance that the individual has little say in.[46]

If you as an instructor want to show that faith is not a reasonable method for gaining any knowledge you'll have to provide a few examples. Examine several paranormal claims first, as I said before. Then afterward, after you get your students to see faith is unreasonable in cases they probably agree with you about, use a few examples from their favored religions. Here are a couple of quick examples with regard to religions.

First argument—regarding the Kalam cosmological argument, which promises to show that some kind of personal God created the universe at some point in time. Infinity is not a number, so the Kalam argument fails. The concept of infinity is a placeholder for a number beyond our finite conceptions. To see this, just think of an infinite set of even numbers. Now add to that set an infinite number of odd numbers. By adding an infinite set of odd numbers to the infinite set of even numbers we have not increased the actual numbers in that set. So an actual infinite set of numbers does not exist. We could even subtract all numbers with zeros in them, or the numbers 1–1,000, or all prime numbers and more, and still have an infinite set of numbers leftover.

The error with the Kalam argument is in thinking infinity is an actual number. Based on this error William Lane Craig says there cannot be an actual infinite number of past events. Well, of course not. That's because infinity isn't an actual number. Precisely because infinity is not an actual number we cannot count an infinite number of past events. The way apologists use infinity incorrectly assumes in advance there was a beginning an infinite time ago. The truth is that an infinite timeline necessarily lies outside of our epistemic horizons. But this tells us nothing at all about whether the universe is eternal.

James Lindsay, who has a PhD in mathematics, wrote the following in his book, *Dot, Dot, Dot: Infinity Plus God Equals Folly*. He says:

> Eternal cosmologies deny the existence of a beginning. Eternal means no beginning and no end. No first moment. No last moment. In an eternal cosmological model, we have to reckon time only from defined moments, and we can imagine a timeline of infinite length in both directions from any point that we choose. The way we conceive of that is not of a beginning infinitely long before or an end infinitely long after but rather as "there's always an earlier moment than any we describe and always a later moment than any we describe. Now the point isn't that we know the universe is eternal. It's that we don't know that it isn't. The whole point, by definition, of an eternal cosmology is that there is no first moment (i.e., no beginning).[47]

In an email to me, he went on to say, "The Kalam is exactly the kind of cosmology we would expect from people who hadn't yet discovered science. . . . It would be absurd if they weren't so embarrassingly serious."

Second argument—regarding the case for the existence of God due to objective morality. The moral argument to the existence of God depends on one's morality. Many Christian theologians and philosophers attempt to make an argument from the existence of objective morality to the existence of their God, who just happens to have the same kind of morality they do, surprise! From the outset it depends on whether or not there is an objective morality. Many atheists are cultural relativists. How can people make an argument to God's existence from morality if cultural relativism is the case? They can't.

The moral argument to a particular Christian God's existence could be shattered in an ethics class, or a history of ethics class, or a global and multicultural class on ethics. Nonetheless, a historical and global understanding of morality would quell such considerations. Take for example the Islamic State (or ISIS). They could make the same moral argument to the existence of their god, using their own morality, where it's okay to rape women, own slaves, chop off heads, and burn people alive. Christians would have to agree with their moral argument, but subsequently disagree with their morals. However, the morals of ISIS are used as evidence that their god exists, just as the specific morals of Christians (depending on the century) are used as evidence their god exists. So certain kinds of morals lead to certain kinds of gods. Or certain kinds of gods are used to justify certain kinds of morals. Which comes first? I'm as sure as sure can be that the morals come first. Where do believers get their morals from? That's as tricky a question as it gets for me. But I can guarantee you Christians do not get their morals from the Bible. For if they did, they would look much the same as the morals of the Islamic State. For in the Bible we see much of the same things, like slavery, holy wars, genocide or ethnic cleansing, and Inquisitions.[49]

Regardless, there is no time in the history of ethics where Christians themselves could not make this argument based on the morals of their day. They could own slaves, sacrifice children to Yahweh, or have sex slaves and be heard to argue at the local pub that their god is the source of objective morals. This argument to god from morals is empty rhetoric without any content.

Since morals come first, I think philosopher Raymond Bradley has produced a good counterargument. Bradley: "If there are universal objective moral truths, then there is no God of the Bible." He then provides some universal objective moral truths that are counter to biblical morality: (1) "It is morally wrong to deliberately and mercilessly slaughter men, women, and children who are innocent of any serious wrongdoing"; (2) "It is morally wrong to provide one's troops with young women captive with the prospect of their being used as sex slaves"; (3) "It is morally wrong to make people cannibalize their friends and family"; (4) "It is morally wrong to practice human sacrifice, by burning or otherwise"; (5) "It is morally wrong to torture people endlessly for their beliefs." He argues that "if we take these moral principles as objective ones, as Christians themselves do, then since we find them commanded and permitted by the God of the Bible, he does not exist."[50]

9. When teaching PoR classes there is no need to grant anything for the sake of discussion. More and more I'm finding that atheist philosophers are granting way too much when dealing with the coherence of such mythological nonsense as the existence of Yahweh, Satan, and hell and the story of the virgin birth, incarnation, and resurrection of Jesus. It's like we skip a very important step, a crucial one in my opinion, when we grant anything to ancient mythical beliefs that don't deserve any respect at all.

I see no reason to grant anything for the sake of discussion. I don't think atheists can do much to change the minds of fundamentalists, for instance. Atheists are the last people to reach fundamentalists. We are not even on their grid. Some of them only read the Bible. So there is usually no reason to grant something for the sake of a discussion with them either. Fundamentalists are most likely to listen to moderates, who are most likely to listen to liberals, who are most likely to listen to deists, who are most likely to listen to agnostics, who are most likely to listen to atheists. So we don't need to be too concerned about this. Others along this continuum are already active, already arguing their cases. We just need to focus on reaching those who are reachable on our side of that continuum.

There is a two-pronged attack we shouldn't neglect. When we're dealing with an ancient religious belief we should first examine it in the context of the mythological past in which it belongs. If it's a nonhistorical myth we don't need to examine the belief philosophically, which is the second prong. So before dealing with the philosophical issues we should place these mythological beliefs where they belong, in the ancient past.

When it comes to the ancient past the ancients did not produce any deity or belief that should be taken seriously, period. For what we find is a bunch of dead deities and sacrificed virgins and children, along with baseless miraculous claims no longer taken seriously by anyone. So if Orthodox Jews or Christians or Muslims say there is one deity that still lives from out of that same prescientific superstitious past, that itself is an extraordinary claim requiring a lot of evidence to support it. In the case of Yahweh, the god most Jews and Christians believe in today is not the Yahweh of the Old Testament. Yahweh and their own god are not the same person.

Anyone who looks into the historical evidence for Yahweh, Satan, hell, virgin births, incarnations, and resurrections will see these beliefs come from the ancient mythological past. The best way to kill such barbaric and utterly ignorant beliefs is to look at their mythological origins, and no appeal to the genetic fallacy can help the honest believer here. All that intelligent people have to do is use the empirical look-and-feel test for myths. If it looks and feels like a myth it is one. If it looks and feels to have an origin in the ancient superstitious past and contains wild and bizarre stories that only ancient people could have believed before the age of science, then it is myth all the way down. When we take seriously a mythical idea we give it some sort of respectability just by doing so. For instance, I doubt very much that philosophers would try to show why Muhammad could not have ridden a horse around the solar system by offering a detailed analysis of physics and horses.

Here is a case in point for illustrative purposes, concerning the barbaric biblical doctrine of hell. How should we treat it? Let's consider how philosophers of religion treat biblical subjects. In his book, *The Problem of Hell*, philosophy professor Jonathan L. Kvanvig mainly utilizes philosophical arguments on behalf of the view that, based upon God's character "in which his love is the primary motivational characteristic,"[51] God will not abandon any person until that person has made a settled, final decision to reject God, under favorable circumstances. Once a person has finally and competently chosen to reject God, then out of respect for that person's autonomy, God allows him or her to be annihilated, as a sort of rational suicide when all other alternatives are too painful or hopeless. He thinks this is the best description of hell, and that it isn't incompatible "with any appropriate theological constraint on an account of hell arising from the authority of the Christian scriptures." But he does admit that his "strictly philosophical investigation of the doctrine of hell does not imply many of the aspects of biblical teaching about hell."[52]

Look what Kvanvig is doing. He's granting the existence of hell and trying to make it pleasant to civilized ears. He's not trying to harmonize his views with the Bible. No, he even admits this somewhat. When his views don't imply all that the Bible does he simply tosses the Bible away. He's making stuff up as he goes. He's an obfuscationist philosopher trying to hide what the Bible really teaches about hell. Creationist Henry M. Morris and Martin E. Clark are at least honest about it. They wrote, "So far as we can tell from Scripture, the present hell, Hades, is somewhere in the heart of earth itself. . . . The Biblical descriptions are quite matter-of-fact. The writers certainly themselves believed hell to be real and geographically 'beneath' the earth's surface."[53] One thing we know about creationists like Henry Morris, and even Ken Ham, is *they are not embarrassed to say what the Bible says.* They should be, but that's besides my point right now. They don't try to soft pedal the truth as the Bible teaches it. So I consider them to be more faithful to what the Bible actually teaches than other believers precisely because of this. Kvanvig and others who get embarrassed with what they read in the Bible are the ones trying to create a revisionist obfuscationist theology to hide their embarrassment. Kvanvig can obscure or suppress biblical truth when it serves him, but then he's not taking the Bible as evidence that hell exists either. He needs to tell us why anyone should bother taking a statement in the Bible about hell to be evidence that it exists? Where's the evidence?

In a 1984 Wendy's fast-food commercial, a little old lady, played by actress Clara Peller, asked, "Where's the beef?" So let's ask, where's the evidence, the sufficient objective evidence, the beef for the existence of hell? We don't find it where it's supposed to be, down in the depths of the earth, as far as oil rigs can drill down. Should we accept a statement about the existence of hell from ancient prescientific people who thought the earth was a flat disk with a firm sky above where the Judeo-Christian god resided on his throne?[54] Just like we haven't discovered hell in the recesses of the earth, we haven't discovered God where he's supposed to be located either, in the sky, just above the mountains in the clouds. We've been above the moon and sent satellites through the solar system and peered into the far reaches of the universe and still haven't found God. Where's this evidence for the biblical God? Lacking that where's the objective evidence that God acted or acts in history? That's what we need. That's what any outsider needs. Evidence. Objective evidence. Sufficient evidence. It simply does not exist. Obfuscationist theology or philosophy will not change this fact.

What do atheist philosophers of religion have to gain by showing Kvanvig's concept of hell is too barbaric to be accepted as true, when he has not produced the evidence that hell exists? Why bother with such arguments until said evidence is produced? This is where P. Z. Myers' *courtier's reply* comes into play. Show me the evidence! No philosopher needs to engage in such sophistry until there is some credible evidence such a place exists. Doing so is to grant such an unevidenced belief a measure of credibility, since it allows Christian theists to appear smart when they respond.

The truth is hell actually does exist, but it's not the hell welcomed by most Christians. The Greek word for hell, *gehenna*, describes a valley outside of Jerusalem where rubbish was burned. I actually visited this place in 1989 and rubbish was still burned there. So when the earliest Christians wanted to talk about punishment in the afterlife, what better image could they use but *gehenna*? It was a garbage heap. In a garbage heap fire and worms (maggots) consume the trash. To literally say sinners go to hell when they die quite frankly means they end up in this garbage heap. That's the image they used to describe a place deep in the bowels of the earth, where no one can go to test that hypothesis.

10. Philosophy instructors who teach religion honestly should treat them all equally, privileging none, without any special pleading. All faith-based claims, all paranormal beliefs should be placed on a level playing surface if we're supposed to play with them correctly. That's what the outsider perspective on faith does. None of them get any special access to the truth because they're believed by more people, or they're more recent, or, in reverse, they have centuries of sophistry in their defense. All that intelligent people have to do is use the empirical smell test for faith. If it smells like a dead fish it is one. If it smells like faith it is

faith. Atheists are better at sniffing for faith than believers are, although believers in different religious traditions have a remarkable ability to smell the dead fishes of other faiths as well as atheists can.

Let me give you a few indicators when faith is on the hook, since we need to identify faith-based claims if we're going to treat them all the same. Faith is certain. It doesn't entertain much doubt at all. Faith refuses to change its mind in the face of good solid evidence. Faith seems to always find that small little hole through which it can still maintain it was not obliterated by the evidence. It has a deer-in-the-headlights look when encountering a good argument to the contrary for the first time.

Probably the best way to figure out if an idea is held by faith, rather than because of the probabilities based on good evidence, is to look at the intersection where faith and science meet. If there is overwhelming support for an idea in the global scientific community, then that idea has the backing of very strong objective evidence. If you object to that idea, you do so based on faith. Evolution is one such idea. The present crisis of human-caused climate change is another one. That vaccines save lives is yet another one. Science delivers the goods. Period. Faith does not.

By contrast to the assured results of the consensus of scientists, if an idea is not agreed upon by religious believers, then to that same degree of disagreement the idea is faith-based, false, and probably unworthy of serious consideration. Moreover, if an idea is only—or largely—held by people in one part of the globe, then to that same degree of global separation the idea is faith-based, false, and probably unworthy of serious consideration. If that idea is only contained in one religious book, or only held by a sect within a sect of a religion, then to that same degree the idea is faith-based, false, and probably unworthy of serious consideration.

Furthermore, if any religion has taught, or still teaches, that its church, mosque, temple, shrine, or holy place sits at the center of the earth, then that faith is false and probably unworthy of serious consideration. If any religion has taught, or still teaches, it's okay to enslave people against their will, or mistreat and rape women, then that faith is false and probably unworthy of serious consideration. If any religion has taught, or still teaches, it's mandatory—or even permissible—to kill homosexuals, witches, heretics, apostates, or people who hold another religion, then that faith is false and probably unworthy of serious consideration. If any religion has taught, or still teaches, that it's okay to brutalize animals due to some kind of dominion mandate, or to dash babies against rocks as the last acts of genocide, then that faith is false and probably unworthy of serious consideration. If any religion has taught, or still teaches, that its God approves of or commands a holy war to defend its sacred truths, to convert people by force, or to steal land from others, then that faith is false and probably unworthy of serious consideration.

Any questions?

Notes

1. Ronald A. Lindsay titled his book *The Necessity of Secularism: Why God Can't Tell Us What to Do* (Durham, NC: Pitchstone Publishing, 2014).

2. Elicka Peterson Sparks, *The Devil You Know: The Surprising Link between Conservative Christianity and Crime* (Amherst, NY: Prometheus Books, 2014).

3. See Richard Carrier, "Christianity Was Not Responsible for Modern Science," in *The Christians Delusion*, ed. John W. Loftus (Amherst, NY: Prometheus Books, 2010), pp. 396–419, and also Richard Carrier, "The Dark Ages," in *Christianity Is Not Great: How Faith Fails*, ed. John W. Loftus (Amherst, NY: Prometheus Books, 2014), pp. 209–221.

4. On climate change, see William Patterson's "Christianity and the Environment," in *Christianity Is Not Great: How Faith Fails*, ed. John W. Loftus (Amherst, NY: Prometheus Books, 2014), pp. 286–302.

5. Rudolf Bultmann, *New Testament Mythology and Other Basic Writings*, trans. Schubert M. Ogden (Philadelphia: Fortress Press, 1984), https://books.google.com/books?id=JhiW3y9HZ7IC&pg=PA145&lpg=PA145&dq=Is+PresupUs+Exegesis+without+presuppositions+Possible&source=bl&ots=YbyY2aFkFf&sig=PY35rfuczSRND6BYO3ItMvF1ZsE&hl=en&sa=X&ved=0ahUKEwjv9LKjzL7NAhUDLB4KHds3CDEQ6AEINTAD#v=onepage&q=Is%20PresupUs%20Exegesis%20without%20presuppositions%20Possible&f=false.

6. See, for instance, "Three Definitive Answers to What It Would Take to Convince Atheists to Believe!" Debunking Christianity, June 9, 2015, http://

debunkingchristianity.blogspot.com/2015/06/three-definitive-answers-to-what-it.html. See also my chapter 7 in "What We've Got Here Is a Failure to Communicate," in *The Christian Delusion*, ed. John W. Loftus (Amherst, NY: Prometheus, 2010), pp. 181–206, and my book *The Outsider Test for Faith* (Amherst, NY: Prometheus, 2013).

7. Michael Shermer in *The Believing Brain* (New York: Henery Holt, 2011), p. 259.

8. See page 3 of his book *The Death and Resurrection of the Beloved Son* (New Haven: Yale University Press, 1995). In that book he argues that "only at a particular stage rather late in the history of Israel was child sacrifice branded as counter to the will of YHWH and thus ipso facto idolatrous" (p. 5).

9. Peter Boghossian, "Is It Ever Reasonable to Agree to Disagree?" *Philosophers' Magazine* no. 59 (2012): 15–16.

10. I actually think such a university class should be a mandatory requirement in all universities, even if a student is majoring in disciplines like philosophy, business, food management, English, and so forth.

11. Regarding comparative religion, David Eller wrote (via email):

> From my experience, "comparative religion" is a much more restrictive discipline or approach. It tends to stick to the Big Five "world religions" (Judaism, Christianity, Islam, Hinduism, Buddhism), and it is much more text- or scripture-oriented. It tends to give generalized and superficial descriptions of the religions, and it tends to take "religion" for granted, without a critical stance on what "religion" is or how the concept evolved— and how it affects contemporary scholarship on "religion." Forgive my bias, but anthropology of religion is dramatically more inclusive, embracing many more religious traditions, including and especially "tribal" or indigenous religions. It also moves away from texts and elite knowledge to the actual practice of religious members (what is increasingly called "vernacular religion"). Further, it is much more critical and analytical of (largely Western and Christian) concepts like "belief" or "ritual," asking where these concepts came from and how they changed over time.

> Regarding psychology of religion, Eller wrote (via email):

> Psychology of religion is tired in two ways. First, it operates with Western psychological concepts, and second, it operates with Western religious concepts. I suppose there is some room in the academy for questions of religious "experience" or "emotions" or whatever—as long as we remember, with William James, that "religious experiences" are just experiences, and "religious emotions" are just emotions. So far, the cognitive theory of

religion has not really dealt with individual psychological experiences too much, perhaps because psychology of religion is already occupying that territory. As you know, cognitive science of religion [CSR] tends to ask how religion evolved out of basic human mental and social characteristics, rather than how religion is practiced and experienced in the present. There has been some generic work on memory and why certain religious ideas "stick" in the mind (from "costly signaling theory" to Whitehouse's two modes of ritual), but up to today CSR has had a narrower mission than psychology of religion. Perhaps CSR will expand to fill the role of psychology of religion, but it also needs to expand to include more than religious "ideas"—again, to grapple with practices, institutions, and other non-mental forms of religion.

12. David Eller, *Atheism Advanced: Further Thoughts of a Freethinker* (Cranford, NJ: American Atheist Press, 2007), p. 233.

13. Ibid., p. 233.

14. Ibid. Emphasis is his.

15. Ibid, p. 232.

16. This is something I've written about in chapter 17 of *Why I Became an Atheist*, pp. 349–369.

17. On this see T. J. Wray and Gregory Mobley, *The Birth of Satan: Tracing the Devil's Biblical Roots* (New York: Palgrave, 2005), chapter 5, "Satan Between the Testaments," pp. 95–112.

18. See Alan Bernstein, *The Formation of Hell: Death and Retribution in the Ancient and Early Christian Worlds* (Ithaca, NY: Cornell University Press, 1996).

19. Ibid., p. 25.

20. Ibid., p 341.

21. Hector Avalos, *The End of Biblical Studies* (Amherst, NY: Prometheus Books, 2007).

22. Hector Avalos, *Slavery, Abolitionism, and the Ethics of Biblical Scholarship* (Sheffield: Sheffield Phoenix Press, 2011).

23. Hector Avalos, *The Bad Jesus: The Ethics of New Testament Ethics* (Sheffield: Sheffield Phoenix Press, 2015).

24. Ibid, p. 342.

25. Norman L. Geisler and Ronald M. Brooks, *Come, Let Us Reason: An Introduction to Logical Thinking* (Grand Rapids, MI: Baker Books, 1990).

26. Stephen Law, *Believing Bullshit* (Amherst, NY: Prometheus Books, 2011), p. 75.

27. Peter Boghossian, *A Manual for Creating Atheists* (Durham, NC: Pitchstone Publishing, 2013), p. 43.

28. Ibid., p. 70.

29. Idid., p. 43–44

30. Ibid., p. 45.

31. Ibid., p. 51.

32. Ibid., p. 72.

33. Ibid., p. 75.

34. Ibid.

35. Ibid., p. 77.

36. Ibid., p. 177.

37. Ibid., p. 220.

38. See my book *The Outsider Test for Faith*.

39. Jerry Coyne, *Faith vs. Fact: Why Science and Religion Are Incompatible* (New York: Viking, 2015), pp. 85–86.

40. Guy P. Harrison, *50 Reasons People Give for Believing in a God* (Amherst, NY: Prometheus Books, 2008), 86.

41. Ibid., p. 108.

42. Ibid., p. 127.

43. Ibid., p. 213.

44. Published by McGraw-Hill Humanities/Social Sciences/Languages in 2013.

45. Published by Scientific American/Farrar, Straus and Giroux in 2014.

46. Harrison, *50 Popular Beliefs That People Think Are True* (Amherst, NY: Prometheus Books, 2012), pp. 251–252.

47. James A. Lindsay, *Dot, Dot, Dot: Infinity Plus God Equals Folly* (Onus Books, 2013).

49. I refer readers to my anthology *Christianity Is Not Great* (Amherst, NY: Prometheus Books, 2014).

50. Raymond A. Bradley, "A Moral Argument for Atheism," http://infidels.org/library/modern/raymond_bradley/moral.html.

51.   Jonathan L. Kvanvig, *The Problem of Hell* (Oxford: Oxford University Press, 2001), p. 136.

52.   Ibid., p. 158.

53.   Henry M. Morris and Martin E. Clark, *The Bible Has the Answer,* revised and expanded (El Cajon, CA: Creation Life Publishers, 1987), p. 312.

54.   See chapter 4 by Victor Stenger, "Christianity and Cosmology" in my anthology *Christianity in the Light of Science* (Amherst, NY: Prometheus Books, 2016), pp. 97–118, and Edward T. Babinski, "The Cosmology of the Bible," in my anthology *The Christian Delusion* (Amherst, NY: Prometheus Books, 2010), pp. 109–147.

7

ANSWERING OBJECTIONS AND OTHER PRACTICAL CONCERNS

Religion is being taught in secular universities and this must end, now! That is the focus of this book. I'm calling for something specific and attainable, the end of the philosophy of religion discipline in secular universities. Maintaining it as a discipline of learning in a secular university is giving these faith-based claims far more credibility than they deserve.

The main goal is to help motivate the influencers, the donors, the university presidents, the chairs of philosophy departments, and the professors themselves to undertake this feat. Beyond this immediate goal, this book should also help readers understand why we should not take religiously motivated faith-based pseudo-philosophy seriously. It does not deserve a place at the adult table in any intellectual discipline of learning that seeks to gain knowledge. Allowing it as a discipline of learning is to allow the pretense of empty sophisticated rhetoric to masquerade as knowledge. Just as surely as secular universities would not grant equal time for a discipline in creation science, they shouldn't grant philosophers of religion equal time with their own subdiscipline.

Having a separate philosophy of religion department in secular universities must end. If this cannot be done immediately then I'm explaining what professors should be doing in the meantime. In the end I'm merely calling for atheist philosophers of religion to be honest with their students and to show them why none of the theistic arguments work. In this chapter I'm going to answer some objections to my position and discuss some practical concerns.

"Believers Do Indeed Use Arguments in the Classroom"

In politics we don't care where a policy proposal or law comes from. It could be something a politician learned from a dream, or from a ghost who appeared in the middle of the night, or from an out of body experience, or from God himself! What we demand are secular reasons to think a policy proposal or law would solve a problem, or a set of problems for our society. No legislator in any secular government would propose banning abortion based on the argument that it's what God wants. It doesn't work like that, even if that's the main motivation for proposing such legislation. Instead, legislators base their proposals on whatever reasons and evidence they could muster in support of such legislation, even if the main motivation is a religious one.

So if we're not opposed to religious motivations in a secular nation, so long as legislators muster up some reasons and evidence for them, why should we be opposed to religious motivations in producing arguments in secular classrooms, so long as some reasons and evidence are presented for them? Good question. Glad no one has asked it yet.

In one sense we really do care if a particular kind of legislation is religiously motivated. When we find that it's religiously motivated it's easier to dismiss it. Remember *Law's law of faith*? If it's religiously motivated we should take a good hard look at the reasons and evidence advanced for a proposed law to see if they're good ones. Many times religion gets in the way of thinking, reasoning, and the evidence. In another sense, though, there is nothing we can do about it. It's what the political process allows. A free society requires it. At least legislators must provide secular reasons for proposed laws and that's a good thing. Not every law, even when religiously motivated, is bad for people. Just think of the commandment not to kill, as one example.

In the classroom it's different. It isn't a place where truth wins by a majority. Students are not making truth proposals where they put it up for a vote at the end of class. Truth is not up for a vote. The truth must be discovered in the process of studying the issues out. One truth is that faith has no merit. Good instructors will teach this to their students. And good instructors are experts in knowing which arguments are obfuscating the faith that lies behind it. They can easily spot them. Because faith requires special pleading and so many other informal fallacies, I can say faith itself is a fallacy. It's certainly a cognitive bias that causes believers to overestimate the probabilities on behalf of faith. For good instructors it's about teaching the truth. What lies behind the stated arguments of faith is faith itself, which is not something students should be allowed to bring into the classroom, since faith-based arguments are bad, really bad arguments. If professors are to teach how to argue correctly on behalf of something the first thing they should do is expose illogical and unreasonable arguments, especially the arguments of faith. In other words, since the arguments that believers utilize in the classroom are based on faith, and since faith is based on insufficient evidence and logical fallacies, the arguments should be exposed by instructors for what they really are, insufficiently evidenced logically fallacious ones.

"This Is a Violation of Separation of State and Church"

If the PoR discipline isn't going away anytime soon then instructors should teach PoR classes correctly by arguing faith has no epistemic warrant, and as such, all religionist PoR is pseudo-philosophy. No religionist will teach any PoR class this way so none of them should teach these classes, especially in a secular university where faith is never allowed as a solution to a question in any other intellectual discipline.

Religionists in PoR departments should not be invited to teach in the first place and they should not be granted tenure. Existing PoR professors should be drummed out of the secular university since they are teaching theology in a secular university, and thus indoctrinating their students, in the same way creationists should not be teaching science classes in the secular university. If a department is dominated by pseudo-philosophers the administrators should be pressured to eliminate that department, just as no creationists should be teaching classes on evolution.

James Lindsay offers the following hard-line suggestions (via email):

There should be no explicit philosophers of religion and no respected philosophy of religion academic journals (that are taken seriously by academics—they should be seen as poison to publish in). There should be an identification that identifies PoR explicitly with theology and the work of other quacks. Current philosophers of religion should be encouraged to shift their focus to more worthy philosophical endeavors, and these shouldn't really include the kinds of stupid metaphysical explorations that they're likely to turn to.

This is not about censorship. It's about the nature of faith-based arguments coming from pseudo-philosophers. As I've been repeating myself for emphasis, faith has no method and never solved any problem. It's an utterly unreliable guide to get at the truth. In fact, faith hinders students from arriving at the truth. It should no more be allowed in the university classroom than creationism. If our universities are to teach the truth then philosophy professors should attack faith as childish and unbecoming of the adults they are soon to be. That's the truth about faith. It has no merit and should not be coddled in our universities.

In the past the truth was censored out of universities. So many capable people were denied a professorship because they were nonbelievers. Some, many, were butchered. Now times have changed. There is no breaching of the First Amendment to the U.S. Constitution by taking religion out of our schools. It's what the Constitution demands. We do it for truth. We do it because of the Constitution.

Is This Proposal Too Offensive? Too Evangelistic? Too Strident?

If atheists draw battle lines in the sand and make it our fight to show faith is not a virtue in the classroom, aren't we being too evangelistic, too aggressive, too offensive?

This is an important concern. However, I see no reason to think professors who teach the evolutionary paradigm are being offensive or evangelistic, nor do I see any reason to think superstition should be placated, especially when we seek knowledge. Knowledge cannot be known by the nonmethod of faith. We live in an era where we need to have knowledge so that the decisions of our governments are good ones. Way too often ignorance reigns with policymakers because they are people of faith. That's because faith and ignorance go together. Faith breeds ignorance. This must end. And if our professors fail us in the universities then they are not doing their jobs.

Faith also breeds intolerance, fear, and hatred. All I would think readers of this present book should need to do is read my anthology, *Christianity Is Not Great: How Faith Fails*, to see, well, how faith fails us. As that book shows, on page after more than five hundred pages, faith fails us at every turn. It fails us not only when it comes to gaining knowledge. It also fails us when it comes to politics, science, and having a good society. It causes a great deal of harm to others, including, of course, people of faith. To fight for truth against faith is to fight for people, real people, people who can and will be harmed by faith. That's worth it.

But won't we lose this battle? If believers get this memo won't they fight back? Since they outnumber us won't they win? Isn't it better to get along for now and fight another day when we're stronger in numbers? Well, believers do outnumber us in most PoR departments, and other disciplines of learning. They have for a long time. And in their positions of influence they are arguing against nonbelief. Isn't it time we present our arguments about faith? They are not going to stop anytime soon. So why don't atheist professors teach the truth about faith, since it's the truth? It's their responsibility as the gatekeepers to our societies. They graduate the movers and the shakers of our societies, so why not teach these students how to get knowledge so they can change our societies for the better? Even if what I'm proposing is partisan to the core, creating an antagonistic atmosphere in our universities and leading to a backlash as Christians decide to be more aggressive in teaching their brand of pseudo-philosophy, I will welcome this. The reason is because if believers decide to be more aggressive, the students will object. This can actually help end the PoR in secular universities since even more college students will in turn reject religion.

How can we lose? The truth about faith is pretty much obvious. How can anyone argue against it once it's exposed for the dog and pony show it really is? I would think all we need to do with most students is inform them about faith, and if they disagree require them to offer reasons why they disagree. When they try they will quickly learn they can't do it.

On Twitter a smarter than your average philosophical amateur named Justin Schieber replied to such a view by implying I'm too strident or extreme when arguing we should treat all faith-based claims the same, privileging none. I had said Scientology is not any better nor worse than Christianity. They both are equally delusional belief systems, or something like that. Schieber responded, "Two words: intrinsic probability." Then this: "Not all wrong ideas are equally plausible." Then he proceeded to educate me, saying, "Read pretty much anything by Draper." Paul Draper? He's been wrong much of the time. Schieber wants to be respected as some sort of philosopher of religion, which motivates him to argue against what I'm saying, even though as of this writing he's an undergraduate in a community college, okay. This isn't the way to do it though. Let me respectfully respond to him.

I see absolutely no intrinsic probability to a virgin who had a baby in the ancient superstitious past, or the resurrection of a false prophet from the dead, or his ascension into the sky from which it was promised he would come again in the generation he was crucified. Further, I see no intrinsic probability that he was/is the incarnate Son of God or that I will suffer an eternal conscious torment in hell if I don't believe the two-, three-, or even four-times-removed conflicting testimonies of people I cannot cross-examine, assembled in doctored-up fourth-century manuscripts over the many other Christian testimonies and stories written and told over hundreds of years. None. None at all. That is a start. And for the record I see absolutely no intrinsic probability to faith. Adults, reasonable adults, think exclusively in terms of the probabilities. When adults think deep enough about what this means they will finally get it. Faith is irrational. It has no epistemic merit at all.

The truth is that when looked at in greater depth there is no such thing as "intrinsic probability." In an online essay discussing the views of Paul Draper, William Briggs makes this case.[1] Briggs has a PhD in statistics, teaches statistics for Cornell University, and is the author of *Uncertainty: The Soul of Modeling, Probability & Statistics*.[2] He said:

> Draper defines intrinsic probability for a hypothesis (proposition) as the "probability independent of the evidence we possess for or against it." Since probability is epistemological and not ontological, and since all probability is conditional of stated premises, I cannot see how this definition makes any sense. There is no such thing as unconditional probability, therefore there can't be "intrinsic" probability.

I think I just need to share one of Briggs's hypothetical counterexamples. "The hypothesis that all arsenic is poisonous to human beings is intrinsically more likely to be true than the hypothesis that, while all observed arsenic is poisonous, all unobserved arsenic is nutritious." Briggs rhetorically asks, "how hard is it to exclude all you already know about arsenic before answering this?" For someone who knows nothing about arsenic at all there is no intrinsic probability that it's poisonous.

There is nothing much to suggest Christianity is more probable than Scientology prior to hearing of them. They are both believed, not known. That's why they're called *faiths* in the first place. Neither of them have the requisite evidence to believe. The only thing Christianity has over Scientology is that there are fourth-century manuscripts that tell us people believed Jesus arose from the dead, stories coming from an ancient superstitious era in which virgins gave births to semi-gods. We have no possible way to externally verify any of these so-called testimonies as we first find them in manuscripts that were tampered with for a few centuries. That's not much. At all!

Does My Proposal Reject Specialization in a Religion?

Philosophers, like other academics, specialize. It's what makes them who they are. They can be the experts among other experts in something. But if I'm saying the best way to approach religion is to treat all faith-based claims equally, privileging none, and that doing so is best done in anthropology of religion or comparative religion programs and classes, how can professors specialize in Christianity, as one example?

Kevin Schilbrak, whom we met up with in chapter 5, responds to this question. He has a traditional philosopher friend who agreed with his proposal for teaching the PoR but who pointed out that "no single philosopher of religion can master the philosophical intricacies of one religious tradition, let alone all of them. Scholarly expertise requires specialization." So his friend asked if there is anything wrong "with specializing, as he does, solely in Christian philosophy of religion?" Schilbrak provides two answers. In the first place, he's not arguing "for a change in the work of any individual philosopher of religion, but rather in our understanding of the task of the discipline as a whole [the PoR as he conceives it] to which that work is meant to contribute. Insofar as philosophers of religion come to see the scope of their work as global, it may have an impact on their teaching and scholarship." It would mean, if nothing else, the department his friend teaches in, which focuses on Christianity, would see "their present coverage in the discipline as one-sided and incomplete."[3]

Schilbrak's second response "is more critical." The flaw in the traditional approaches to PoR is the assumption that theism and naturalism are the only two "live" options. They're not. So "those philosophers of religion who do want to demonstrate the superiority of their faith need to engage with rival religious philosophies. Simply put, one cannot make comparative claims about the superiority of one's position unless one actually compares. Consequently, those who want to defend their faith cannot succeed at their task if they do not take into account the full range of religious options, which is to say that they ought to agree to the proposal of this book."[4]

Schilbrak writes from a position of faith but what he says is good. I would add one additional thought to his. While no one can specialize in all religions I think people can specialize in faith. That's what I'm talking about. To be a specialist in faith is to know why human beings evolved to have it, why so many of us seem to need it, how it blinds so many people from seeing the cold-hard objective evidence to the contrary, and how we can wean people off of it. Being an expert in faith requires just enough examples from all sorts of paranormal claims to see it. Peter Boghossian is a specialist in faith.

Responding to Keith Parsons

Lest anyone think I'm unnecessarily picking on Keith Parsons, I think he's not entirely wrong. It's just hard to figure him out. Even though I have master's degrees in the PoR, I'm arguing the PoR discipline doesn't deserve a place in secular universities. I've said why in this book. One of my criticisms is that PoR doesn't usually deal in concrete biblical examples, and when it does, it takes for granted what no reasonable person should. I prefer to deal in terms of concrete biblical examples by far, so I cannot grant for the sake of argument most of the things philosophers of religion do. I prefer Jaco Gericke's approach, who wrote, "The trouble with William Lane Craig and Alvin Plantinga is that their philosophy of religion conveniently ignores the problems posed for their views by the history of Israelite religion. They might as well try to prove Zeus exists. People sometimes forget 'God' used to be Yahweh and it is possible to prove from textual evidence that 'there ain't no such animal.'"[5]

In their PoR classes Christian instructors assume their particular god exists, and then make a case that believing in that god is rational, and that he probably exists, without examining the so-called biblical evidence itself. In their PoR classes they'll assume miracles have taken place in the Bible, and then make a philosophical case that miracles are possible and even probable, without examining the so-called biblical evidence itself. They'll assume there's a trinitarian God and a guy in the first century who was 100 percent man and 100 percent God without losing any essential divine nor human qualities, and try to make rational sense of it all, without examining the so-called biblical evidence. The same things go for discussions of prayer and the problem of evil. They'll assume, for the sake of their PoR classes, that petitionary prayer works and try to make rational sense of it, without looking at the scientific studies showing prayer works no better than chance. They'll assume their god is supremely good, without looking at the biblical evidence describing a barbaric and uncaring God. They are doing philosophy of religion they'll say. Those other issues are for biblical scholars. But it's all special pleading since they take for granted what no reasonable person should, that science does not undercut their faith, and that the Bible is considered evidence for the god they believe in. Wait just a minute? you'll hear me ask. Why bother talking about the properties and supposed activities of Zeus unless there is evidence to think he exists, and that he's acted in the world? Until these philosophers of religion pony up, so to speak, we're wasting our time. And until they deal in terms of concrete biblical examples they are special pleading their case.

In an online essay for the Secular Outpost, Parsons expertly did just that by showing us how to do the PoR correctly, using a concrete example, the case of the genocidal biblical texts concerning the Amalekites. The options are not good for Christian apologists, to say the least. Philosophy of religion, if it's to be done right, should do so by examining the source of these religious beliefs. When done correctly there is no good reason to elevate the PoR as a separate discipline in the secular universities. In this case Parsons is looking at the problem of suffering for a good all-powerful deity using as his example the genocidal texts in I Samuel 15. Parsons concludes with a rhetorical understatement: "I Samuel, chapter

15 presents the apologist with a number of options. None of them sounds very good.[6]

In the Appendix I've included a written interview I conducted with Parsons (with his permission). When interviewing him my purpose wasn't to argue with him but rather to get a clearer understanding of his views. To be clear, I'm still unclear what he thinks. Is the case for theism dead or not? What exactly is the role of reason if he thinks it can't help us to know the truth about religion, such that it can be used to support both sides? Where does evidence come into play for him? I didn't see him saying anything about that. To what degree would he say it's probable he could be wrong? When he says he wants religion to be taught in his college how should it be taught? We just don't know.

Let me respond here to some of the points he made in the interview, which I've excerpted as block quotations below.

> I am teaching a philosophy of religion class because I consider it an important part of our philosophy curriculum. Students find the issues and the readings interesting, and they are introduced to a number of important philosophical concepts, tools, and topics, such as possible worlds and modal concepts, the principle of sufficient reason, Hume's critique of miracles, probability and Bayes' Theorem, teleology and function explanations, naturalism/physicalism, epistemological foundationalism and its critics, etc.

Anti-intellectualism is never the solution, so gaining knowledge for the sake of knowing is always valuable. Ignorance is never justifiable. However, something considered interesting may not be important, or useful, or helpful. That's my point. A number of these philosophical tools are important, yes, as explicated in Julian Baggini and Peter S. Fosl's book *The Philosopher's Toolkit: A Compendium of Philosophical Concepts and Methods.*[7] It does not mean these tools are best learned or used in debating the God question. A number of them are used by believing obfuscationist philosophers to obfuscate ideas we probably shouldn't take seriously.

> As Hume observed in the first chapter of his *Enquiry Concerning Human Understanding*, the only cure for bad philosophy is good philosophy, and bad philosophy will proliferate if good philosophy abandons the field.

This is definitely true. But bad philosophy is the kind that takes ancient superstitious myths seriously that shouldn't be taken seriously. Believers and nonbelieving atheists who take ancient superstitious myths seriously are doing bad philosophy. What we have is more of the same. We need to change how we treat these myths, as I argued in chapter 6.

> The theistic arguments remain very interesting, if only because it is extremely instructive to see just where they go wrong. Actually, much of philosophy is like that. We still read Descartes's *Meditations,* though it is pretty much universally agreed that he failed in his object of putting knowledge on foundations of absolute certainty. When very bright people try something very big and fail, it is highly instructive to see just how they went wrong and what that failure means. I still think that natural theology has run its course and that, as living philosophical effort, it is finished. However, as an object for postmortem analysis, it remains quite fascinating!

I'm interested in knowing which arguments failed and why they failed, yes. It helps us become better critical thinkers, and that's worth some effort, sure. It helps us make good decisions as we face choices in life. What else it helps us with is something unclear to me. Why, for instance, would anyone from Asia need to know about Descartes except as a curiosity or to understand Western history? What would he or she learn that was important about any matter of fact from doing so? Nonetheless, what Parsons says here, even though he denies it later, is that PoR classes are exercises in critical thinking. The difference is that the subject matter concerns religious arguments. But I think we can teach critical thinking without having whole classes dedicated to religious arguments. Why should we do so if religion has nothing going for it? Doesn't this elevate faith to a virtue, the very thing we should reject? And why single out for consideration the failed project of natural theology? Religion has failed so many times at discovery, explanation, and justification that the problem Parsons should focus on is faith itself.

Take for example a class on the history of science. Such a class would not focus on falsified scientific hypotheses. What can we learn from studying any failures of science that isn't better spent learning about its many successes? Focusing on the successes of science teaches us much more than focusing on those times when some accepted scientific theory was falsified by the science of its day.[8]

The problem is that in PoR one finds very little to count as a success. In fact, in PoR there aren't any successes. Not one of the many PoR arguments of the distant past is accepted as put forth in its original form by modern philosophers of religion. This includes anything from Socrates, Plato, Aristotle, Anselm, Descartes, or the lot of them.[9] All of the previous arguments in PoR lacked some important distinction, or failed to handle future objections adequately or needed to be revised due to the discovery of new evidence. So in order to understand the current state of PoR, budding philosophers of religion must study only its failures, because that's all they've got to study! The whole discipline is a failure. Why then is it important to study Descartes if we want to gain knowledge about matters of fact? It has some minimal historical value to it, sure. But the PoR has never produced a fact.

> I am a physicalist. I hold that all that has substantial existence (which I construe as being capable of acting or being acted upon), is physical. I do not think that there is a supernatural or transcendent aspect or element of reality. I do not believe in any gods, ghosts, souls, spirits, demons, demigods, angels, vital essences, occult powers or animistic forces. Full stop. But I could be wrong. . . . Though zealots on both sides hate the thought, I agree with [John] Hick that reason does not dictate which side you come down on. One may rationally opt for a naturalistic or supernaturalistic interpretation. . . . I find the arguments for atheism very strong. However, I do not regard them as so strong as to preclude rational dissent.

I am neither a knave nor a fool, but there is something lacking in what Parsons writes. Evidence. Sufficient objective evidence. Convincing evidence. He talks instead in terms of arguments and reasons. I just don't think talking about evidence comes to his philosophically trained mind, not that it's unimportant to him. It is very important to me. Yes, I agree, reason can find a way to support almost anything given *Law's law of faith* (one more time): "Anything based on faith, no matter how ludicrous, can be made to be consistent with the available evidence, given a little patience and ingenuity."[10] People use reason to support so many bizarre beliefs we need to demand cold hard objective evidence for them, especially extraordinary claims. If the evidence is inconclusive, we should withhold judgment. If it isn't sufficient we should reject the claim. If the evidence is woefully lacking it's unreasonable to hold to that belief. We must proportion our assent according to the strength of the evidence, per David Hume. Not doing so is unreasonable. No reasonable person should say that which is unreasonable is reasonable.

> What would we say of an atheist who refused even to look at the arguments for theism? Do I want to convince my students of anything? Sure. I want to convince them of the profound value of reasoning about important things and not simply trusting their "gut." Yes, one of the aims of any philosophy course is to encourage a less gullible and more skeptical attitude. However, it has to be an informed skepticism.

In the next chapter I answer this view of Parsons. It's enough just to be right, even though I prefer that people know they are right by far. But what should atheists know they are right about? What is an informed skepticism? Must atheists know the details of fundamentalist Christianity, or Scientology, or Eastern Orthodoxy, or Hinduism, or Islam in all its sects before they reject religion? I see no reason to think so. All atheists have to be informed about is that faith is an unreliable way to gain knowledge about anything. Any faith examples will do, not just the ones Parsons is an expert in.

> Honest skepticism is nothing other than to adhere to Socrates' dictum to follow the argument wherever it leads.

I just highlighted this statement to showcase again that Parsons does not think in terms of evidence, but rather argument. In doing so he has a misplaced focus, which strengthens my case against PoR since that's what philosophy has led him, a seasoned philosopher, to focus on. However, several times I insisted he talk about the evidence so he did.

> I do not think that there is any scientific evidence for religious claims at all. The same applies to all sorts of metaphysical claims. There is no scientific evidence for Platonic Ideal Forms or Cartesian minds.

This is a good admission with which I agree. I don't think he understands the implications of this admission though, for he goes on to say,

The question of rationality is larger than the question of what is answerable by science at any given time. Philosophy deals with worldviews, and worldviews are not decidable by appeal to science. Rather, one's view of the authority and scope of science is dependent on worldview. In a worldview where faith is primary and empirical evidence is secondary, no degree of empirical evidence can dislodge the claims of faith. Such a view is highly antithetical to mine, but, obviously, it cannot be critiqued with empirical evidence, but only with philosophical argument.

Parsons is talking pragmatically here, about why rationality appears to be larger than empirical evidence. He intellectually inhabits the realm of reason, which is what people use to interpret the available evidence. He already admitted there is no scientific evidence for religious claims. Now he's talking about how to convince believers of this who use reason to disagree with him about the evidence. In the process Parsons ends up agreeing with believers who disagree with him about the evidence. He says the evidence is not there to believe. They disagree. He grants that it's rational to disagree even though the evidence is not there. Sounds reasonable, right? To whom? Not to me.

I don't think it's rational to disagree with the evidence. And I think the evidence is conclusive. It's just that believers won't allow themselves to see the evidence. Valerie Tarico, a psychologist who wrote the book *The Dark Side: How Evangelical Teachings Corrupt Love and Truth*, tells what's really going on in the minds of believers. Tarico claims "it doesn't take very many false assumptions to send us on a long goose chase." To illustrate this she tells us about the mental world of a paranoid schizophrenic. To such a person the perceived persecution by others sounds real. "You can sit, as a psychiatrist, with a diagnostic manual next to you, and think: as bizarre as it sounds, the CIA really is bugging this guy. The arguments are tight, the logic persuasive, the evidence organized into neat files. All that is needed to build such an impressive house of illusion is a clear, well-organized mind and a few false assumptions. Paranoid individuals can be very credible."[11] This is what believers do, and this is why it's hard to shake off one's faith, in her informed opinion.

So the so-called rationality that believers have in defending the indefensible with obfuscationist philosophy against the evidence is not praiseworthy at all, but based on a delusion of faith. I detailed in chapter 6 how best to dislodge faith from believers, and one way not to do it is to say they're treating the evidence reasonably when they refuse to acknowledge the evidence. What we need to do is help force believers to see how faith is the antithesis of reason in that it keeps them from seeing the evidence. We need to show them why faith causes them to be closed-minded to the evidence. David Eller (via email) tells us why, in that believers have "a different set of eyes than we do, and they cannot see what we see. Criticizing them, even poking them in the eye, simply does not improve their vision. They are deep inside a Christian box, and until they see the box and the world outside of it, their view is fatally limited." This is what describes believers I have no doubt. It also describes what Parsons is trying to deal with when acknowledging believers see things differently with their own worldviews. It says nothing about whether they're reasonable to live in that box though. They're not. Parsons says a largely Christianized worldview "is highly antithetical to mine." Okay, then, tell us why you think so. Argue your case. Don't be shy. What's holding you back?

> The question is whether there are any interesting questions left for PoR that science cannot settle. Surely there are. Is the question of theism/atheism one that is straightforwardly empirical? Some (you, John) will say yes and lots of others will say no. If you debate the point you will be doing PoR.

Am I doing PoR now? Let's step back a bit. Philosophy proper must not be considered equivalent to reasoning, otherwise there is no content to the discipline of philosophy. Scientists must reason to be scientists, but that isn't the same thing as discussing Aquinas. The mere use of logic and the avoidance of fallacies shouldn't be considered philosophical reasoning in and of themselves. Philosophy helps by discovering the rules we debate the issues with, but not everything discussed using these rules is to be considered philosophy. The same thing can be said of PoR. People aren't doing PoR just because they are reasoning.

Parsons argued in his book, *It Started with Copernicus: Vital Questions About Science*,[12] that Darwin engaged in philosophical questions so perhaps he should be considered a philosopher:

In *The Origin of Species*, Darwin frequently addresses philosophical as well as scientific questions. For instance . . . he devotes considerable space to examining the hypothesis of special creation as a theory competing with natural selection. He realizes that special creation is, of course, more than just a purportedly scientific claim, and impinges on deep philosophical and religious commitments. In addressing special creation, therefore, Darwin often speaks the language of philosophy and even theology. Darwin's remarkably comprehensive intellect, his background that encompassed both theology and natural science, and his sensitivity to cultural context, made him a particularly qualified commentator on the relation between science and religion.[13]

What does Parsons say is the criteria for when someone is engaging in philosophy, as opposed to science? He says this:

In cases . . . where the evidence will not settle the dispute, scientists must employ philosophical arguments. And they do. Therefore, the suggestion that science can simply replace philosophy is wrong for the reason that, as [Thomas] Kuhn observed, scientific debates often embed—or are embedded within—philosophical debates. These philosophical differences often cannot be settled by straightforward empirical means, but must be addressed with philosophical argument. Science cannot replace philosophy because philosophy is an essential part of the scientific enterprise. Kuhn was wrong about many things, but on this point he was absolutely right.[14]

I'm simply not persuaded that scientists are doing philosophy when reasoning about the evidence. What would the distinction be between reasoning and philosophy at that point? I think we should agree that mere reasoning is not equivalent to philosophy, or PoR, so scientific reasoning is not necessarily doing them either. We should also agree that we don't need to wait until everyone agrees that a particular dispute has been settled by science before we can say scientists are no longer doing philosophy when reasoning about the evidence. The dispute over evolution has been settled in our day. I think the implications about evolution are settled too. What Parsons needs to do is show why anyone should wait until evolution deniers agree that this dispute has been settled before we can say evolutionists are not doing philosophy or PoR. I see no reason to accept that criteria with regard to his specific example.

And if reasoning is called for, as opposed to plopping the evidence down on a table for all to see, then by all means let's reason about it. Where there's a stalemate then we have a stalemate, at which time we should suspend judgment and wait for further evidence. Without further evidence I see no reason why we should even debate an issue, although I can admit it's fun to conjecture. We know people of faith can find justifications for a great many unevidenced and underevidenced claims. If the evidence doesn't settle the dispute then what makes anyone think nonscientists can settle it? Have any nonscientists settled a scientific dispute? I know of none. After all, philosophers, especially philosophers of religion, are not in the business of discovering data. Philosophers can bring out the implications of the available evidence, and that's welcomed, of course. But to date, given the woeful lack of evidence for any superhuman beings or their actions in our world, the implications of this lack of evidence are easily seen. Anyone can see them.

Parsons utters the same kind of criticism of Peter Boghossian offered by Graham Oppy, a criticism that I find to be misguided.[15] Oppy said Boghossian's rejection of PoR "seems to be expressing views in the philosophy of religion." This reminds me of the criticism thrown at atheists that we believe even though we don't, or that we're religious because we take a position on religion. But using reason to reject the PoR is not the same thing as doing PoR, just as using scientific reasoning to reject creation science is not doing creation science. It's reasoning, not PoR. Reasoning is not to be equated with philosophy or PoR. Just consider how someone could argue to end PoR if it cannot be done without doing it? The only alternative is to stop saying anything at all about the PoR, which is an unreasonable demand if one wants to end PoR.

We could even bite the bullet and agree we're doing PoR, if merely to end it. I see no problem with that response either. We'd be doing so pragmatically in hopes our arguments succeed in ending PoR. This wouldn't strictly be doing PoR but rather meta-philosophy of religion. The meta-distinction is legitimate in other disciplines like ethics, so it's legitimate here as well.

As another way to look at this, if we need to do so, there is a distinction between theologians and atheologians, which I think was first introduced by Alvin Plantinga. Theologians do what theologians do, by obfuscating theology to make it palatable to an evolving community of modernized believers. Atheologians are atheists who are critical of obfuscationist theology, which is the only kind of theology that exists. Can it really be said that atheologians are doing or participating or practicing or explicating theology when arguing as atheologians? I think not. They are arguing against theology, not doing theology. So believing philosophers who teach religion are to be considered *philosophers of religion,* whereas atheist philosophers who argue against religion are to be considered *aphilosophers* of religion. *Aphilosophers* of religion seek to disabuse philosophers of religion of their religion. They are not to be considered doing PoR. They are arguing against PoR. Period.

I don't think there should even be aphilosophers of religion though. This title, just introduced for the first time with all that it entails, must not be embraced by anyone who argues for the demise of that discipline. Dealing with religion should be taken away from aphilosophers of religion and given to the disciplines that can more adequately deal with the phenomena of religion. Aphilosophers of religion should bow out. Or they should argue faith has no basis in the secular university, or argue against the merits of faith in every class. Aphilosophers of religion are largely doing a disservice to those of us who think faith-based claims should all be treated equally.

When Should We Engage Religious Arguments?

James Lindsay brings to our attention an important consideration that needs to be addressed:

> So long as believers peddle nonsense, someone will need to shoot it down, even if we shouldn't lose ourselves in the weeds in the process.
>
> Figuring out when we should ignore and when we should address piffle is a perennial problem, particularly with its religious brands. Engaging it legitimizes it in a way, even if doing so eventually embarrasses it. Ignoring it enables it to fester and spread unchecked, a problem for infectious ideas, especially ones that prey upon vulnerability. The matter is also context dependent: a conversation with one's cousin or mother, for instance, might admit a lower threshold for engagement than impersonal discussions on national or international stages. Deciding when to expose crap for what it is can be a difficult problem.
>
> Theism sometimes bothers to be specific enough to shoot at, and the

circumstances sometimes warrant it. In those cases, we should sometimes take aim and fire. Note, however, that taking theism seriously enough to shoot it down has to have a shelf life. As theism becomes less and less meaningful culturally, antitheism becomes less and less appropriate. There is little reason to argue against something that most of us don't take seriously. Ignoring it, scoffing at it, and outright making fun of it are sufficient to the task at that point.[16]

I like his ideas here. I need to add just one consideration in the context of writing online essays and books and producing podcasts and YouTube videos. When doing these activities we should focus on faith as an utterly unreliable process, and not on the arguments from faith, nor the dogmatic content of faith. The dogmas are fodder for the real point to be made that faith is something reasonable adults should never trust to get at the truth. Once this is understood it won't be too hard to know when to raise the issue of faith and when not to do so. Raise it whenever someone else does. Raise it all of the time if needed. Provide examples, lots of them, from a wide variety of sources, including the plethora of paranormal claims, including as many examples from as many religions as you can. Take aim. Shoot faith down. At every opportunity if you're so inclined. For faith in all of its manifestations is the main target.

Concluding Thoughts

Not all secular philosophers try to disabuse their students of faith. So if I can get more of them to do more of that, without losing their jobs in the process, they would do their students a service and be more in line with the rest of the disciplines in a secular university, where God explanations are not allowed to solve problems.

I agree we should try to understand religion, most emphatically. Mine isn't an either/or proposal. The questions up for debate are whether religion should be approached philosophically and whether or not other disciplines in the university would be better suited for studying religion. When secular philosophers of religion merely seek to help students understand the philosophical arguments, rather than critique them by arguing against faith, they are doing their students a disservice. They have to first choose which God or gods to do this for. And how do they choose? What's the criteria? Well, so far as I can tell these secular philosophers choose whatever God or gods are currently believed within their parochial districts. That privileges those particular gods just by taking them seriously.

If you want people to see that religious faith has no merit, other disciplines are best for this. Science destroys religion, especially evolutionary science. At that point there would be no need to philosophically examine the arguments for God or gods or religions, since they are seen for what they are, based on faith. In epistemology classes alone, secular philosophers worthy of their position should focus on disabusing students of faith as a virtue. Once that's done properly there's no need to examine the philosophical arguments of faith. When was the last time anyone examined the philosophical arguments for the Canaanite religion and child sacrifice in any class? That's the point. There would be no reason to do so.

So if my proposal is not viewed as feasible or practical, then I don't consider that a serious criticism, since Nietzsche called for and predicted the death of God. If he did nothing wrong then I'm not doing anything wrong when I call for the end of the philosophy of religion. In fact, calling for its end can help speed it up. So hopefully my call for the end of the PoR discipline can help end it in some small tiny way. Hopefully it can at least raise awareness of the need to excise religious PoR in our universities, which is a worthy goal in itself.

As to my young atheist critics, I say, don't be afraid to think outside the box. Many times young people who have been taught to think a certain way by older experts tend to think within the box just like the older experts. They usually have a knee-jerk reaction to something new without understanding that there was a time when that which they were taught to accept was not always accepted. And the older experts usually have a vested interest in keeping the status quo intact for personal reasons unrelated to the arguments. So even though young atheist critics may still reject what I'm proposing, they should at least give it some deep thought. What are its merits? In doing so tell me if Nietzsche was wrong when he predicted and called for the death of God. You do realize that his prediction came true for the Death of God theologians in the sixties? And it's coming true in Northern European countries too. Be sure you're not on the wrong side of history, that's all, even if we may not live long enough to see it.

Notes

1. William Briggs, "There Is No Such Thing as Intrinsic Probability," May 30, 2014, http://wmbriggs.com/post/12617/.

2. William Briggs, *Uncertainty: The Soul of Modeling, Probability & Statistics* (Springer, 2016).

3. Kevin Schilbrak, *Philosophy and the Study of Religions: A Manifesto* (Malden, MA: Wiley-Blackwell, 2014), pp.12–13.

4. Ibid., pp. 12–13.

5. John W. Loftus, "Jaco Gericke: Fundamentalism on Stilts," Debunking Christianity, December 12, 2009, http://debunkingchristianity.blogspot.com/2009/12/jaco-gericke-fundamentalism-on-stilts.html.

6. Keith Parsons, "The Amalekites and Options for Apologists," Secular Outpost, October 14, 2014, http://www.patheos.com/blogs/secularoutpost/2014/10/14/the-amalekites-and-options-for-apologists/.

7. Julian Baggini and Peter S. Fosl, *The Philosopher's Toolkit: A Compendium of Philosophical Concepts and Methods* (Malden, MA: Blackwell Publishing, 2003).

8. For an interesting read on this see Mike McRae, *Tribal Science: Brains, Beliefs and Bad Ideas* (Amherst, NY: Prometheus Books, 2012), especially chapter 6, "The Science Graveyard," pp. 161–190.

9. I am unsure whether Thomas Aquinas's argument to God's existence from contingency is one of them. I know his argument is defended by current Catholic philosophers of religion and others. What I'm a bit unsure about is whether his argument lacked some important distinction, or failed to handle future objections adequately, or needed to be revised due to the discovery of new evidence. I strongly suspect, though, that this is the case, or that his argument became obsolete with the rise of modern science. Galileo's magisterial book *Dialogue Concerning the Two Chief World Systems* (published in 1632 in Italian) was a big blow to Aristotelian science, which was the foundation upon which Aquinas depended for his argument (Aquinas called Aristotle "The Philosopher").

10. Stephen Law, *Believing Bullshit* (Amherst, NY: Prometheus Books, 2011), p. 75.

11. Valerie Tarico, *The Dark Side: How Evangelical Teachings Corrupt Love and Truth* (Lulu.com, 2006), pp. 221–222, and reissued as *Trusting Doubt: A Former Evangelical Looks at Old Beliefs in a New Light* (Oracle Institute Press LLC, 2010).

12.   Keith Parsons, *It Started with Copernicus: Vital Questions About Science* (Amherst, NY: Prometheus Books, 2014).

13.   Ibid., p. 355–356.

14.   Ibid., pp. 357–358.

15.   "Armchair Atheism, Ep. 2—Why Philosophy of Religion? with Graham Oppy," video, uploaded July 23, 2014, https://www.youtube.com/watch?v=Yv3DVvxgo5E.

16.   James A. Lindsay, *Everybody Is Wrong About God* (Durham, NC: Pitchstone Publishing, 2015), p. 70.

8

IT'S ENOUGH TO BE RIGHT!

I argue in this chapter that in many cases it's enough to be right about something. My focus is on religious beliefs as a subset of paranormal beliefs, of which Christianity is my main target, but I think the case can be made about many other issues. While reasonable people would certainly want more than to just be right, when it comes to solving important problems, alleviating suffering, and doing what is good, being right is good enough.

Here's an example: People may come to the correct conclusion that we should not discriminate against gay marriages because the Constitution grants gay people that right, not because people are born gay. Why should anyone care too much that these people are ignorant here, so long as they come to the correct conclusion?[1]

Here's another example: Some Christians accept and defend the separation of church and state because they think state support for the church is bad for the true *invisible* church (the one only their god can see), which contains true Christians who are faithful witnesses, as opposed to lukewarm and hypocritical believers who play the part of faith because it's better to be thought of as Christians. The right reason to support the separation of church and state is because reason demands it, not because it helps weed out the tares from the wheat (see Matthew 13:24–30).[2] Why should anyone care too much what their reasons are, so long as they come to the correct conclusion?

189

Here's another example: The fate of our planet hangs in the balance when it come to climate change.[3] So I would rather that someone gets active to do something about climate change even if she or he does so because of a nightmare one night. Dreams and nightmares are not reliable ways to learn anything.

Here's an analogy: Consider the difference between being given some food to eat and knowing how to grow crops to feed ourselves. It's good enough to get something to eat one day even though learning how to grow our own crops is better in the long run (although it's not better in the short run). Being fed is good enough when hungry. Being fed is sufficient for that day.

People can come to the right conclusions for wrong reasons when it comes to matters of fact. People can come to the right conclusions for wrong reasons when it comes to treating people with respect and dignity. Learning how to follow the evidence wherever it leads, and knowing how to reason about the available evidence, is much, much better of course. For when one has a reliable means to come to the correct conclusions it can be used across the board in every area of life. Nonetheless, coming to the correct conclusions is still good enough in many cases, when solving important problems, alleviating suffering, and doing what is good. In those cases, having the right conclusions for ignorant or bad reasons is good enough. It is sufficient to be right.

Many Christian apologists argue they can skip the process of reasoning and get to the right conclusions because of the subjective influence of the spirit of their god in their lives. For the record I'm not skipping anything. Reasoning based on science is always what rational people should rely on. There is no other alternative if we want objective knowledge about matters of fact. We should never punt to faith, as it's an unreliable way to know anything except by luck. But, when people get lucky to be right, that is enough on many issues. It's a start. It's a beginning. It's not wrong to be right. It is sufficient.

When it comes to religious claims think on these lines. Doubt comes easy. We all do it. Arguing that one particular viewpoint is correct out of the myriad of claims being put forth is the hard part. Doubt is therefore more likely than not to be right since there are so many conflicting and inconsistent claims to faith. It isn't the case that atheists are adding one more religious claim to the many others being put forth from which to choose from. It's doubt versus everything else, and the odds are on doubt, even for bad reasons.

Now, if I can make this case on a mundane level, how much more so can it apply when the Christian god is placed in the mix. I'm arguing human beings can be right that a god does not exist for the wrong reasons, even though the best way to know this is to learn how to think critically, skeptically. This is especially forceful if there's a god who demands belief unto salvation, for if such a god exists he should do something to help ignorant people reason correctly or to keep them from having experiences or dreams that lead them astray. By failing to help nonbelievers, if this god really exists, s/he is knowingly allowing ignorant people to go to hell (however conceived). So people who are born ignorant, who may be so ignorant they don't even see the value of an education (and critical thinking classes), are condemned to go to hell on Christian assumptions, by the very fact of being born.

In the game of 8-Ball there's a saying that goes like this: "Better be lucky than good." It's usually said after we get a lucky roll on a shot, or win a game due to some good luck. It's not that pool players don't depend on skill to win. We do. It's just that luck can overcome the best opponents in ways skill cannot, especially when playing against a better opponent. Playing with good skill and good luck on a given day is the optimum scenario. Playing below our skill level on a given day with bad luck is the worst scenario. If we had a choice we would always hope for luck no matter how we're playing on a given day. Without it we couldn't beat better players. Without it we might even lose to lesser skilled players. So better to be lucky than good, although being good is the goal of our practice and our play since we cannot practice for luck. Similarly, dumb luck can lead to the right conclusion no matter the method for making the conclusion.

Would you rather have more people who vote for Democrats, even if they vote for Democratic candidates for the wrong reasons? Would you rather have more atheists in society, even if they arrived at their atheism because of dumb luck? I am as sure as sure can be that Christians would rather have another Christian, even someone who believes for the wrong reasons, over another non-Christian. In the end, higher numbers of people on the right side of an issue are good enough, especially when the other side is demonstrably wrong and causes harm to people, the world, and the environment.

Another way to think of this is to ask how many Christians have looked into the apologetic cases made for Islam, whether by the traditional Sunni and Shia branches, the many Sufi orders, or one of the newer reform movements, such as Salafism. To the degree Christians have not considered these cases they are counting on being right without knowing they are right. And yet they are right to reject these sects, since they are all faith-based religions lacking the requisite evidence needed. How many of us ever considered the case for the existence of Zeus and the gods and goddesses in his pantheon? It's the same thing. Anyone who rejects the ancient Greek pantheon has done so rightly, even if they never studied it out. Same thing goes when it comes to ancient paganism.

This is not the place to argue for these things, but I consider them to be true from all that I know, and I know more than I can tell. I think this about all religious faiths even though I have not studied most of them for myself. I know enough about many of them to know people are inherently religious and adopt religious faith fantasies because of the need to believe. They will adopt religious fantasies without the reasonable request for evidence, or with no evidence worthy of the label "evidence" at all.

Let's say a recognized expert on cats claimed a cat talked. People do not have to be experts in cats to say they need to see the evidence. Nor do any of us need a theory of knowledge to doubt it. But if you believed the cat talked you would have to come up with a whole lot of intellectual gymnastics in order to make such a claim seem respectable to others. Lesson: It does not require understanding a whole lot of epistemology or sophisticated theology to doubt the existence of God either. In fact, even a child can do it.

What I'm getting at has to do with the burden of proof. People making an extraordinary, or an out-of-the-ordinary claim, must produce the evidence that what they claim is true. Until that happens others can ignore their claim. In a YouTube video Hemant Mehta, editor of the Friendly Atheist, pulls no punches, saying it this way: "We're just calling out bullshit where we see it. . . . You don't need to be an expert to state the obvious. The burden of proof is on religious people to justify their wacky beliefs. We're not the bad guys for saying, 'That wasn't really a miracle.' . . . You just need to, like, reach the age of six."[4]

Alvin Plantinga in Reverse

Alvin Plantinga's so-called contributions to epistemology include an argument that is called Reformed epistemology because he traces it back to the Protestant Reformers in the sixteenth century, most notably John Calvin. According to Plantinga, belief in the existence of his particular god can be rational and justified without any argument or evidence at all. Belief in his particular god can be justified independently of any evidence and requires no argument. He can be within his epistemic rights when sharing a belief in his particular god without any evidence at all. It all depends upon whether or not his particular god exists. Of course, Scientologists can be rational and justified without any argument or evidence at all, if body thetans exist. So can Muslims, if Allah exists.

I don't think Plantinga's cognitive faculties are functioning properly. They are infected with a host of cognitive biases due to the manner in which our brains have evolved, too many to mention. Faith is one of them, which takes on the form of confirmation bias, a bias Michael Shermer calls, as earlier noted, "the mother of all biases."[5] This bias is a like a parasite of the mind, turning even the most sophisticated intellectuals of today's world into zombies who believe in absurdities, act on them, and defend them. This bias can and does forbid its host to arrive at evidence-based, reasoned conclusions. It forces feeble-minded people to accept its conclusions, unaware they are even being ruled by such a parasite. It has taken over people like Plantinga himself, who, despite having a formidable intellect, is even made unaware that faith does this to him.

In what follows I'll offer a counterargument to Plantinga's Reformed epistemology by arguing people are within their epistemic rights *not to believe in his particular god* even without an argument and even without evidence. Their nonbelief in a god can be rational and justified even without arguments or evidence. In a way, Plantinga and I are fighting over the uninformed and the ignorant among us. Who can claim them in our pursuit of truth? Plantinga says he can. His particular god has an app for that. They can be rational to believe in his god without evidence or argument, he argues. But I have an app as well. These people can be rational not to believe in his god without evidence or argument, I will argue.

On the most basic level what I'm arguing should be acceptable by just analyzing the terms involved. Since Plantinga has the burden of proof then nonbelievers just need to be given sound arguments based on the required sufficient evidence. Until those arguments based on the evidence are put forth, nonbelievers are rational when they don't believe. Since the reason we are nonbelievers is because there isn't sufficient evidence to believe, then we are rational to be nonbelievers precisely because there isn't evidence. End of story.

Argument from Ignorance

Surely people have heard of the *argument from reason*, which attempts to show God exists. I hereby advance the *argument from ignorance*. I will attempt to show that nonbelief is justified based upon the fact that as human beings we are ignorant, and we are ignorant because we are profoundly limited and immature as human beings. I take David Hume's principle as axiomatic, that the wise person should proportion his or her conclusions to the available evidence. Going beyond the probabilities of the evidence is unreasonable. That's what faith does when we embrace it. Faith takes believers beyond the probabilities. Faith is an irrational, unevidenced, or misplaced trust in something or someone. If faith is trust then we have no good reason to trust in faith. So I put this in the form of a dilemma. On the one hand, there is a woeful lack of evidence to conclude any theistic god exists. But on the other hand, even if there was a sufficient amount of evidence, many if not most nonbelievers are still warranted in not believing any theistic god exists. How much more so is this the case since there isn't sufficient evidence to believe? I'm saying it's good enough to be right and that no further justification is necessary.

Christian people have said of me that, "Of the many atheist and theist blogs that I follow I would have to say that you are the best at consistently coming up with interesting topics and arguments even though I disagree with almost everything you say." Okay then, here goes.

Let's see if I can make my case by taking an absurdly ignorant argument against Christianity and show why it's still a good reason for rejecting the Christian faith. Keep in mind that my target is evangelical, conservative, Bible-thumping Christianity, the kind that would accept this *doctrinal statement*:

There is an omniscient, omnibenelovent, omnipotent God who sent Jesus to atone for the sins of all who believe in him. This same God desires everyone should be saved and that no one should be lost (see 1 Timothy 2:4; 2 Peter 3:9).

Evangelicals believe more than this doctrinal statement, but at a minimum they believe it.

Keep in mind I'm also speaking of the reasons people personally have for rejecting Christianity rather than the arguments constructed to convince others. I don't think people must be able produce an argument that will convince others of something before it can be said they have good reasons for what they think. A farmer may have good reasons to think aliens have abducted him even though he cannot convince anyone else. A lawyer may have good reasons to think someone is a con-artist even though she cannot produce an argument that will convince anyone else. People who have been victimized by someone may not be able to see their victimizer in a good light. They have good reasons for what they think even if others don't agree. Counterintuitively, people may have bad reasons for conclusions that end up being true.

Is there a legitimate distinction then between someone's having good personal reasons and having bad objective reasons for believing something? Again we're not talking about arguments constructed to convince others, for the rules of logic dictate which arguments are good ones from bad ones. We're talking instead about the personal reasons people have for accepting or not accepting something as true. How do we really know that what we think is justified? Do we really understand how many cognitive biases affect most all of us most of the time? Do we have a clue at how many arguments are constructed to defend what we have come to believe based on personal idiosyncratic irrational reasons? Marx, Freud, and Nietzsche, known as the three masters of suspicion, taught us to be suspicious of all arguments because most people constructing them have ulterior self-serving agendas.

Do people in different cultures have good reasons for what they believe? Did people in different eras in human history have good reasons for what they believed? Is the whole concept of good reasons vs. bad reasons culturally relative? What exactly is a good personal reason for accepting something as true? Some things just appear to be true to us and we cannot bring ourselves to think differently.

What about someone who has a low IQ or someone who lacks emotional intelligence? What about someone who is brain damaged in some way, or who has suffered a stroke, or suffers from Alzheimer's disease? What about a child, or an adult who has never grown up? What if, as I strongly suspect, that belief is overwhelmingly involuntary, if not completely involuntary? Is it all just a lucky coincidence if we get something right? If any of these conditions obtain then the distinction between having good personal reasons and bad personal reasons basically flies out the window. If nothing else, there are certainly many cases where we cannot even say what it means for some people to have good personal reasons for what they believe. What we can say with virtual certainty is that people who believe something is true think they have good personal reasons for why they believe it is true (at least on a conscious level).

So, given the doctrinal statement above, what personal reason could be a bad reason for rejecting Christianity? Let's say a guy named Pat thinks Christianity is false because he had a strange dream where Patricia, his dead Christian mother, tells him it's all a ruse, that no matter what people believe when they die, God is sending everyone to hell anyway. Kinda like the parable of the rich man and Lazarus with a different slant.

Would Pat have good personal reasons to reject Christianity? I think so. This is not about convincing others with an argument. It's about him believing his mother's message in a dream, despite the lack of an evidence-based argument, despite his ignorance about the real nature of dreams, and despite any attempts by us at convincing him that he's wrong.

This is ultimately about who we are as human beings and the nature of the doctrinal statement. They are incompatible with each other. Now for my money quote: If God desires Pat to be saved, and if God knows Pat will be convinced by his dream because his God-given cognitive faculties are such that he would accept its message as true, then God should not have allowed Pat to have had such a dream in the first place. Allowing a vulnerable ignorant person like Pat to have had such a dream, knowing it would lead him to reject Christianity, makes that God just as culpable as if he himself caused Pat to reject Christianity.

What about an insincere reason, one whereby people lie to themselves about the real causes for rejecting Christianity? In the subconscious regions of their brains they believe Christianity is true but they suppresses this truth so it never reaches the conscious regions of the brain, much like

Paul writes about (see Romans 1:18–32). Paul, of course, knew nothing about the subconscious mind and how it controls our conscious thinking. We didn't know about such a thing until basically Sigmund Freud's time. Paul is describing people who consciously know the truth and knowingly choose to believe and act on that which they know is a lie. Such a claim is much too bold to be taken seriously by anyone after the rise of psychology.

Since consciously lying to oneself seems not to be likely in the least, or even impossible, what about a person who subconsciously lies to himself? What about self-deception? A lie is a lie is a lie, right? No, not necessarily. We deceive ourselves almost every waking hour. It's who we are. It keeps us sane. It keeps us encouraged to get up in the morning and go about trying to live a good life. It keeps us from being depressed with the realities of life that bear down on us. We probably cannot do otherwise, and if we do, then it's rare. A good little article about it can be found at The Skeptic's Dictionary.[6] It's a real problem for human beings. Unless people are properly trained they cannot do otherwise but to think illogically, based upon self-deception. This science is not something we even knew about until the last few decades. People don't even know enough to know that they are deceiving themselves. Let that sink in. Again, people don't even know enough to know they are deceiving themselves.

Since we have this strong propensity for self-deception, not just in regard to religion but also in regard to almost everything that involves us, our family, and friends, then, given the doctrinal statement, the very fact that some people do subconsciously deceive themselves into not believing is a good reason not to believe after all. For when we deceive ourselves we don't know that we are deceiving ourselves. We're just doing what we do. We probably can't even do otherwise in most cases, even knowing who we are as human beings. So, if someone is deceiving themselves into nonbelief, then that can no more be a bad personal reason for rejecting Christianity than when we deceive ourselves about anything else.

Now for another money quote: Deception, after all, is deception. The deceived do not know they are being deceived, even if it's self-deception. Get it? So just as in the case of Pat above, if God allows us to deceive ourselves into nonbelief when we don't know this is what we're doing (and we don't), then we can no more be held accountable for this self-deception than Pat can be held accountable for his ignorance. Just as Pat has good personal reasons to reject Christianity, even though they are ignorant, so too some people who deceive themselves into nonbelief can have good personal reasons for their nonbelief, because they are ignorant of their own self-deception.

Furthermore, I don't even think conscious rebellion against the God hypothesis is a bad personal reason to reject Christianity. We are all rebelling against all other deities anyway. I state for the record, and for all to read, that I am rebelling against Allah, who is presumably pleased with militant Muslims willing to fly planes into buildings, if called upon to do so.

I think this is a good reason to reject Allah, don't you, by rebelling against his moral codes in a civilized society? Or, must I have better reasons? If these are good enough reasons then why can't I rebel against Yahweh for allowing, no, demanding, child sacrifices, slavery, the denigration of women and homosexuals, and for rejecting the freedom of conscience, freedom of assembly, freedom of speech, and freedom of religion, something akin to the First Amendment of the U.S. Constitution? I can and I do.

So there isn't a bad personal reason to reject the Christian faith given the doctrinal statement. That means some people, maybe most of us, cannot be held accountable for being ignorant about Christianity, or the "evidence" that is supposed to convince us it's true.

Two Atheists Object

I've found that the more well-known an atheist becomes then the more often atheists criticize him or her for this, that, or the other. I don't like it but it comes with the territory. It's a sign of some kind of success, believe it or not. Atheists disagree with each other quite a bit anyway, but in my case I have put out thousands of pages over the last eight years, so atheists who want to nitpick at this, that, or the other can find plenty of nits to pick, especially since I like being a provocateur from time to time. One atheist critic of the argument I put forth in this chapter is Jeffery Jay Lowder, who graduated in 1995 with a BS in computer science from Seattle Pacific University, yet goes around deceptively calling himself a "philosopher," something I don't even call myself since that's for others to judge.

First of all, Lowder agrees with me that it is normally rational for people who had a unique (or extraordinary) personal experience of some kind to believe such an experience actually happened. But that's where the agreement ends. Lowder goes on to point out the obvious. He says it doesn't follow that it's rational for someone to believe just anything based upon a unique (or extraordinary) personal experience. He says no personal experience can make it rational for someone to believe that the moon is made out of green cheese, since no unique (or extraordinary) personal experience can do this.

Why is it that when we're talking about private subjective experiences someone always brings up obvious public objective examples as counter examples? Christians repeatedly do this. Lowder did the same thing. I offered an example of what I was talking about—a dream by a guy named Pat. Then I related the evidence showing that we deceive ourselves. These processes take place in the private subjective recesses of the mind. Lowder's response is basically to say that obvious public objective examples are in a different category than private subjective experiences.

Not to be too harsh on him, but thanks Jeff for this noninsight, mirroring how Christians argue. The question for us, however, is whether private, subjective, ignorant, irrational, rebellious, and self-deceptive reasons to reject Christianity are good ones given the doctrinal statement above. My argument is that even these "bad" reasons for rejecting Christianity are still good reasons. *Bad reasons are good ones. Or, to state it better, bad reasons are not bad reasons after all, while good reasons are still good ones.*

I think that what makes any given belief rational is a complex subject. Yes, yes, it involves sufficient evidence, but it's really interesting how rational people can basically evaluate the same evidence and come away with opposite conclusions. One major reason is because our abilities to reason are extremely bad. It's because of the haphazard evolution of the human brain, as Gary Marcus expertly shows in his book, *Kluge: The Haphazard Evolution of the Human Mind.* The only antidote to our poor reasoning abilities is science.

Matt DeStefano objects to my argument. He's an atheist who is a graduate student at the University of Arizona, having earned a master's degree in philosophy from the University of Missouri–St. Louis. DeStefano presented a scenario that is supposed to be the exception to my blanket claim that there isn't a bad personal reason to reject Christianity. If an exception can be found then my blanket claim is false. So let me say first of all that even if DeStefano's counterexample works it doesn't undercut anything else I'm arguing. It only means there is an exception or two. Nonetheless, I don't think his scenario works.

DeStefano initially suggested this scenario of a person who rejects Christianity:

> If Christianity were true, I would be rationally obliged to significantly alter my lifestyle. I do not wish to significantly alter my lifestyle. Therefore, Christianity is not true.[7]

Left unresolved is whether this change of lifestyle is for the good or bad, that is, whether it will require such a person to do harm or do good to oneself and others. Presumably DeStefano is assuming that the lifestyle change required but rejected is to be a better person who does good rather than harm, and additionally that Christianity is a religion of peace, justice, brotherhood, and good will toward all men(!). But it is not the case that Christianity makes better people and it is not the case that Christianity is a religion of peace.[8] But why is this to be presumed? There is nothing in his scenario that requires it. If the lifestyle change is to do harm to oneself and other people then I think this is most definitely a good personal reason to reject Christianity. Who, for instance, would not reject Yahweh's voice commanding us to kill and burn as a sacrifice our only son, as Abraham supposedly was commanded regarding Isaac? I would. I would not think the heavenly voice came from a loving God, that's for sure. I would sooner question my sanity than think it was really from a good God. And if I thought it was from an evil deity I would have no choice but to disobey him and take the consequences, since after all, a God who could command such a thing will eventually do whatever he wants to me anyway. So let's just get the pain and suffering of his punishment for disobeying him started immediately, rather than doing what my conscience cannot allow. My moral intuitions are such that I refuse to worship such a barbaric God. Period. The objective evidence for the truth of Christianity must be overpowering to overcome these personal moral intuitions of mine.

There is an additional question that needs to be answered. In DeStefano's scenario does such a person think there are strong objective reasons to embrace Christianity or not? If such a person does not think there are strong objective reasons for the Christian faith, that should settle the question. For the truth should not be settled by whether or not a given religion is personally considered to be a peaceful, good, neighborly one. For if so, there are better religions to choose from. However, if such a person thinks there are strong objective reasons for embracing the Christian faith, then that person would be irrational not to believe. Objective evidence and reasons take precedence over subjective evidence and reasons, hands down, no ifs, ands, or buts about it. I never said otherwise.

So the person DeStefano supposes as the exception turns out to be an irrational person. What's a God represented in the doctrinal statement above to do about an irrational person? Does an irrational person have good personal reasons for rejecting Christianity? Why not? I see no reason to think that an irrational person can think rationally about such matters. So why is he not supposed to conclude whatever an irrational mind concludes? His cognitive faculties are not functioning properly and God should know this about him. Since God wants to save him (given the doctrinal statement) then God could snap his omnipotent fingers so that the person can logically connect the dots. It's not about forcing him to believe at all. Given this scenario it's merely about helping such a person think rationally, that's all.

So unless DeStefano can show why an irrational person does not have good personal reasons for thinking irrationality and that the God in the doctrinal statement is under no moral obligation to help him think rationally, his exception is not an exception to what I'm arguing at all.

Christian Apologist Dr. Vincent Torley Objects

Vincent Torley writes for Uncommon Descent, a creationist site run by William Dembski. He understood my argument fairly well, so I'll comment on his objections.[9] Dr. Torley, describing me as a "secular philosopher," offers three criticisms of my argument.

> Loftus' argument bears a strong resemblance to the old philosophical argument (dating back to the ancient Greeks) that there is no such thing as *akrasia*, or weakness of will: no-one would ever willingly choose what they knew was bad for them, as we can only will what is good for us. As Plato's Socrates declared in the Protagoras: "No one who either knows or believes that there is another possible course of action, better than the one he is following, will ever continue on his present course" (Protagoras 358b-c). Philosophers continue to debate how weakness of will occurs, at the psychological level, and there is an interesting article about it here in The Stanford Encyclopedia of Philosophy. But the fact that it occurs is

something I consider to be self-evident. It is a simple fact, after all, that people break their New Year's resolutions all the time, even though they know perfectly well that they shouldn't. If we acknowledge that people can sometimes do things that they know they shouldn't, then we have to allow that they might sometimes choose to believe pleasing but ultimately pernicious ideas, even though they know they shouldn't.

Yes, to sum up ancient Socratic Greek thought, "to know the good is to do the good." And yet, even people who know the good don't do it. To what then can we attribute the weakness of the will? It has to do with our fleshly appetites, yes, but all of us have these appetites built in our DNA. So there's more to it than that. We might consciously know we shouldn't eat more chocolate when on a diet, but we just can't stop ourselves. The reason we eat more of it anyway is because our will has a subconscious component that overrides what we consciously think we want. Located in our subconscious mind is what we really want. We want more chocolate. We want it now. The problem of the weakness of the will then becomes the problem of how our conscious mind can override our subconscious mind.

So the issue for us is how our subconscious mind has arrived at its conclusions, the ones that really motivate us. And the answer is simple, from our DNA and from everything we have experienced in life, along with any conclusions we arrived at from our experiences, all of them. Most of our early childhood experiences in life formed the attitudes that have shaped and subsequently are used to manage all of the ideas we arrive at, and this occurs at such an early stage in life that no one holds children accountable for this. Let that sink in.

Torley continues along the same lines with his second criticism:

This brings me to the ultimate flaw in Loftus' argument that there can be no bad personal reasons for rejecting Christianity—or more generally, for rejecting a God Who punishes people for their unbelief. Loftus is assuming that when people come to believe that Christianity is false, their belief is caused in a deterministic fashion by their cognitive faculties. And Loftus' point is that people can't be blamed for the way in which their cognitive faculties work: that would be like blaming Sam for being Sam, or for that matter, blaming Sam for being human. Sam is what he is, and he is who he is. Nobody can blame him for that.

Loftus' argument implicitly assumes that we have no control over the way in which our cognitive faculties work—in other words, that free will (and here, I'm talking about the libertarian variety) plays no role in the formation of our beliefs. "Well, why should it?" I hear you ask. "You didn't choose to believe Pythagoras' Theorem, do you? The logic of the argument compelled you to accept it." But this is a highly atypical case. The vast majority of our beliefs do involve an element of choice, and our cognitive faculties do not normally work in a deterministic fashion. People often believe things that they find pleasant, or aesthetic, or morally uplifting, or intellectually congenial, or currently fashionable, or politically convenient, or what have you. The point I'm making here is not that they should or shouldn't be forming their beliefs for these reasons, as they're not all bad ones—science, for instance, is often guided by aesthetic considerations. The point I'm making is that beliefs typically involve an element of choice.

This objection of his is based upon an unevidenced assertion about something I never said. Apart from these two flaws what remains is excellent! Never mind there isn't anything that remains. ;-)

My real argument is not based upon determinism. I can demonstrate that even granting libertarian free will we human beings don't have much of it at all, if we have any of it. Just read this thoughtfully. That's all I need to make my present argument. To read some good arguments that we have no free will, though, I recommend Jonathan Pearce's book, *Free Will?: An Investigation into Whether We Have Free Will, or Whether I Was Always Going to Write This Book.*

Torley's third criticism of my argument is just as flawed.

[I]t assumes that God knows all possible counterfactuals. . . . it assumes that God has knowledge of each and every counterfactual, relating to human choices. For instance, God knows what I would do if I were offered a bribe, or if I suddenly lost my sight, or if I won the lottery, or if I dreamed about snakes. It's absolutely vital to Loftus' case that God should possess this kind of knowledge.

Nope, this is not the case at all. Just as it does not depend on determinism neither does it depend on God knowing each and every counterfactual. All we need for the argument to work is simple divine omniscience, the kind Torley argues for stemming from Boethius, but which is rejected by other

Christian philosophers (so I'll let them duke it out, and when they settle it among themselves I'll debunk the consensus, if that ever happens *cough*).

Does Torley really think that a God with simple divine omniscience cannot tell in advance what Pat will conclude if he had a dream as I described? If God cannot know what Pat will conclude from such a dream then omniscience means nothing at all. At a bare minimum omniscience should entail that a God with it could predict with nearly 100 percent certainty what a person's next act will be. Likewise such a God could predict with near certainty what a person's next thought will be. The problem of whether such an omniscient being could predict subsequent future acts and thoughts of a person is not a problem for my argument. For I'll grant that with simple divine omniscience such a God will be less and less likely to predict what will happen as time moves into the future, since the counterfactuals will begin to pile up quickly and muddy the waters. Even then, if God has simple omniscience then he is still the master chess player and can predict the moves of people like chess pieces so far out in advance that it should stun us if he had such an ability. Apparently Torley isn't stunned by such an ability at all. Ho-hum, he yawns. Such a God cannot predict what Pat will conclude from a given vivid dream, so there. Poof, Loftus has no argument.

Sheesh. What a cheap notion of omniscience Torley has. I would love to see him use that same cheap notion of omniscience in explaining away why there is so much intense and ubiquitous suffering in our world. But I digress as well.

The point is that even Pat's own brothers and sisters could predict in advance what he would conclude if he had such a dream. Doesn't omniscience mean God has more knowledge than brothers and sisters or not? If not, give up the notion entirely. If so, my argument stands. His choice. I care not what he chooses.

Concluding Implication: The Importance of Persuasion When Reasoning Fails

There is a very important implication from this *argument from ignorance*. If brain studies mean anything, we know that people are persuaded into thinking differently. They aren't just reasoned into it. Persuasion counts when reasoning doesn't. Spock doesn't exist in reality. He never did. None of us are like him. So we shouldn't treat people as if they are like Spock, especially believers who believe for other reasons than having good solid evidence. We must use reasons and tout the objective evidence whenever we're dealing with believers who are not so blind that they can reason with us on an issue or two, but we should also seek to persuade them if we want to effect change in their lives, change for the good. So in the interests of persuading believers, rather than continually driving down one dead-end road after another chasing them down, I simply try a different tactic, a reasonable one based on solid evidence that believers do not reason about their faith. People can claim what they want to about how I roll. It's just that I can better persuade my opponents by using several different ways of seeing the same truth rather than following them down the rabbit hole where we will not agree in the end anyway.

We see things differently. I know this. Others don't seem to. That's the difference. For me it's not always about more detailed arguments with time-consuming in-depth reasoning. It's about helping those who disagree with me see things my way. It takes a conversion, a new way of seeing the evidence, much like a lawyer who becomes a prosecutor in the midst of the same trial. That's the genius of what I do (if I have any at all), although for this I am railed against in places. Still I know what I'm doing. The facts are the facts. Kick against these goads all you want to. I have a properly basic belief that God doesn't exist. The only thing left is to persuade. ;-)

The alternative is for someone to tell me how to reach brainwashed people. You cannot reason with them for the most part at all. Most all of them are impervious to reasoning. They always have an escape clause much like the guy who thought he was dead, was convinced dead men don't bleed, then upon being cut with a knife concluded dead men do bleed after all! So what I'm advocating is to treat the patient in ways appropriate to the illness.

Christians don't like this. I understand. Many atheists don't either. But then I don't write to win friends more than I do to change minds. I've come to the conclusion most all believers cannot be reasoned out of their faith because they were never reasoned into it in the first place. So sometimes all one can do is be like that child in the crowd who sees the promenading emperor without any clothes on and yells out, "Hey, he doesn't have any clothes on." This is the level at which some Christians are in my judgment. They need to be shocked into seeing they are unjustly brainwashed to believe. At that point I am no longer interested in arguing with them but in persuading them, challenging them, provoking them to see things differently, to see things my way. One college textbook I used in my critical thinking classes has a whole chapter on persuasion that I highly recommend. The authors argue that "exaggerated, slanted, or misleading language is compatible with perfectly good reasoning. A claim or an argument that is couched in emotionally charged language is not necessarily a false claim or a bad argument. Slanted language should not be a reason for rejecting a claim or dismissing a piece of reasoning, but neither should it be a reason for accepting a position on an issue."[10]

I try to persuade believers by overwhelming them with a plethora of arguments. But given the fact that believers must be convinced their faith is nearly impossible before they will ever consider it to be improbable, this is what their faith forces me to do if I want to convince them they are wrong. You see, I know a lot more than I can tell. Based on everything I know, I know Christianity is a delusion. The only thing left to do at that point is to convince Christians they are wrong. And they are. It's not that I don't try as best as I can to be accurate by reasoning with believers as much as I can to show them they believe without evidence, or sufficient evidence. I do, most empathically. The very reason I cannot believe anymore is because I would have to be ignorant to do so. It's just that lacking the ability to reason with Christians I also seek to persuade them they are wrong.

David Eller argues this is what Christians have been doing on behalf of their faith for a long time.[11] They seek to persuade. And they have been doing it a lot longer than atheists. I've just learned from what they are already doing.

In an article for *American Atheist* magazine based on his book, *Atheism Advanced: Further Thoughts of a Freethinker*, David Eller says what I'm saying:

> Dale Carnegie offered advice on *How to Win Friends and Influence People*. Since then we have learned a great deal more about how beliefs and attitudes are formed and changed—and theists at least have put these methods into practice, long before the 20th century. They fully appreciate that religion is not a matter of argumentation and certainly not a matter of constructing convincing cases. It is, rather, literally a battle for the mind, as numerous Christian websites clearly illustrate.[12] Apparently, we atheists are in a battle for the mind, whether we fully know it or not, and that reality calls for a new orientation as well as new tactics.

As rationalists, we value facts and logic and we expect everyone else to respect them. However, all of the research into belief/attitude change indicates that facts and logic are not the decisive elements in bringing people around to a new way of thinking. We love to argue, and we think that arguing is effective, but experience supports the conclusion of Carnegie: "You can't win an argument." Instead, "Nine times out of ten, argument ends with each of the contestants more firmly convinced than ever that he is absolutely right." While we do not have to follow all of Carnegie's suggestions, we must take seriously the possibility that our current approach is not the best approach—if, that is, we want to actually change people to our way of thinking on the god-question and not merely entertain ourselves with our cleverness and outrage ourselves with the purported stubbornness and stupidity of our opponents. In a word, we need to learn what works and apply it, to treat the theist/atheist encounter as an exercise in applied psychology, of persuasion, of influence.

Atheists are obliged to educate themselves on the most successful techniques of attitude-change, what Robert Cialdini in his book *Influence: Science and Practice* calls "compliance tactics" or "weapons of automatic influence." I can hear many atheists objecting already, complaining that persuasion or influence is beneath them, even dishonest, akin to advertising or indoctrination. Indeed, the techniques that Sargant, Carnegie, Cialdini, and many others advocate are akin to advertising, but that is beside the point: they work. We can be noble and unsuccessful, and wallow in our frustration that people don't get our finely-crafted arguments, or we can be practical and successful. I assure you that, despite all their high-minded rhetoric, theists employ all of the possible tactics of influence and reap the rewards thereof. In the battle for the mind, atheists have so far been unarmed and disorganized, and our results speak for themselves.

Eller then shares Cialdini's six-part plan for effective attitude change.

1. "People are more likely to do or think what you want if you give them something first. Giving creates 'a sense of future obligation' (p. 20), making it difficult to refuse the supposedly generous giver. That is one reason why religions focus on doing 'good works' or handing out free things like bibles: once someone has done a good turn for you, it is harder to deny their requests."

2. "*Commitment and consistency*. 'Once we make a choice or take a stand, we will encounter personal and interpersonal pressures to behave consistently with that commitment' (p. 52). . . . Getting them to commit verbally and in person is good; getting to them to commit in public and in writing is even better."

3. "*Social proof* . . . holds that 'We view a behavior as correct in a given situation to the degree that we see others performing it' (p. 99). People are persuaded by other people, not by facts—or, other people's belief is a fact. 'The greater the number of people who find any idea correct, the more a given individual will perceive the idea to be correct' (p. 108–9)."

4. "An obvious but important facet of influence is *liking*: people are more inclined to think and act like people whom they find pleasant and agreeable. . . . Not for nothing do churches and many otherwise non-enjoyable activities feature lunches and potlucks and pizza parties. It would behoove atheists to *be nice*."

5. "*Authority*, which has been demonstrated again and again. We are more likely to follow and to comply with people in authority, who have power and/of expertise. Humans are, as well as imitative, inherently obedient. And this authority could and should be symbolized with titles, official-looking clothing, and the other 'trappings' of status and knowledge. This is why religions include elaborate robes or decorative altars or imposing architecture."

6. "Cialdini mentions *scarcity*, because 'opportunities seem more valuable to us when they are less available' (p. 200). People are motivated when something is limited in supply and time, or when they are afraid of losing something they already have, or especially when something is in high demand. Religions of course often claim to be dealing in scarce goods, like salvation or remittance of sins. If there are more people than can get into heaven, the (alleged) fact inspires competition for the few remaining spaces."

Notes

1. For what I consider proof that people are born gay read Veronica Drantz's chapter, "The Gender Binary and LGBTI People: Religious Myth and Medical Malpractice," in my anthology *Christianity Is Not Great* (Amherst, NY: Prometheus, 2014), pp. 242–263.

2. On this see Ronald A. Lindsay's book, *The Necessity of Secularism: Why God Can't Tell Us What To Do* (Durham, NC: Pitchstone Publishing, 2014).

3. On this read William Patterson's chapter "Christianity and the Environment," in my anthology *Christianity Is Not Great* (Amherst, NY: Prometheus, 2014), pp. 286–302.

4. "You Don't Need a PhD to Criticize Religion," The Atheist Voice, video published on May 10, 2016, https://www.youtube.com/watch?v=YPeG8vbv55o.

5. Michael Shermer, *The Believing Brain* (New York: Times Books, 2011), p. 259.

6. "Self-Deception," http://skepdic.com/selfdeception.html.

7. John Loftus, "There Isn't a Bad Reason to Reject the Christian Faith, Part 1," Debunking Christianity, February 1, 2013, http://debunkingchristianity.blogspot. com/2013/02/there-isnt-bad-reason-to-reject.html#comment-786962209.

8. See my anthology *Christianity Is Not Great*.

9. Vincent Torley, "John Loftus' Faulty Logic on Free Will," Uncommon Descent, February 2, 2013, http://www.uncommondescent.com/intelligent-design/john-loftus-faulty-logic-on-free-will-theres-no-such-thing-as-a-bad-personal-reason-for-disbelief-in-the-god-of-the-bible/.

10. See Brooke Noel Moore and Richard Parker, *Critical Thinking* (New York: McGraw-Hill Humanities/Social Sciences/Languages, 2008), chapter 5, "Persuasion Through Rhetoric: Common Devices and Techniques."

11. David Eller, "How to Win Friends and Introduce People to Atheism," *American Atheist*, September/October 2009, pp. 18–20.

12. As examples, Eller directs the reader to http://www.ucgstp.org/lit/vt/ vt05/mind.htm; http://www.joycemeyer.org/OurMinistries/EverydayAnswers/The+ Battle+In+Your+Mind/default.htm; http://www.sw-mins.org/battle_of_the_mind. html; and http://www.hissheep.org/deliverance/the_battle_for_the_mind.html.

9

ON JUSTIFYING RIDICULE, MOCKERY, AND SATIRE

My view of ridicule, mockery, and satire is that human beings may be so bad at reasoning that persuasion is all that matters. We are not like Spock of *Star Trek*. No one is. Far, far from it. If this even has some modicum of truth to it, and I think it does, then that alone justifies the use of mockery. Christians, for instance, were not usually reasoned into their faith. They were persuaded into it. They were persuaded to believe by the circumstances of their upbringing or the likability of a significant person in their lives. Based on this human propensity of ours, mockery might actually be more effective than thought, for if Christians were persuaded into their faith, then maybe they can also be persuaded out of it.

I Changed My Mind about Ridicule

I've previously mentioned changing my mind about some important things. I want my readers to know this changing of mine has all been in the same direction. The pattern has been from conservative Christian to liberal Christian to agnostic to atheist—more specifically, from a weak or an agnostic atheist to a strong atheist—along with all that entails. What you're reading in this book is a jaded Loftus, one who has tried reasoning with believers on a daily basis without achieving much success relative to my efforts. I figure if I cannot reach very many of them the problem is with belief itself. It has no merit at all. Believers do not reason well because they are blinded by faith in their culturally inherited fantasies.

More than a decade ago, in 2006, I agreed with Christian philosopher of religion Victor Reppert when he said, "I really dislike ridicule, from either side of the fence." I wrote at the time, "I'm not saying there isn't a place for some of it in some forums specifically addressed to the proverbial 'choir' for venting and/or entertainment purposes. It's just not something I pander to here at DC [Debunking Christianity] from either side of the fence."[1] Two years later, in 2008, in reference to the taunts of atheist Pat Condell, who said, "Provide evidence or expect mockery and ridicule," I wrote, "I try to carry on a reasonable discussion with people who disagree with me. . . . I agree with him that Christian beliefs are ridiculous. And I know many Christians think atheism is ridiculous. What if both sides in this debate approached each other as Condell suggests? Many of them do."[2] Just five years ago, in 2011, I penned a comprehensive post titled, "I Still Want a Respectful Educated Discussion of the Ideas That Separate Us," where I described my changing attitude about ridicule.[3] I wrote:

I am gravitating to the dark side, having argued with fundamentalists for about five years online now. It's just that such an approach has a justification and it's needed. And it's not as if [Richard] Carrier or I don't also have the arguments to back up our ridicule, either. Just consider this on a continuum. Perhaps I've been too polite and need to move in that direction. On August 8, 2010 Phil Plait weighed in by decrying the use of ridicule, to which I responded with "Don't Be a Dick, Phil Plait."[4] There I argued that "Ridicule in a social grouping does have it's effect because we are social human beings. There are some beliefs we can never argue people out of because they were never argued into them in the first place. Religion is one of them. So ridicule and social approbation do have their effects." And I laid down this principle: If skeptics want to argue believers out of their religion then when addressing believers skeptics need to treat believers and their beliefs with a good measure of respect and dignity.

This should be non-controversial I would think, once we grant the distinctions. If however, you don't think a particular believer can be argued out of his or her religion (and I've known plenty of believers like this), or, if you need to vent (which I've also done when totally frustrated), or if you are speaking to other skeptics in front of believers in order to encourage these skeptics, then what Plait argued for simply does not apply.

In some ways my gradual change has been because it has to do with my audience. When I wrote that in 2006 I was aiming at a respectful discussion with respectful believers. When discussing these issues with a believer whom I respect as an intelligent person, I treat that person with respect without any ridicule at all. I am the same person. What changes me is the people I deal with. I adjust my responses to the overall perceptions I have of the people who argue against me. So I still want a respectful educated discussion of the ideas that separate us, but reality hit me in the face. I cannot have a reasonable discussion about the issues surrounding faith. So my change was in response to the way believers themselves think and write.

Everyone ridicules beliefs in Zeus, Ra, Hathor, Baal, Thor, and Odin. I see no reason not to do the same thing to the Christian belief in their god Yahweh. I still don't think we should personally ridicule people to their faces, for that will not effect any attitudinal changes. We should do so, though, in public venues in their hearing. As more people think Yahweh is no longer a credible god then more of us should ridicule such a belief. That's how gods die. Being able to ridicule any particular god is a sign that god is dying or already dead. Surely faithful believers in each culture whose god died didn't like the ridicule, but it came anyway. People no longer feared them or their priests so they ridiculed them. So what we're potentially seeing is the beginning of what Nietzsche predicted long ago, the death of God, like what has largely happened in Europe. Whether America's God dies soon or not is another story. But I welcome it, and that's one reason I do ridicule the dominant God of our culture, because I want to help it die. There's nothing at all ignorant or bigoted about my doing so. I can back up my claims.

No wonder some Muslims kill when their prophet or god is ridiculed. They know what it means. Their religion is under attack.

Historical Examples of Effective Ridicule and Mockery

I know believers don't like their beliefs mocked. I get that. So it's no surprise they would object to ridicule by saying it doesn't cause them to change their minds, that it makes them dig their heels in deeper, and that it just makes them think less of the one doing the mocking. You would expect them to say this. The facts however are different. Ridicule and mockery have been very effective in any cultural war and they will forever be effective and necessary.

There have been some very famous satires in history. Here are five important ones:

1. Aristophanes's Greek comedy *The Clouds* portrays Socrates as a buffoon and a deceiver of the young. It was the first comedy "of ideas" and was a contributing factor in the trial and death of Socrates.

2. In 1509 Desiderius Erasmus wrote *In Praise of Folly*, one of the most notable works of the Renaissance and considered to be a catalyst for the Protestant Reformation. In it Erasmus praises self-deception and madness and proceeds to highlight both with regard to the abuses of the Roman Catholic Church.

3. In 1729 Jonathan Swift wrote *A Modest Proposal for Preventing the Children of Poor People From Being a Burden to Their Parents or Country, and for Making Them Beneficial to the Publick*, where he mocks the English mistreatment of the Irish poor (a subject dear to my heart being of Irish descent). Swift sarcastically suggests the solution for the impoverished Irish was to sell their children as food to the rich.

4. In 1759 Voltaire's *Candide* effectively mocked Leibniz's theodicy that "all is for the best in the best of all possible worlds."

5. Thomas Taylor wrote a satire of Mary Wollstonecraft's book *A Vindication of the Rights of Woman* (1792). Her book was the first defense of women's rights in Western English literature. She attacked gender oppression and argued for equal educational opportunities, justice, and equality for all humanity. Taylor mocked her ideas with *A Vindication of the Rights of Brutes*, arguing that if women have rights, then animals also have rights, but that was preposterous to him and to his readers at the time. The irony of Taylor's satire is that he provided some of the first arguments for animal rights that are used today (by those who also condemn his sexism).

Now, does anyone think these satires convinced the people who disagreed, the ones who made the case that was being mocked by these satires? I highly doubt it. I doubt they changed any minds among the ones who thought differently, who knew Socrates personally, who were archbishops in the Catholic Church, who considered the Irish to be garbage, who agreed with Leibniz, or who thought women were second-rate human beings. These people cannot be convinced by satire, so satire is not written to change their minds. It's written to marginalize them by laughing at them. It persuades people who don't yet have a settled opinion on the issue, in part by using social pressure. No one wants to be a laughingstock. No one wants to be the butt of a joke. If people are laughing at a particular view it pressures the undecided to distance themselves from it. It draws a line in the sand, so to speak. It can also silence people who think otherwise, for they won't want to speak up in a class on behalf of something most others will laugh at.

Isn't using laughter an informal fallacy known as *appealing to ridicule*? It sure is. Shouldn't all intelligent people denounce using an informal fallacy then? Shouldn't they instead take the moral and intellectual high ground? No, not at all. In some ways we just cannot help ourselves since some ideas seem that preposterous. When something cannot be taken seriously it deserves our laughter. We all do it, all of us. Should we hide our laughter so as not to offend? I think not. It's a way to "come out of the closet," so to speak, to let others know they will be laughed at if they espouse certain ideas with a straight face. There is power in social pressure. There is power in numbers.

Ridicule also shows people just how bad we think the case is for something. The worse we think the case is then the more our ridicule shows people what we really think of it. Laughter is an entirely appropriate response to a person who suggests women are inferior to men. That's how bad the case is for sexism or homophobia. And the more studied a person is on a particular issue then the more force that person's ridicule has on others. I'm ridiculed almost daily by believers who are usually ignorant of their own ignorance, so their ridicule shouldn't matter at all. By contrast, I have spent forty years studying Christianity and my conclusion is that believers who seek to defend it are worth being laughed at. I laugh almost daily when reading something written by one of the top Christian apologists. They remind me of the story of the emperor who has no clothes on, really. I'm not kidding. Been there, done that myself. I'm never going back to that nutty nudist camp for the mentally challenged who are all infected with the same virus of the mind.

The use of ridicule can be justified pragmatically. It works well under the right circumstances, depending on the issue and the potential effectiveness of using it. It is best used when the arguments are there to back it up, and when more people agree against the ideas that are being ridiculed. So satire, ridicule, and mockery are weapons that should be in our arsenal in this important cultural war of ideas.

Ridicule expresses a type of peer pressure that changes minds. We know that peer pressure changes minds, even against what seems quite clear to someone with a different opinion. We KNOW this! If a person says she doesn't agree with belief A, that tells you something important, even if this is all she says. But if she laughs at belief A, that tells you she doesn't have any respect at all for belief A. Now imagine most of the people you know laughing at belief A. That would get your attention and could indeed change your mind. Peer pressure works. Ridicule is a type of peer pressure. Ridicule changes minds. Ridicule from lots of people has more power to change minds. It's quite simple really, such that anyone who disagrees is ignorant. There are other questions to address, but let's start with baby steps. Ridicule is both helpful and necessary. Someday in the future people will treat Christianity just like all of the other dead gods and religions are treated today. We mock them. In the future, anyone who learns about Christianity in a history book will mock it like all the other dead religions.

Nothing I've written should lead anyone to think all we need is mockery. Far from it. I will continue reasoning with believers as always. It's just that mockery is effective, necessary, and justifiable in this cultural war. It's one of the weapons we need to change the religious landscape.

Some Further Examples of Effective Ridicule and Satire

Good ridicule must be based on some truth, otherwise it wouldn't be funny. It must also bring home an important point. Some of it is gentle humor while some of it is quite mean-spirited. Some people focus on ridicule while others focus on elaborately reasoned arguments. If you think ridicule is unbecoming of an atheist, or anyone for that matter, then you cannot like the comedy style of Stephen Colbert, Jon Stewart, Bill Maher, or even Jay Leno or David Letterman. Look at the following good examples and then try to honestly tell me ridicule has no place in our cultural wars.

Socrates

If you have ever read Plato's Dialogues, you know Socrates ridiculed his opponents. Anyone who has read the ending of the Euthyphro dilemma sees this plainly:

Socrates: Were we not saying that the holy or pious was not the same with that which is loved of the gods? Have you forgotten?

Euthyphro: I quite remember.

Socrates: And are you not saying that what is loved of the gods is holy; and is not this the same as what is dear to them—do you see?

Euthyphro: True.

Socrates: Then either we were wrong in former assertion; or, if we were right then, we are wrong now.

Euthyphro: One of the two must be true.

Socrates: Then we must begin again and ask, What is piety? That is an enquiry which I shall never be weary of pursuing as far as in me lies; and I entreat you not to scorn me, but to apply your mind to the utmost, and tell me the truth. For, if any man knows, you are he; and therefore I must detain you, like Proteus, until you tell. If you had not certainly known the nature of piety and impiety, I am confident that you would never, on behalf of a serf, have charged your aged father with murder. You would not have run such a risk of doing wrong in the sight of the gods, and you would have had too much respect for the opinions of men. I am sure, therefore, that you know the nature of piety and impiety. Speak out then, my dear Euthyphro, and do not hide your knowledge.

Euthyphro: Another time, Socrates; for I am in a hurry, and must go now.

Socrates: Alas! my companion, and will you leave me in despair? I was hoping that you would instruct me in the nature of piety and impiety; and then I might have cleared myself of Meletus and his indictment. I would have told him that I had been enlightened by Euthyphro, and had given up rash innovations and speculations, in which I indulged only through ignorance, and that now I am about to lead a better life.

Boghossian's Tweet

On June 15, 2014, philosopher Peter Boghossian (@peterboghossian) tweeted: "Being published in the philosophy of religion should disqualify one from sitting at the adult table." This is the tweet that woke me from my dogmatic PoR slumber. As I considered it, the more I thought about it the more I liked it. It was genius as an example of ridicule with a point. Even as someone who knows a lot about the PoR myself, who takes that discipline seriously, I think he has raised an important issue via ridicule. He has raised awareness about the claims of religious faith. These claims either have no evidence for them or they lack sufficient evidence. While Boghossian's tweet was only a few words long, I think it merits an honorable mention along with some very famous historical satires.

Lindsay's Short Play

James Lindsay wrote an excellent example of ridicule. He's the author of *Everybody Is Wrong About God* and has argued theism is done and won't last into the future, just as I do. Victor Reppert responded by saying a bit sarcastically: "Oh yeah, theism is losing adherents, it's down to 74% in the latest Harris poll." Then Lindsay responded, well, ya gotta read his short play:

> *Fool*: The craft is definitely sinking, sir. We are falling steadily and have been for some time.
>
> *Victor*: Nonsense! Are we not still aloft?
>
> *Fool*: Yes, sir, we are, but . . .
>
> *Victor*: No but! Are our engineers not still manning the engines of our mighty craft?
>
> *Fool*: Yes, sir, but . . . But it appears we have lost our only source of lift, and we're gliding ever downward. We are going to crash.
>
> *Victor*: Nonsense! Insubordination!
>
> *Victor*: [checks altitude gauge]

Victor: Our altitude is at 74%! How can we be crashing, Fool?!

Fool: Sir, we have no means of generating lift. We've been dropping steadily . . .

Victor: Nonsense! As long as the craft is an inch above the ground, we're still flying!

Fool: Yes sir! I'll rearrange the deck chairs, then, shall I?

Victor: Yes, and take mine away from the window. I grow weary of looking outside.

Fool: Yes sir!

:Exeunt:

Saudi TV Series Deploys New Weapon Against ISIS: Satire

People hate ridicule. But if you want to get their attention like nothing else then ridicule them. There's just something about it, and Saudi TV is using it against ISIS. Michael Rubin, formerly a U.S. State Department official, agrees with this approach: "Islamists cannot handle free thinking in the best of times, but ridicule is their kryptonite, for it shows that the would-be caliphs have no clothes. . . . Hence it should be an essential part of any strategy." [5]

The Onion *Satirizes Evangelical "Scientists"*

The title says it all: "Evangelical Scientists Refute Gravity with New 'Intelligent Falling' Theory." [6]

Sacrilegious Graphic (Comic) Books for the Young

A young friend showed me a couple of great looking and very funny R-rated graphic comic books he's beginning to collect. They are sacrilegious, extremely well done, and funny. One is called *Battle Pope* and the other is *Jesus Hates Zombies*. There is a generation of young people who think the Pope and Jesus are objects for ridicule. No argument here. Just ridicule. And they find these books funny. To me THAT is funny. We no longer have to debunk Christianity with arguments. Just get them hooked on these comic books! ;-)

The Top 10 Satires Against Religious Faiths

1. Bill Maher's mockumentary *Religulous*

2. George Carlin's "religion is bullshit" routine

3. Julia Sweeney's monologue *Letting Go of God*

4. *Penn & Teller: Bullshit!*—episode titled "Creationism"

5. Mr. Deity's "Episode 1: Mr. Deity and the Evil"

6. DarkMatter2525's video "Sodom and Gomorrah"

7. NonStampCollector's video "Context!!!"

8. Edward Current's video "Checkmate, Atheists!"

9. The character Betty Bowers, "America's Best Christian"

10. The "Top Ten Signs You're a Christian Fundamentalist" list, modeled on Jeff Foxworthy's "You might be a redneck if . . ." jokes.[7] For those who haven't seen the list, which has been spread widely on social media, I'll share it here:

You might be a fundamentalist if . . .

10—You vigorously deny the existence of thousands of gods claimed by other religions, but feel outraged when someone denies the existence of yours.

9— You feel insulted and "dehumanized" when scientists say that people evolved from other life forms, but you have no problem with the Biblical claim that we were created from dirt.

8—You laugh at polytheists, but you have no problem believing in the Trinity.

7—Your face turns purple when you hear of the "atrocities" attributed to Allah, but you don't even flinch when hearing about how God slaughtered all the babies of Egypt in "Exodus" and ordered the elimination of entire ethnic groups in "Joshua"—including women, and children.

6—You laugh at Hindu beliefs that deify humans, and Greek claims about gods sleeping with women, but you have no problem believing that the Holy Spirit impregnated Mary, who then gave birth to a man-god who got killed, came back to life, and then ascended into the sky.

5—You are willing to spend your life looking for little loopholes in the scientifically established age of Earth (4.55 billion years), but you find nothing wrong with believing dates recorded by Bronze Age tribesmen sitting in their tents and guessing that Earth is a couple of generations old.

4—You believe that the entire population of this planet with the exception of those who share your beliefs—though excluding those in all rival sects—will spend Eternity in an infinite Hell of Suffering. And yet consider your religion the most "tolerant" and "loving."

3—While modern science, history, geology, biology, and physics have failed to convince you otherwise, some idiot rolling around on the floor speaking in "tongues" may be all the evidence you need to "prove" Christianity.

2—You define 0.01% as a "high success rate" when it comes to answered prayers. You consider that to be evidence that prayer works. And you think that the remaining 99.99% failure was simply the will of God.

1—You actually know a lot less than many atheists and agnostics do about the Bible, Christianity, and church history—but still call yourself a Christian.[8]

Atheists Who Agree We Should Ridicule Ridiculous Beliefs

It's not just the so-called new atheists like Richard Dawkins, Bill Maher, and P. Z. Myers who advocate ridicule. I do too. So does Richard Carrier, as does Stephen Law, Keith Parsons, and many others. Keep in mind we don't advocate ridicule as the only response, nor do we advocate doing it to a believer's face, nor do we advocate using it against believers as individuals but rather against their ridiculous beliefs.

Here's a sampling of quotes in defense of ridicule:

Thomas Jefferson in defense of mockery: "Ridicule is the only weapon which can be used against unintelligible propositions."[9]

British atheist and freethinker George William Foote (1850–1915): "Goldsmith said there are two classes of people who dread ridicule—priests and fools. They cry out that it is no argument, but they know it is. It has been found the most potent form of argument. Euclid used it in his immortal Geometry; for what else is the reductio ad absurdum which he sometimes employs? Elijah used it against the priests of Baal. The Christian fathers found it effective against the Pagan superstitions, and in turn it was adopted as the best weapon of attack on them by Lucian and Celsus. Ridicule has been used by Bruno, Erasmus, Luther, Rabelais, Swift, and Voltaire, by nearly all the great emancipators of the human mind."[10]

Bertrand Russell's orbiting teapot was an example of ridicule. He also backed his ridicule up with reason and evidence. The orbiting teapot example caught people's attention precisely because they knew he was not stupid. He earned the right to ridicule. The teapot example also educated people. There was information to be gleaned from it, a discussion to be had based on it. Per Russell, it is indeed possible to simultaneously ridicule, inform, and convince others. There are times to ridicule and times to argue, and the same person can do both, even in the same lecture, and convince others!

Walter Sinnott-Armstrong: "Our best hope for progress is for atheists to speak out and (as politely as possible) tell any theists who will listen why religious beliefs are ridiculous."[11]

James Lindsay elevates the use of laughter as one of three tools that can uproot faith (along with Boghossian's street epistemology and my outsider test for faith):

> The power of effective satire is to take the puff out of the sails of faith and expose it as a false virtue that people will want to avoid. It does so by breaking the powerful taboo on profaning the allegedly sacred (this being a point understood in moral terms). Once sacredness falls away, the belief in question can more easily be reconsidered and, in many cases, revised. The ideological, including the religious, we must note, are anything but unaware of this fact. Indeed, they sometimes go to great lengths, some murderous, in order to protect their core beliefs from "blasphemous" satire.[12]

Hemant Mehta: "We should absolutely mock religion. . . . Bad ideas deserve to be criticized. And mockery is a form of criticism. I think it provides a more useful way to get people to rethink their beliefs. So have at it. Religion's basically a long setup just waiting for a punchline. . . . Ridicule is a good response to ideas that are ridiculous."[13]

Keith Parsons joins with others in advocating ridicule. He advocates this as one response to fundamentalism:

> "A single belly-laugh is worth a thousand syllogisms," said H. L. Mencken. Fundamentalism and fundamentalists should be ridiculed in the media, by comedians, or wherever. You don't have to worry about fairness, since, as Poe's Law famously notes, no satire can possibly be more absurd than the real thing. Come on. You just can't come up with anything more ridiculous than someone who honestly thinks that all human woes stem

from an incident in which a talking snake accosted a naked woman in a primeval garden and talked her into eating a piece of fruit. Again, most ridicule would consist of pointedly drawing attention to what they really believe. Nothing could be fairer than that. As a sign admonished on *The Simpsons*, put the fun back in fundamentalism. Laugh it to death.

Richard Carrier: "By and large the minds of the ridiculous can't be changed. It's their flock we're talking to. But even the ridiculous change under ridicule . . . some respond by getting more ridiculous (and those are the ones who could never be swayed even by the politest methods), but others accumulate shame until they see the error of their ways (I've met many ex-evangelicals who have told me exactly that). Thus, ridicule converts the convertible and marginalizes the untouchable. There is no more effective strategy in a culture war."[14]

Faisal Saeed Al Mutar lectures on Muslim issues around the world. His focus is on Islamic problems in the Middle East and how they can be solved. On Facebook he wrote: "If you hold ridiculous beliefs, your beliefs deserve to be ridiculed. You have rights, your beliefs don't."

Doug Krueger is the author of the excellent book *What Is Atheism?* On Facebook he wrote: "We should ridicule the ridiculous. This is sometimes more effective than arguments because believers often substitute emotion for argument, which is why they are so resistant to evidence."

Keith Parsons on Rules for Using Ridicule

Keith Parsons has proposed some helpful rules of ridicule:

1. Never ridicule the reasonable. Just because you have strong, visceral, even vehement disagreements with someone, is not a sufficient justification for ridicule. So long as the other person is willing to address the issues dividing you in good faith and with rational argument, then ridicule is inappropriate. You do not have to consider your opponent's arguments to be good arguments. The fact that they are making an honest effort to engage in open and serious debate is honorable. Anyone making such an effort deserves respect, not ridicule. When you ridicule someone you are making the judgment that they have repudiated rational discourse.

2. Ridicule only those who are both unreasonable AND dangerous to others. There are many forms of harmless stupidity. Other forms only harm the

ones being silly. Being a snooty, smarty-pants liberal college professor, I regard NASCAR, monster truck rallies, and professional wrestling as low-brow pastimes (college football, however, is sublime). However, getting cheap laughs by lampooning the devotees of such entertainments would make me feel cheap. No, to be worthy of ridicule, something has to be both irrational and harmful to others. If creationism were only practiced among consenting adults, it would deserve nothing worse than the occasional dismissive wisecrack. However, creationists have always been very aggressive in promoting their nonsense in the public arena. They want your children to be taught that stuff, not just their kids. Because creationism taught as science in the public schools IS harmful, creationism is fair game for ridicule.

3. Insofar as possible, direct your ridicule at the ridiculous ideas, not the persons who promote those ideas. It is possible, and indeed more effective, to ridicule creationism without depicting creationists, a la H. L. Mencken, as backwoods buffoons. Laugh at the Triceratops outfitted with a saddle at Ken Ham's museum. Why a saddle? So that Adam and Eve could ride it around the Garden of Eden. Duh. Gotta have a saddle. Could you imagine riding a Triceratops with just your bare butt? Yee-ow! No need to call Ham names. Do like Frank Capra when he made the "Why we Fight" propaganda films for the Army in WWII. That is, use their own words and claims against them. When dealing with many silly and harmful things there is an algorithm for ridiculing them: Quote them.

4. In sum: Restrict your ridicule to that which is truly ridiculous. The truly ridiculous is not only unreasonable, it is in defiance of reason; it is anti-reason. True stupidity is not committed by those with low-I.Q.s. Real stupidity is committed by smart people who have a big ax to grind.[15]

While Parsons offers some good overall rules about the use of ridicule, I think every one of his rules has exceptions to them, especially if we just consider the venue. For instance, comedians can break all of his rules if they can get a laugh. No one holds comedians to those high standards. By contrast, consider a face-to-face personal discussion/debate. I have never ridiculed friends in person when discussing their faith nor do I think this is good to do, even if they are being unreasonable. Nor do I think we should do that. Still, these rules are a good starting place for discussion. For my part, I defend those who ridicule or satirize ridiculous beliefs, although I don't do it often at all, especially since I'm not so good at it myself.

The fact is that no one has to justify the use of ridicule. Ridicule is self-justifying. The justification of ridicule is in the laughter from like-minded people, along with the existence of a real target audience that it targets. If no one laughed, or if the targeted audience didn't exist, then ridicule would be unjustified. It would fall flat. It would fail to achieve any results. No one would get it. For no one would laugh and no one would feel targeted. This is not hard to see.

Stephen Law on Five Morals for Debating Believers

Stephen Law proposed five morals to guide both atheists and believers in our debates.[16] I found his essay to be something I agree with completely. So it's refreshing to me personally, having participated in daily discussions/debates with believers for ten years now. So here they are in block quotations followed by my comments. His focus is on calling attention to issues that might cause offense and potentially shut down debate. (Note: He uses the name Peter to refer to a Christian believer.)

1. There's a tendency among the religious to take offence at comparisons drawn by atheists between religious belief and other supernatural beliefs such as belief in ghosts, fairies, etc. No doubt some atheists do just want to belittle and bait the religious by making such comparisons. However, it seems to me that drawing such a comparison can be very appropriate. I certainly intend no offence by drawing it. I don't think the religious should take offence.

The point of these comparisons is to express the need for hard, cold evidence for all of these supernatural entities. The kind of evidence required to accept ghosts and fairies should be there for God. That's all. Analogies like these are appropriate even if believers don't like them. Please don't take offense at them. We're just being honest. You can take our honesty and pick it apart if you can. At least we put it out on the table.

Believers have comparisons that might seem equally offensive to atheists as well. They may say atheists cannot explain morals or consciousness until we can explain why rocks don't have them, since life came from inanimate matter. I'm not offended when they say such ignorant things, if it's what they believe. In appropriate circumstances they should be honest and say it, so we can have a discussion about it.

2. Atheists should not suggest that religious folk are stupid. Unfortunately, many do. While there is some evidence that a lower IQ correlates with increased religiosity, the fact is that most popular religions—even the most absurd—can boast adherents at least as smart as myself. I count among my close friends Christians with impressive intellects. They aren't fools.

I've gone on record as saying it takes a great deal of intelligence to be a Christian apologist, in that they are more intelligent than I am, since that's what it takes to defend the indefensible. But more to the point, most religious believers are not stupid. Many of them are smarter than I am. I'm just better educated than most, that's all, and the things that I know from being better educated lead me to say most believers are ignorant. Ignorant does not equal dumb. The smartest scientist in the world may not know that Plato was Aristotle's teacher, or anything about the Nag Hammadi library, the Qumran Dead Sea Scrolls, nor be able to read a dead language like Koine Greek. So he or she could be ignorant about many facts and yet be recognized as one of the top intellectuals in the world.

This same point of Law's should be recognized by believers. Atheists are not stupid either. Of course, many believers have a hard time with that one, since their faith convinces them God is as obvious as the nose on one's face. For believers to admit this fact may be a problem, as an argument by J. L. Schellenberg illustrates:

> If there is a God, he is perfectly loving.
>
> If a perfectly loving God exists, reasonable nonbelief does not occur.
>
> Reasonable nonbelief occurs.
>
> No perfectly loving God exists (from 2 and 3).
>
> Hence, there is no God.

3. I suggest honesty is the best policy. Christians who, like William Lane Craig, think the sin of rejecting God is so momentous that atheists deserve to burn in hell ought not to attempt to hide that opinion for fear of causing offence. First off, most atheists have thick skins. We know we're a highly distrusted minority. Secondly, I for one would much rather understand what my intellectual opponent really believes about me than have them disguise it. After all, if a Christian really believes

that, as an atheist, I am hell-bound, they surely have a moral duty to warn me. I understand and appreciate that. I think we atheists should be similarly honest. I consider Christian belief of the sort defended by Peter to be pretty ludicrous: scarcely less ludicrous, in fact, than many other religious belief systems that Peter himself would probably find ludicrous (such as Mormonism and Scientology, for example). I think I should be honest about that, rather than disguise my opinions for fear of "causing offence". For obvious reasons, dialogues between belief systems where the participants try to disguise their beliefs and deal in half-truths are unlikely to be helpful in terms of getting at the truth. Nor am I convinced such deceit is even the best policy when the aim is merely getting along. If Peter tells me he believes that, being an atheist, the depth of my moral depravity is so deep as to qualify me for eternal damnation, I'll be a little shocked. But I'll be happy to discuss that with him. If, on the other hand, he chooses to hide this assessment from me, then there is a good chance that I'll nevertheless detect his attitude.

Again, spot on. I too think Christianity is ludicrous and a delusional belief system comparable to Scientology, and I have said so. This is a matter of honesty. No Christian needs to take offense at this in the same way as I'm not offended when they tell me I'm hell-bound.

4. A little mockery and leg-pulling is, in some circumstances, entirely appropriate. No one should abandon a belief because others laugh at it. Nor should any religious person or atheist be mocked merely to cause them distress. However, while humour should not take the place of rigorous criticism, it can enhance the latter's effectiveness by breaking the spell of deference and "respect" that belief systems are capable of casting over us. In Hans Christian Andersen's "The Emperor's New Clothes," the small boy who points and laughs breaks the spell: he allows everyone else watching the naked Emperor to see how they have been duped, to recognise the absurdity of their situation.

Exactly! I've written a great deal on the use of ridicule. The flip side is that atheists should be able to take a little ridicule too. Again this is about honesty. What does each person think of the views of their opponent? Let's put that on the table so we know how far we're apart.

5. Atheists should understand the often good motives of those who evangelize. After all, Christian evangelists really are trying to save us atheists. The stakes couldn't be higher. If I could only save someone from a dangerous fall by rudely grabbing them and shouting my warning in their face, I would. I will generally forgive those who strive, by behaving with similar urgency, to save me from a fate literally worse than death. I certainly don't expect the religious to keep their beliefs to themselves.

Yes, if you as an atheist are upset by proselytizing believers, then at least recognize they are just trying to do what their god commanded them to do, and that they probably care about you (I don't know which motive takes precedence, especially those who bellow out "God hates fags"). The flip side is that believers need to recognize atheists also care. We care for the personal lives of believers, their families, their communities, their states, their countries, and the world as a whole. You can see this for yourselves in my anthology, *Christianity Is Not Great: How Faith Fails*.

Atheist Jeffery Jay Lowder Responds

Jeffery Lowder has joined with Christian philosophers Victor Reppert and Randal Rauser in rejecting the need for and value of ridicule. Lowder was even interviewed for chapter 4 in Rauser's book, *Is the Atheist My Neighbor?: Rethinking Christian Attitudes toward Atheism*.[17] They all seem to have the same objection to the use of ridicule. Reppert expresses it from time to time on his blog Dangerous Idea, as does Lowder at Secular Outpost. Rauser wrote an earlier book expressing it, titled *You're Not as Crazy as I Think: Dialogue in a World of Loud Voices and Hardened Opinions*.[18] In that book he argues we need more dialogue between opposing sides, rather than more vitriol. Rauser comes down hard on evangelicals and atheists alike. There is way too much vitriol between atheists and evangelicals, he argues. We're not as crazy as each side tends to think of the opposition. So we can and will learn from each other if we stop treating our opponents as "Others."

I can see Lowder's disregard for ridicule in that I have read most of his online writings in the last several years, and very few times if ever have I seen any real attempt at humor in anything he wrote. Maybe he's just a lackluster type of fellow? I don't know since I have never met him. He doesn't even seem to recognize humor. Take for instance one of a few posts he began doing on what he calls "stupid atheist memes." Lowder attacks them as if they are expressing an argument rather than ridiculing beliefs.

One such "stupid atheist meme" Lowder criticized was this one: "If you could reason with religious people, there would be no religious people." He says of it:

> At best, this meme is an unsupported generalization. Even if you think you know with absolute certainty that God doesn't exist, it doesn't follow that every religious person on the planet is unreasonable. An additional argument would be needed to justify the universal generalization implied by the meme. And I have no idea how a finite being would go about gathering such information about every other theist on the planet.
>
> But I think this meme is worse than an unsupported generalization. I think it's false. There are religious people and then there are religious people. Say what you will about the "average believer" (whoever that is), I think the existence of professional philosophers like Richard Swinburne and Daniel Howard-Snyder, both of whom are theists and very reasonable people, clearly refute this meme.[19]

How one views something should be according to its genre. You cannot deal with an argument in the same way as you deal with ridicule. They are to be judged differently. All that is required of ridicule is that there is some truth to it. Otherwise no one would laugh. The more truth to it the better. There is definitely some truth to this atheist meme. That's the point of ridicule. We don't demand of ridicule to make an ironclad case.

For the record, and in defense of this atheist meme, I think faith is always present to some degree whenever there is religion, and that faith is always unreasonable. There is at least one logical fallacy in the way the mind of the believer reasons when embracing religion. So if we could reason with religious believers and they accepted reason, there would be no religious believers.

Anyway, Lowder offers probably the main objection to the use of ridicule when commenting on Rauser's blog:

> As a philosopher who happens to be an atheist, I think the suggestion that we should ridicule religious belief is, well, self-defeating. There are many brilliant theists working in philosophy, including philosophy of religion, who have made profound insights about arguments for and against God.

I have profited from reading their work. Some of the insights for my case for atheism only came about as a result of reading these theists. I think that if I had adopted the ridicule approach, I never would have taken theism seriously enough to get these insights, and so my case for atheism would have been weaker as a result.

For the record, my primary motivation for reading theists is the search for truth, not atheist apologetics. But for those like Loftus who are engaged in atheist apologetics, I would think they want to be in the business of building a better case for atheism.

Besides, who wants to have their cherished beliefs ridiculed? I don't want people ridiculing what I think and I don't ridicule what others think.[20]

First off, I must say Lowder is no philosopher. As noted, he holds only a bachelor's degree in computer science from Seattle Pacific University. More importantly, even if he's considered as such by others, he should not run around saying he is one. That's quite presumptuous of him. It gets him some undeserved credibility. One of the reasons I have publicly exposed Lowder's deception is because he has successfully convinced people into thinking he's a philosopher when he is not. No atheist philosopher I have encountered has shown himself to be so ignorant about so much, so it does matter that people see who he really is. For if he's considered a fully credentialed philosopher with a PhD, then what he says is taken more seriously than, for example, what I say. His cheerleaders say there have been many philosophers in the past who didn't have PhDs, like Socrates, Aristotle, Descartes, and Aquinas, which I know all too well. That's irrelevant. I'm arguing Lowder lacks the breadth necessary to be on par with someone who has earned a PhD in philosophy.[21]

Now on to my response. There are plenty of beliefs worthy of nothing but ridicule if not disgust, namely, misogyny, racism, flat-earth "theory," alien abductions, homeopathy, young-earth creationism, faith healing, hell-fire fundamentalism, and the teachings of many cults too strange to entertain seriously. Now if anyone disagrees with this think specifically instead of the KKK, ISIS, Kahanism, Scientology, John Frum cargo cults, and those guys claiming to be Jesus right now (like José Luis de Jesús Miranda). Or, think of Ken Ham, Pat Robertson, Benny Hinn, or Ray Comfort.

Lowder says he's searching for truth. Then he needs to tell us how seriously he would take these beliefs or the groups and people I've just mentioned. Why does he single Christianity out as worthy of respect from the many other faith-based claims? Why does he not treat all of them the same? He's being hypocritical to single out Christianity, if he does. But he certainly cannot take all faith-based claims seriously, which is the point. Some are way too bizarre to entertain. He must have a filter to choose which ones should be taken seriously. What is that filter? Despite Paul Draper's views, as discussed earlier, a genuine search for truth begins the day people reject faith-based answers, not before. Until they do so they fail to have a reliable method for knowing the truth about existence, the nature of nature, or which religion is true, if there is one. That's the filter Lowder lacks.

I think all faith-based answers are worthy of ridicule given the right moment in the right venue. We shouldn't ridicule ridiculous beliefs all of the time. Ridicule should be used sparingly, but it should be used on occasion just so the undecided will know what we think of faith-based answers, all of them. Thinking adults should think exclusively in terms of the probabilities. Period. In that same vein one can read several of my attempts to ridicule beliefs, with titles like, "Ebola Is Coming! Praise God!"; "Praise God for the Candiru Parasite! Isn't God Good?"; "Praise God for the Disaster in Haiti! Isn't God Good? Thank You Jesus!"; "God Loves Cho Seung-Hui."[22]

So how can we ridicule another's beliefs and yet carry on a polite, civil discussion with representatives of that belief at the same time? See Stephen Law's five morals for debating believers, which I quoted above. I have civil discussions all of the time. For instance, in *God or Godless?*, which I cowrote with Randal Rauser, I respectfully engaged Randal even though I think his faith is bizarre, no different from Scientology. Why did I respectfully engage? For the same reason I ridicule those very beliefs. I know Rauser isn't going to change his mind. I'm writing for the undecided. I argue my case so the undecided can see that my ridicule is justified. There is nothing inconsistent about this, or self-defeating. It's simply being honest and restrained at the same time. It's honest because that's what I think of Rauser's faith. It's also restrained to a large degree, because if I really told him what I think we couldn't discuss his faith at all.

Finally, for the record, I have spent my whole intellectual life pondering and reading on these issues, and I still do, so please don't suggest that I should "be in the business of building a better case for atheism" when I already am. *Shesh* . . . Lowder is projecting upon me his own lack of knowledge methinks.

Here's another atheist meme. Try this on for size: "The Bible: Because a book written by a bunch of guys that didn't know where the sun went at night must have all the answers." Is it stupid? No!

Daniel Dennett on Avoiding Caricaturing One's Opponents

I'm including Daniel Dennett's discussion here so my critics can see quite plainly I have not and will not give up on reasoning with believers. As I argued in a previous chapter, I reason with them in the most effective way though. Dennett offers what he calls "the best antidote [for the] tendency to caricature one's opponent." While I defend the use and need for ridicule as an effective weapon in disabusing believers of their faith, what I do is not characterized by ridicule. Most of the time I deal with the arguments of believers respectfully until it appears they are unwilling to think. Sometimes I can spot them quickly with the first comment on my blog. They will mindlessly quote-mine from the Bible or the theology based on it. These are people who come to preach to me rather than learn from me. I've said it before and I'll say it again; there is nothing significant believers can tell me that I have not considered before. It takes a great deal of my time before they will realize this about me. I'll even tell them to read my books but hardly any of them are interested. It doesn't occur to them I have more to teach them as a former believer and an intellectual than they could ever teach me. In many cases after dealing with the same believers for months or years, I lose respect for them and turn to ridicule. In my mind they are beyond hope. But after regrouping and readjusting, with some time off from them, I start being respectful again, until it becomes clear all over again they are unwilling to think. This is a vicious cycle. Nonetheless, what Dennett writes serves as a good reminder to us all *if we wish to personally interact with believers.*

How to compose a successful critical commentary:

1. You should attempt to re-express your target's position so clearly, vividly, and fairly that your target says, "Thanks, I wish I'd thought of putting it that way.

2. You should list any points of agreement (especially if they are not matters of general or widespread agreement).

3. You should mention anything you have learned from your target.

4. Only then are you permitted to say so much as a word of rebuttal or criticism.[23]

Doing so can on rare occasions transform our opponents into being more receptive to our criticism, which can further our discussions.

Notes

1. "Reppert on Ridiculing One's Opponents," Debunking Christianity, August 15, 2006, http://debunkingchristianity.blogspot.com/2006/08/reppert-on-ridiculing-ones-opponents.html.

2. "Pat Condell: Provide Evidence or Expect Mockery and Ridicule," Debunking Christianity, December 28, 2009, http://debunkingchristianity. blogspot.com/2008/11/pat-condell-provide-evidence-or-expect.html.

3. "I Still Want Respectful Educated Discussion of the Ideas That Separate Us," Debunking Christianity, February 16, 2011, http://debunkingchristianity. blogspot.com/2011/02/i-still-want-respectful-educated.html.

4. "Don't Be a Dick, Phil Plait," Debunking Christianity, August 21, 2010, http://debunkingchristianity.blogspot.com/2010/08/dont-be-dick-phil-plait. html.

5. Alma Al Turkmani, "Saudi TV Series Deploys New Weapon Against ISIS: Satire," CNN.com, June 22, 2015, http://www.cnn.com/2015/06/22/ middleeast/anti-isis-satire/?sr=cnnifb.

6. "Evangelical Scientists Refute Gravity with New 'Intelligent Falling' Theory," *The Onion*, August 17, 2015, http://www.theonion.com/article/ evangelical-scientists-refute-gravity-with-new-int-1778.

7. These ten examples can be seen in a blog post of mine: "Examples of Ridicule," Debunking Christianity, November 19, 2014, http:// debunkingchristianity.blogspot.com/2014/11/examples-of-ridicule.html.

8. "Top 10 Signs You're a Fundamentalist Christian," https://www.reddit. com/r/atheism/comments/352b8k/top_10_signs_youre_a_fundamentalist_ christian/.

9. "Thoms Jefferson on Christianity and Religion," compiled by Jim Walker, http://www.nobeliefs.com/jefferson.htm.

10. George William Foote, "On Ridicule," in *Seasons of Freethought: The Collected Works of G. W. Foote*, ed. Tristan Vick (Regolith Publications, 2013), p. 260.

11. Walter Sinnott-Armstrong, "Overcoming Christianity," in *Philosophers without Gods*, ed. Louise Antony (New York: Oxford University Press, 2007), p. 78.

12. James A. Lindsay, *Everybody Is Wrong About God* (Durham, NC: Pitchstone Publishing, 2015), p. 189.

13. "Should We Mock Religion?" The Atheist Voice, video published on November 27, 2014, https://www.youtube.com/watch?v=tVMPS-P11Qs.

14. In an email to author.

15. Jeffery Jay Lowder, "If You Think Atheists Should Ridicule Theistic Beliefs, Read This," Secular Outpost, November 21, 2014, http://www.patheos.com/blogs/secularoutpost/2014/11/21/if-you-think-atheists-should-ridicule-theistic-beliefs-read-this/#comment-1710027336.

16. Stephen Law, "How Should the Religious and Atheists Approach Each Other in Discussion? Five Morals," The Outer Limits with Stephen Law, December 14, 2015, http://www.centerforinquiry.net/blogs/entry/how_should_the_religious_and_atheists_approach_each_other_in_discussion_fiv/.

17. Randal Rauser, *Is the Atheist My Neighbor?: Rethinking Christian Attitudes toward Atheism* (Eugene, OR: Cascade Books, 2015).

18. Randal Rauser, *You're Not as Crazy as I Think: Dialogue in a World of Loud Voices and Hardened Opinions* (Colorado Springs, CO: Biblica Publishing, 2011).

19. Jeffery Jay Lowder, "Stupid People Meme #1: If You Could Reason with Religious People . . . " Secular Outpost, May 18, 2015, http://www.patheos.com/blogs/secularoutpost/2015/05/18/stupid-atheist-meme-1-if-you-could-reason-with-religious-people/#sthash.Qccd88xT.dpuf.

20. Randal Rauser, "Contempt for Dissenting Opinion," Tentative Apologist, November 16, 2014, http://randalrauser.com/2014/11/contempt-for-dissenting-opinion/#comment-1695520001.

21. "Vic Reppert on the Fundamental Divide Between Jeff Lowder and Me," Debunking Christianity, August 18, 2015, http://debunkingchristianity.blogspot.com/search/label/Lowder%20Ignorance.

22. "Ebola Is Coming! Praise God!" Debunking Christianity, October 14, 2014, http://debunkingchristianity.blogspot.com/search/label/Praise%20God.

23. As quoted by Maria Popova in "How to Criticize with Kindness: Philosopher Daniel Dennett on the Four Steps to Arguing Intelligently," Brain Pickings, https://www.brainpickings.org/index.php/2014/03/28/daniel-dennett-rapoport-rules-criticism/.

APPENDIX A

My Interview with Keith Parsons

Keith M. Parsons is on the faculty of The University of Houston–Clear Lake, where he is associate professor of philosophy. He has written a number of books and essays and was the founding editor of the philosophical journal *Philo*. He also did very well in two debates against William Lane Craig. Keith has honored me with the opportunity to interview him on the philosophy of religion, a topic I'll be writing about in a book titled *Unapologetic: Why the Philosophy of Religion Must End*. What prompted this interview was that I noticed he was teaching a philosophy of religion (PoR) class after saying he wouldn't teach these classes any longer, or so it appeared.[1] I wanted to let him clear the air in case he changed his mind (his prerogative if he so chooses), or correct any misunderstandings readers might have. Going beyond this I want to get his present perspectives on the PoR discipline.

The following interview, shared with permission, took place as I asked Keith a question via email, to which he responded as his time allowed. Then I would ask him another one, and so on. It was not a debate, because I was restricted to asking questions. Even though I threw a few hardballs it wouldn't be fair to characterize this as anything more than a discussion. I interviewed him for the purposes of learning his views more or less, and that's it.

* * * * *

John: The first question I must ask is why are you teaching a PoR class? Is it just one class, or are there others? Didn't you say you would no longer do so?

Keith: 1) I am teaching a philosophy of religion class because I consider it an important part of our philosophy curriculum. Students find the issues and the readings interesting, and they are introduced to a number of important philosophical concepts, tools, and topics, such as possible worlds and modal concepts, the principle of sufficient reason, Hume's critique of miracles, probability and Bayes' Theorem, teleology and function explanations, naturalism/physicalism, epistemological foundationalism and its critics, etc. So it is eminently justified merely from a pedagogical perspective. More broadly, so long as religion remains a core human concern (for the foreseeable future), then, like all other vital human concerns (e.g. knowledge, morality, politics) it will invite philosophical reflection. This is why philosophy of religion, in some form, will, and should, be around as long as there is religion. Put another way, philosophers would be derelict in their professional duties if they refused to reflect rigorously on the issues raised by religion. As Hume observed in the first chapter of his *Enquiry Concerning Human Understanding*, the only cure for bad philosophy is good philosophy, and bad philosophy will proliferate if good philosophy abandons the field.

2) No, this is the only course in philosophy of religion at our university. However, I would very much like to see a whole program of religious studies taught here.

3) Yes, I did say that I would not teach philosophy of religion any longer. I changed my mind. When I made that announcement I was suffering from severe ennui brought on by having to slog through many bad, ax-grinding, and tedious arguments for theism. However, after taking a couple of years off from teaching PoR, I got a second wind. Reading John Hick's *An Interpretation of Religion* convinced me that my focus had been too narrow, and that there are many issues that are still of considerable interest. Even the arguments for the existence of God, if properly presented, retain considerable interest. I discovered Yujin Nagasawa's *The Existence of God*, and found his lively, lucid, judicious, and appealing presentation of the

arguments to be just the ticket for rekindling interest (both mine and my students'). The theistic arguments remain very interesting, if only because it is extremely instructive to see just where they go wrong (and, as Nagasawa shows, many of the standard "refutations" might at least need more work). Actually, much of philosophy is like that. We still read Descartes's *Meditations,* though it is pretty much universally agreed that he failed in his object of putting knowledge on foundations of absolute certainty. When very bright people try something very big and fail, it is highly instructive to see just how they went wrong and what that failure means. I still think that natural theology has run its course and that, as living philosophical effort, it is finished. However, as an object for postmortem analysis, it remains quite fascinating!

* * * * *

John: Excellent answers Keith, as I expected they would be! Just so readers don't misunderstand you, I should ask about John Hick's views before going any further. As you know, he was one of the most important philosophers of religion in the past century. One of his main arguments in the book you mentioned is that, "The universe is religiously ambiguous in that it is possible to interpret it, intellectually and experientially, both religiously and naturalistically. The theistic and anti-theistic arguments are all inconclusive, for the special evidences to which they appeal are also capable of being understood in terms of the contrary worldview." (p. 12). Are you saying you've changed your mind about the force of theistic arguments, that you now lean more toward agnosticism than atheism? On agnosticism readers should now Bertrand Russell had a different view than Thomas Huxley who originated the term.[2]

Keith: You quote from John Hick's *An Interpretation of Religion:* "The universe is religiously ambiguous in that it is possible to interpret it, intellectually and experientially, both religiously and naturalistically. The theistic and anti-theistic arguments are all inconclusive, for the special evidences to which they appeal are also capable of being understood in terms of the contrary worldview." (p. 12). Then you ask: "Are you saying you've changed your mind about the force of theistic arguments, that you now lean more toward agnosticism than atheism?"

No, I am most definitely an atheist. I disbelieve in God. I think that there is no good reason to believe that God exists and several good ones for holding that he does not exist. Further, I am a physicalist. I hold that all that has substantial existence (which I construe as being capable of acting or being acted upon), is physical. I do not think that there is a supernatural or transcendent aspect or element of reality. I do not believe in any gods, ghosts, souls, spirits, demons, demigods, angels, vital essences, occult powers or animistic forces. Full stop.

But I could be wrong.

Hick is undeniably right that an experience of the numinous or sacred is an integral and pervasive aspect of the human experience. Very, very many humans have, at times in their lives felt, in Wordsworth's words:

. . . a sense sublime
Of something far more deeply interfused,
Whose dwelling is the light of setting suns,
And the round ocean and the living air
And the blue sky, and in the mind of man.
A motion and a spirit, that impels
All thinking things, all objects of all thought,
And rolls through all things . . .

The ambiguity of reality that Hick speaks of is how we are to interpret such experiences, i.e. encounters with the numinous. I interpret these experiences pantheistically; I view the natural universe as the proper object of awe and wonder. But, again, I could be wrong. Other people, no less rational than myself, take the "depth" experiences as pointers to the transcendent, to a reality that is deeper than or more inclusive than the physical. Though zealots on both sides hate the thought, I agree with Hick that reason does not dictate which side you come down on. One may rationally opt for a naturalistic or supernaturalistic interpretation. This is not a wishy washy relativism that says that there is no objective truth here. No, either there is a transcendent reality or not. I say not, and, though I can give reasons for saying what I say, I have to admit that these reasons are not decisive and that they might be rationally rejected. Again, fundamentalist theists and fundamentalist atheists will hate to admit it, but there are eminently reasonable and rational people who violate no epistemic duties in holding opposite views. Indeed, the ones who really have egg on their faces are the ones who think that those who disagree with them on these matters must either be knaves or fools.

* * * * *

John: Very Interesting! It sounds like you're a weak atheist to me. If true, we differ on the strength of the evidence. Everyone has some sense of deep wonder at existence, or they should.

It's clear from the course objectives to your PoR class that you kindly sent me, you want students to become better critical thinkers, and to better understand and argue the subject matter. Is your class more or less an exercise of reasoning and logic that just so happens to use PoR as the subject matter? Or do you want to convince your students of something? Do you want them to develop a skeptical disposition too?

Keith: I don't know what you mean by a "weak atheist." If you mean that I must regard the arguments for atheism as weak, or as establishing only a slight priority of evidence over theism, that is not my view at all. I find the arguments for atheism very strong. However, I do not regard them as so strong as to preclude rational dissent. It is similar to political convictions. I am a true-blue, old-fashioned, tax-and-spend liberal. I consider the weight of morality and rational argument to be on the side of liberalism. Further, it is unquestionably the case that much howling madness now passes for "conservatism." However, I see no justification for saying that there cannot be rational conservatives who hold their views in good faith and without committing any epistemic or moral sins. In short, it is entirely possible to (a) hold one's convictions firmly and even passionately, and (b) admit that rational disagreement is possible. There is nothing "weak" about such a position.

Do I want my students to learn to be better critical thinkers? Sure. When my university adopted a "critical thinking" initiative I pointed out that every course that I taught was a course in critical thinking. Indeed, "critical thinking" is a fair definition of what philosophy is. Is the aim of the class just to teach critical thinking and PoR is only the vehicle for doing that? No, I want them to understand the content as well. I think that all philosophy students need to be acquainted with the issues of PoR, both the traditional and the newer ones. For instance, I think that they need to be acquainted with the arguments both for and against the existence of God and their strengths and limitations. What is the alternative? Ignorance? What would we say of an atheist who refused even to look at the arguments for theism? Do I want to convince my students of anything? Sure. I want to convince them of the profound value of reasoning about important things and not simply trusting their "gut." Yes, one of the aims of any philosophy course is to encourage a less gullible and more skeptical attitude. However, it has to be an informed skepticism. It cannot be a sort of reverse dogmatism like that of the so-called "climate skeptics" who will not be convinced by any arguments for human-caused climate change. Honest skepticism is nothing other than to adhere to Socrates' dictum to follow the argument wherever it leads.

* * * * *

John: Readers might be interested in knowing to what degree you might push your students toward a more skeptical attitude, but that seems hard to quantify. So let me ask instead if you find the arguments against the so-called revealed religions and most all paranormal claims strong enough as to preclude rational dissent? Isn't that what we're almost always talking about? A noninvolved or deistic god-concept doesn't produce much to be excited about at all, nor do we need such a hypothesis in science. Or do we? Why should we take those claims seriously, except for the fact that many people believe them? As far as teaching students the content of the PoR goes, what would you say about requiring classes on biblical literature, since knowing of it in the Western world is to be considered literate? What is so essential about the *content* of Western PoR that immigrants from Asian, Middle Eastern, and Southern hemispheres should understand?

Keith: Could you limit it to three more questions? Sorry, but duty calls.

* * * * *

John: I'm going to publish my last set of questions and your reply that "duty calls." I hope this isn't considered by you to be some sort of dig at you, or your position. I just want readers to know I asked those sets of questions which I consider important for the case I'm going to make in my book, even if you didn't have time to answer them.

Okay, three more questions.

Keith, here are three statements you made when you quit teaching the PoR:

> "In teaching class I try to present material that I find antithetical to my own views as fairly and in as unbiased a manner as possible."

> "I have to confess that I now regard 'the case for theism' as a fraud and I can no longer take it seriously enough to present it to a class as a respectable philosophical position—no more than I could present intelligent design as a legitimate biological theory."

> "I just cannot take their arguments seriously any more, and if you cannot take something seriously, you should not try to devote serious academic attention to it."

You say that you must teach PoR in an unbiased manner, then you say you cannot take theistic arguments seriously, and so you conclude you should no longer teach it. It all makes sense. If professors must teach PoR in an unbiased manner, and if they cannot take theistic arguments seriously, then they should quit teaching it. Got it.

But why did you think—and still think—that PoR professors must teach their discipline in an unbiased manner? What other disciplines are taught that way? And what would you say to professors of PoR who agree with your former self that theistic arguments can't be taken seriously, and yet they disagree with your notion that they must teach the PoR in an unbiased manner?

Keith: Why teach PoR, or anything, in an unbiased manner? I guess I will shift the burden of proof here: What could one possibly say in favor of teaching anything in a biased manner? Maybe you don't mean "biased" in the sense of "prejudiced" or "bigoted" but only in the sense of refusing to maintain a faux neutrality when the subject matter does not warrant it. For instance, if I tried to teach the arguments of "intelligent design" theorists in an absolutely neutral way without indicating that they are, in fact, dreadful arguments, then I would be doing a disservice to my students, failing in my responsibility to critique shoddy thinking and bad science.

It can never be biased to tell the truth. Of course, I could be wrong, and I always invite students to challenge my conclusions when they suspect that I am wrong. How many courses are taught this way? I hope that all of them are. A university class is not your bully pulpit nor a soapbox for partisan hectoring. You present arguments that you oppose as fairly as you can and you critique them as fairly as you can, while, again, inviting disagreement. As for the question about what I would say to colleague who said, as I did five years ago, that the theistic arguments are unworthy of scholarly attention, and so unworthy of consideration in a university classroom? Well, first of all, if we only taught "good" arguments in philosophy, we would have to leave out a very great deal of it. As I said before, there is often pedagogical value in teaching arguments that fail, precisely because it is instructive to see how clever and often intuitive arguments go bad.

But are not some things so egregiously bad, so absolutely unworthy of consideration and so intellectually vacuous so as not to merit inclusion in a university course? Sure. For instance, I just could not imagine taking time to study, say, John Hagee's opinions on the imminence of the "rapture." So, the question is, where, along the scale of intellectual respectability, do we put the theistic arguments. Are they frauds as I said five years ago? As I said immediately afterwards, I do regret having used the term "fraud" since that inevitably implies conscious and intentional deception—the marketing of goods known to be shoddy. That was wrong. I do think that the arguments fail, considered both individually and cumulatively (obviously, since I am still an atheist), but I do not think that they are fraudulent or that they are egregiously bad—like Hagee's dimwitted effusions. After all, the arguments are the products of some extraordinarily intelligent and articulate people. Whatever you think of Alvin Plantinga, Richard Swinburne, William Lane Craig, Ed Feser, J.P. Moreland (not to mention Aquinas, Leibniz, and Descartes), you have to admit that these are very smart and well-informed people. To write them off as mountebanks or inept would indeed be bias, in a pejorative sense. Do I think that natural theology has a future as a viable and possibly productive intellectual enterprise? No, I do not. I think that the theistic arguments, in their most sophisticated formats, have been subjected to deep and incisive criticism and that there is little prospect that some future re-re-re-re-re-revision of, say, the ontological argument, will actually work. Saying this, however, does not mean an end to PoR, nor does it mean that there is no pedagogical value in teaching the theistic arguments.

* * * * *

John: What scientific evidence do you find unpersuasive when it comes to the claims of religion such that it would justify continued philosophical discussions by amateurs (i.e., not scientists) about it? Where does that evidence leave us with regard to religion? Is there any fault with the method (or methods) of science that needs supplemented by religious faith?

Keith: I do not think that there is any scientific evidence for religious claims at all. The same applies to all sorts of metaphysical claims. There is no scientific evidence for Platonic Ideal Forms or Cartesian minds. Scientific evidence cannot settle whether David Lewis or Alvin Plantinga offers the more cogent interpretation of possible worlds. Does that mean that we cannot have rational discussion of such topics? The logical positivists, of course, said that any discussion of metaphysical matters is meaningless, but I think that the last logical positivist died circa 1959. If we accept that metaphysics may be discussed in respectable circles, then it would be special pleading to exclude the metaphysical claims of religion. There is no fault at all with scientific methods, nor do they need to be supplemented by religious faith. That is not the question. The question of rationality is larger than the question of what is answerable by science at any given time. Philosophy deals with worldviews, and worldviews are not decidable by appeal to science. Rather, one's view of the authority and scope of science is dependent on worldview. In a worldview where faith is primary and empirical evidence is secondary, no degree of empirical evidence can dislodge the claims of faith. Such a view is highly antithetical to mine, but, obviously, it cannot be critiqued with empirical evidence, but only with philosophical argument.

Perhaps you only mean to suggest that natural theology, the attempt to establish the existence and nature of God by natural reason alone, is no longer a viable intellectual project. I agree. That was the point of my posting in 2010. I think that the theistic arguments, as a form of aggressive apologetics, have been thoroughly and effectively critiqued. There seems to me little prospect that some new version of the traditional arguments will carry the day. But the retirement of natural theology by no means spells an end to rational discussion of religion. Is religious belief rational only if some version of the ontological, cosmological, or design argument succeeds? To argue "yes" or "no" is to do philosophy of religion.

* * * * *

John: Last question, thanks for bearing through this.

In your wonderfully enlightening book, *It Started with Copernicus: Vital Questions About Faith*[3] and for a blog post[4] you argued that Darwin engaged in philosophical questions. Your point is that Darwin was also a philosopher. The criteria to determine when someone is doing philosophy (in this case PoR) as opposed to science you say:

> In cases . . . where the evidence will not settle the dispute, scientists must employ philosophical arguments. And they do. Therefore, the suggestion that science can simply replace philosophy is wrong for the reason that, as [Thomas] Kuhn observed, scientific debates often embed—or are embedded within—philosophical debates. These philosophical differences often cannot be settled by straightforward empirical means, but must be addressed with philosophical argument. Science cannot replace philosophy because philosophy is an essential part of the scientific enterprise. Kuhn was wrong about many things, but on this point he was absolutely right.

And I have no bone to pick with philosophy per se. But this raises an interesting question. I think we can agree that mere reasoning is not equivalent to philosophy otherwise there is no content to the discipline of philosophy. So scientific reasoning is not necessarily doing philosophy. Scientists must reason to be scientists, but that isn't the same thing as discussing Aquinas. The mere use of logic and the avoidance of fallacies shouldn't be considered philosophical reasoning in and of themselves. We should also agree that we don't need to wait until everyone agrees that a particular dispute has been settled by science, before we can say scientists are no longer doing philosophy when reasoning about the evidence. This was the case in Darwin's day, but the dispute over evolution has been settled in our day. I think the implications about evolution are settled too. What you need to do is to show why any scientifically literate person should wait until evolution deniers agree that this dispute has been settled before saying evolutionists are not doing philosophy of religion. Can you?

Keith: I am not completely sure I see what you are getting at here. You seem to be asking when a question is no longer philosophical, but becomes straightforwardly empirical. Is evolution now just a scientific fact? Sure. Absolutely. It is not a topic of debate whether the diversity of life is due to a natural process of descent with modification, as Darwin called it. Nor is there any reasonable basis for denying that natural selection has been the main driver of evolution. Case closed. What is the relevance of this for PoR? Well, it seems to indicate that there is not much point in discussing "intelligent design" unless to draw lessons about how bad philosophy can be used to prop up bad science. What is the relation to PoR in general? I do not see any. Again, you may be meaning to imply something that is not registering with me.

* * * * *

John: My book, *Unapologetic: Why Philosophy of Religion Must End*, will be arguing something specific about this. If all we need to do is point to the evidence then there is no additional need to use PoR to address bad philosophy. Just point to the evidence. In other words, science has taken over the role of the PoR on this question, so what reason is there for philosophers in general to bother with it? If the only philosophy to be taken seriously is scientifically informed philosophy, then aren't most theistic PoR arguments dead, irrelevant, and inadequate? Alvin Plantinga's *Evolutionary Argument Against Naturalism* and Victor Reppert's *Argument From Reason* are not scientifically informed arguments, since if they really understood evolution they would not make those arguments. What do you think about this?

Keith: Have we reached the point where religious claims are now defunct, disproven by science? Are we at the point where there is no more need for philosophy of religion since all of its important questions have now been answered scientifically? Well, that would certainly seem to be a VERY broad claim to me, and one hard to support. Even if we restricted "philosophy of religion" just to the question of whether the theistic God exists, it is hardly clear that this is, or even, in principle, can be settled by science. Some of the standard theistic arguments are *a priori*, and so, of course, cannot be settled empirically. Even the ones that depend on empirical content, like the "fine tuning argument" (FTA), also appeal to premises that are not empirical. Robin Collins, for instance, defends the application of the classical interpretation of probability to the FTA. Neither do the data adduced by the fine tuners yet have a scientific explanation. There is not yet a "theory of everything," and it is not clear that, even if there were, that it would solve the problem. It seems to me that *any* ultimate posit, i.e. *anything* posited as an ultimate, logically contingent state of affairs will, *qua* contingent, be just one of an infinite number of possible ultimates that conceivably *could* have existed instead. If the answer to why we could have been so lucky as to have a Goldilocks universe is God, then we have to ask why we should have been so lucky as to get God instead of any number of other possible ultimate realities, the *vast* majority of which would not or could not have given a damn about us or had any power to "fine tune" the physical constants.

But I digress. The question is whether there are any interesting questions left for PoR that science cannot settle. Surely there are. Is the question of theism/atheism one that is straightforwardly empirical? Some (you, John) will say yes and lots of others will say no. If you debate the point you will be doing PoR. Besides, surely there are many, many interesting issues to talk about besides the case for or against theism. John Hick rejects the arguments of natural theology, but argues that theism and naturalism are each legitimate responses to the "religious ambiguity" of the universe. Is he right? In what sense is the universe "ambiguous" with respect to the existence of the transcendent? What about a revival of paganism. In Reykjavik, Iceland they are building a temple to the old Norse gods, who will be worshipped for the first time in a thousand years. Is neo-paganism a rational and viable prospect? What about the human experience of the numinous? What is the significance of the sacred? Is nothing sacred? If the standard philosophical apologetic fails, is there reason to support a historical apologetic, one based on historical claims like the resurrection? What about noninferential religious belief? Could it be the case, as Plantinga has argued extensively, that belief in God requires no evidence or arguments at all? Can naturalism account for all phenomena? What about qualia? Is the "hard problem" of consciousness insoluble? I thought of these just off the top of my head, and more extensive reflection could surely turn up many more. So long as religion remains a central element in human life it will invite philosophical reflection. Sorry, John, but I think your announcement of the death of philosophy of religion is greatly exaggerated.

* * * * *

John: Thank you so much for your time and this interview!

Notes

1. Keith Parsons, "Goodbye to All That," Secular Outpost, September 1, 2010, http://www.patheos.com/blogs/secularoutpost/2010/09/01/goodbye-to-all-that/.

2. "Thomas Huxley vs. Bertrand Russell on the Definition of Agnosticism," October 19, 2010, Debunking Christianity, http://debunkingchristianity.blogspot.com/2010/10/thomas-huxley-vs-bertrand-russell-on.html.

3. Keith Parsons, *It Started with Copernicus: Vital Questions About Faith* (Amherst, NY: Prometheus Books, 2014), pp. 354–358.

4. Keith Parsons, "Darwin the Philosopher," Secular Outpost, September 14, 2015, http://www.patheos.com/blogs/secularoutpost/2015/09/14/darwin-the-philosopher/.

APPENDIX B

Robert Price's Rebuttal to William Lane Craig

Dr. Craig often appeals to the consensus of New Testament scholars on behalf of conservative views. By contrast, I am glad to confess that the opinion of the majority of scholars makes no difference whatever to me. In fact, in the Gospels, after all, it's the consensus of scholars in the Sanhedrin that condemns Jesus to death. As Francis Schaeffer used to say, "You can't settle the question of truth by majority vote." I think Martin Luther and Galileo and others knew that, too.

If I am interested in a question, I must examine the issues for myself. I reject, for example, Velikovsky's astronomy, not because the academy sneers at it, which I guess they do, but because his methodology seems flawed to me, as I understand it. And forgive me, but so does Dr. Craig's.

First, let me call attention to two fundamental axioms of Dr. Craig's work. The first is what strikes me as a kind of double-truth model. The second is the old red-herring attempt to evade the principle of historical

Note: This is a portion of their 1999 Ohio State University debate on the question "Did Jesus of Nazareth Rise from the Dead?" The audio of the debate was published on YouTube on October 17, 2013, https://www.youtube.com/watch?v=l1vaqsnhgJY. Used with permission.

analogy, by means of the claim that critics reject miracle stories only because they espouse philosophical naturalism. The second follows from the first, and both commit the fallacy of ad hominem argumentation, even while projecting it onto the opponent.

I think he tips his hand at the end of the first chapter of his book *Reasonable Faith*. He draws a distinction there between *knowing* Christianity is true and *showing* that it is true. He says,

> What, then, should be our approach in apologetics? It should be something like this: "My friend, I know Christianity is true because God's Spirit lives in me and assures me that it is true, and you can know it too because God is knocking at the door of your heart, telling you the same thing. If you are sincerely seeking God, then God will give you assurance that the Gospel is true. Now, to show you it's true, I'll share with you some arguments and evidence that I really find convincing. But should my argument seem weak and unconvincing to you, that's my fault, not God's. It only shows that I'm a poor apologist, not that the Gospel is untrue. Whatever you think of my arguments, God still loves you and holds you accountable. I'll do my best to present good arguments to you, but ultimately you have to deal not with arguments, but with God himself." (page 48)

A little further on, he saith,

> Unbelief is at the root a spiritual, not an intellectual, problem. Sometimes an unbeliever will throw up an intellectual smokescreen so that he can avoid personal, existential involvement with the Gospel. (pages 49–50)

Dr. Craig then freely admits his conviction arises from purely subjective factors. To me, it sounds no different in principle from the teenage Mormon doorknocker. He tells you he knows the Book of Mormon was written by ancient Americans because he has a warm, swelling feeling inside when he asks God if it's true.

Certain intellectual questions have to receive certain answers, then, to be consistent with this revivalistic, heartwarming experience, so Dr. Craig knows in advance, for example, that Strauss and Bultmann must have been wrong, and by hook or by crook he'll find a way to get from here to there. His enterprise is circular, since he grounds Christian belief upon a subjective state described already in Christian theological terminology: God's Spirit dwelling in his heart, etc.

Dr. Craig seems to admit that he holds his faith on purely subjective grounds, but maintains that he's lucky to discover that the facts, objectively considered, happen to bear out his faith. Whereas, theoretically, his faith might not prove true to the facts, in actually—whew!—it does. In any case, it's obvious from the same quotes that the arguments are ultimately beside the point. If an unbeliever doesn't see the cogency of Dr. Craig's brand of New Testament criticism, the same thing exactly as his apologetics, it can only be because the doubter has some guilty secret to hide and doesn't want to repent and let Jesus run his life. If one sincerely seeks God, Dr. Craig's arguments will mysteriously start looking pretty good to him.

Dr. Craig's frank expression to his fellow evangelists and apologists is quite revealing. He tells you to say to the unbeliever that you find these arguments really convincing, but how can Dr. Craig simply take this for granted unless, as I'm sure he does, he knows he is writing to people for whom the cogency of the arguments is a foregone conclusion. They're arguments in behalf of a position his readers are already committed to as an *a priori* party line.

His is a position that exalts voluntaristic decision above rational deliberation. Rational deliberation, though good, is by itself not good enough for the evangelist because it can never justify a quick decision, such as Campus Crusades' booklet "The Four Spiritual Laws" solicits. Every one of Dr. Craig's scholarly articles on the resurrection implicitly ends with that little decision card for the reader to sign to invite Jesus into his heart as his personal savior. He's not trying to do disinterested historical or exegetical research; he's trying to get folks saved. I know the feeling. I used to be the president of an Inter-Varsity chapter.

Note how he characterizes people who do not accept his version of the historical Jesus as "unbelievers" who merely cast up "smokescreens" of insincere carping. But this functions as a mirror image of his own enterprise. His apparently self-effacing pose—"If my arguments fail to convince, then I must have done a poor job of explaining them"—just reveals the whole exercise to be a sham. The arguments are offered cynically, whatever it takes. If they don't work, take your pick between brimstone—"God holds you accountable"—and treacle—"God still loves you."

I'm not saying Dr. Craig is wittingly distorting the truth to win his point; obviously he's not. But he is so committed to a dogmatic party line that he cannot see truth as meaning anything but that party line, just as Kelly a moment ago said that "Truth ought to mean a person, not an abstract concept." In Dr. Craig's lexicon, you look up truth, and it says, "See 'Gospel.'" To borrow Francis Schaeffer's terminology again, for the apologist, truth becomes merely a connotation word. Just as liberal theologian Albrecht Ritschl said, "Jesus has the value of God for us," the apologist might say, "Christianity has the value of truth for us." Just as William James said that righteous endeavor was the moral equivalent of war, for apologists, Christianity is the moral equivalent of truth.

Only it doesn't work. For Ritschlianism, Jesus was in fact not God. For William James, moral endeavor was not in fact war. Even so, anything that substitutes for the truth may be preferred to the truth, but then it's a fiction.

If the charge that unbelievers are hiding behind a smokescreen is a mirror image of the apologist's own strategy, then the "naturalistic presuppositions" business is a specific instance of such childish "I know you are, but what am I?" tactics. Does it take a blanket presupposition for an historian to discount some miracle stories, like Elisha's axe head on the one extreme or the resurrection of Jesus on the other, as legendary? No, because as Bultmann recognized, there is no problem accepting reports even of extraordinary things that we can verify as still occurring today, like faith healings and exorcisms. However you may wish to account for them, you can go to certain meetings and see scenes resembling those in the Gospels, so it is by no means a matter of rejecting all miracle stories on principle.

Biblical critics are not like Carl Sagan or James Randi, going into every investigation already convinced that the paranormal must be a fraud. No, they take miracle stories on a case-by-case basis. But such a selective, piecemeal, and probabilistic acceptance of miracle stories is not what apologists want. They take umbrage that biblical critics do not wind up accepting *any and all* biblical miracles. So, if it would not require a blanket principle to *reject* the historicity of particular miracle stories, we must ask if it would take a blanket principle to *require acceptance* of all biblical miracles. Clearly, it would, and that principle cannot be mere supernaturalism, that is, openness to the possibility that miracles can occur. One can believe God capable of anything without believing that he actually did everything anybody may say he did. One can believe in the possibility of miracles without believing that every reported miracle must have occurred. No, the requisite principle for accepting all biblical miracles is the principle of biblical inerrancy, the belief that all biblical narratives are historically accurate simply because they appear in the Bible. After all, it will not greatly upset Dr. Craig any more than it upset Warfield to deny the historical accuracy of medieval reports of miracles wrought by the Virgin Mary or the sacramental wafer, much less stories of miracles wrought by Gautama Buddha or Apollonius of Tyana.

Supernaturalism is not at all the issue here. The issue is whether the historian is to abdicate his role as a sifter of evidence by accepting the dogma of inerrancy, even if clandestinely. I know Dr. Craig says he is sticking only to the elements of the Gospel story accepted as historical by most scholars, but this is only tactical. He's shortening the apologetical line of defense. Once he has you in the fold, he'll press on to full inerrantism.

Nor is naturalism the issue when the historian employs the principle of analogy. As F. H. Bradley showed in *The Presuppositions of Critical History*, no historical inference is possible unless the historian assumes a basic analogy of past experience with present experience. If we do not grant this, nothing will seem amiss in believing stories that A turned into a werewolf or B changed lead into gold. "Hey, just because we don't see it happening today doesn't prove it never did!" One could just as easily accept the historicity of Jack and the Beanstalk on the same basis as long as one's sole criterion for historical plausibility is "Anything goes." If there are ancient parallel legends about other saviors and sages rising from death or ascending into heaven, but there is no present-day instance, is the historian to be maligned as a narrow dogmatist or a moral coward refusing to repent if he judges the story of Jesus' resurrection as probably a legend, too?

The historical axiom of analogy does not dogmatize. Critical historians are not engaging in metaphysics and epistemology as if they could hop into a time machine and pontificate, "A didn't happen, B did!" Again, Dr. Craig and his brethren are just projecting. It is they and not critical historians who want to be able to point to sure results. Imagine a creed: "If thou shalt confess with thy mouth the Lord Jesus and believe in thy heart that God hath probably raised him from the dead, thou shalt most likely be saved." Now, who's the joke on there? Historians don't have creeds. They frame hypotheses. Sure, you can find some hidebound prof, some small-minded, insecure windbag who will not budge from a pet theory because he has too much personally invested in it, but you have no trouble recognizing such a person as a hack, a fake, a bad historian who ought to know better: Holocaust deniers, for example. The last thing you do is to emulate such behavior and make it into an operating principle. But apologists do; again, it's projection.

It reduces to this: At the end of the "Four Spiritual Laws" booklet, there's a cartoon diagram showing a toy locomotive engine labeled "Fact" pulling a coal car labeled "Faith," followed in turn by a superfluous caboose tagged "Feeling." The new convert is admonished to let faith rest on fact, not to allow faith to waver with feelings. But one must suspect that it is the caboose that is pulling the train, and pulling it backward. Faith is based "firmly" on *feeling*, and certain notions are postulated as fact and defended as such because of the security they afford the sick soul who seeks a port in the existential storm.

Dr. Craig has had occasion to cross swords with John Dominic Crossan. One need not agree with Crossan—I seldom do—to appreciate that he is however an innovative and creative New Testament scholar, that he marshals his vast learning in an attempt to find out new things from the Gospels. Crossan is concerned to advance the state of knowledge; contrast him with Dr. Craig who uses his own formidable erudition in one vast damage control operation. Every effort of Dr. Craig's is to squelch new theories that threaten to cast doubt on the traditional picture of the storybook Jesus. One feels that Dr. Craig would sooner put his efforts elsewhere than putting out fires lit by Bultmann, Strauss, and Crossan. If he had his way, he'd be occupied with something more edifying; at least that's the feeling I get.

Evangelicals think they've got the truth in their back pocket, so they can't be trying to find what they think they've already got. Novelty is the devil. They expend great time and efforts mastering the skills of Greek and Hebrew exegesis. Witness the unparalleled excellence of Dallas Theological Seminary in these areas. But for what? All their efforts at exegesis are the laborings of a mountain to bring forth a mouse. If one of them really comes up with something new theologically, it will result in immediate charges of heresy. The effort is solely to hold the fort against the advance of intellectual history.

Dr. Craig everywhere presupposes a precritical picture of the Gospels as straightforward records of reporting, without tendential bias. He tries to make the Markan empty tomb tale a piece of sober contemporary history. We're told that the story is unvarnished history, since it betrays no signs of theological tendency. No theological coloring? In a story told to attest the resurrection of the Son of God from the dead? What else *is* it? Isn't it *all* varnish, Formica instead of wood?

Charles Talbert (by the way, no God-hating atheist, but a Southern Baptist), in his book *What Is a Gospel?* has no trouble adducing abundant parallels from Hellenistic hero biographies, in which the ascensions into heaven of Romulus, Aeneas, Hercules, Aristaeus, Empedocles, Apollonius, etc., are inferred from the utter failure of their searching disciples to find any vestige of their bones, bodies, or clothing where they might be expected to be found. Sometimes, they make a postmortem appearance to their grieving and worshipful followers. These stories, like all ancient miracle tales, include the element of initial skepticism by the disciples, who are then convinced despite themselves. It's just a narrative device. None of them are factual reports.

Talbert concludes that the empty tomb and resurrection stories in the Gospels would have been familiar genres to ancient readers, as of course they were. Pagan critics hastened to point out the similarities, and Christian apologists lamely countered that Satan had counterfeited the Gospel episodes in advance to throw unbelievers off the track.

Contra Dr. Craig, the empty tomb story is theological through and through. If we're truly interested in history, how can we dismiss other ancient "vanished body and postmortem appearance" stories, making an exception in the single case of Jesus who just happens to be the founder of our religion? And once we recognize the Gospel resurrection narratives to be cut from the same cloth, all questions of whether the women went to the wrong tomb, or if the disciples stole the body (or borrowed it or whatever!), or whether the Sanhedrin could have produced it with dental records to prove who it was, or whether the disciples saw hallucinations, or a case of mistaken identity, are all seen to be moot.

APPENDIX C

The Demon, Matrix, Material World, and Dream Possibilities

I know as sure as I can know anything that there is a material world and that I can reasonably trust my senses. I conclude that the scientific method is our only sure way for assessing truth claims. These things I know to be the case.

Christian philosopher Alvin Plantinga argues that there are countless things we have proper warrant to believe without proof or evidence, such as the existence of other minds; the continuous existence of the world, even when we don't perceive it; that we have been alive for more than twenty-four hours; that the past really happened; that we aren't just brains in a mad scientist's vat; that we can trust our minds and our senses about the universe; that cause and effect are laws of nature; that nature is ordered, uniform, and intelligible; and so on. So Plantinga rhetorically asks why the belief in God is in a different category that needs evidence for it.

Christian apologist and philosopher of religion William Lane Craig uses some conjectures to argue as Plantinga does. Dr. Craig writes:

Note: Excerpted with slight edits from my book, *The Outsider Test for Faith* (Amherst, NY: Prometheus Books, 2013), pp. 134–144; 219–221; 223–226.

Most of our beliefs cannot be evidentially justified. Take, for example, the belief that the world was not created five minutes ago with built-in memory traces, food in our stomachs from meals we never really ate, and other appearances of age. Or the belief that the external world around us is real rather than a computer-generated virtual reality. Anyone who has seen a film like The Matrix realizes that the person living in such a virtual reality has no evidence that he is not in such an illusory world. But surely we're rational in believing that the world around us is real and has existed longer than five minutes, even though we have no evidence for this. . . . Many of the things we know are not based on evidence. So why must belief in God be so based?[1]

Christians apologist and philosopher of religion Randal Rauser does the same thing:

Our sensory experience leads us very naturally to believe in the external world. So it is for the Christian's experience of God. To believe in God is not some arbitrary, top-down explanation we force onto life. Rather, like our experience of matter, it's a natural, ground-level description of our experience of the world. . . . To put it another way, belief in the external world of matter can be believed rationally without evidence or reasoning. My challenge to you is to explain why belief in the external world is properly basic but belief in God cannot be.[2]

I have come to the conclusion that all these scenarios are not good defeaters of the demand for sufficient evidence. Take for instance the Cartesian demon hypothesis. Descartes conjectured that there could be an evil demon that deceives us about everything we think is true, and consequently there would be no evidence that could lead us to think otherwise. Is the evil demon hypothesis possible? Yes. Is it probable? Not by a long shot. Descartes used his extreme method of hypothetical doubt like a massive sword. The mere possibility that there is such a demon was enough to cast doubt on his knowledge about the material world. But why must we base what we think on a mere possibility? Once again, probability is all that matters. There is no reason and no evidence to suppose that such a being exists. If looking for and not finding such a demon does not constitute grounds for denying his existence, then looking for and not finding the elves of Iceland, the trolls of Norway, the Loch Ness monster, the abominable snowman, bigfoot, the tooth fairy, Santa Claus, satyrs, ghosts, goblins, unicorns, mermaids, or hobbits does not constitute grounds for denying their existence either. Even if such a demon exists I should still conclude what I do because of the lack of evidence.

Michael Martin argues that if there is an evil demon that deceives us, then we would have to say that no belief is rational, and as such "it would seem to entail that we could never be justified in thinking that it was."[3] Such a possibility undercuts any hope of knowing anything at all, and that's a pill no reasonable person should swallow. Martin adds that it's more reasonable to think we can come to correct conclusions based on the evidence than that such an evil demon exists, because it's a much simpler view without adding entities unnecessarily (Ockham's razor), and he argues that there is no reason to accept the demon possibility because it is unfalsifiable. He also argues that the demon hypothesis cannot explain the survival of the human race, since in order to survive in this world human beings have needed to act on correct conclusions derived from the world around us. So this is strong evidence that we are not being deceived by that demon.

Descartes searched for certain knowledge, a goal that was long ago abandoned by most philosophers. But a lack of certainty does little to undercut the need for sufficient evidence before accepting a proposition about the nature of our experience in this world. All we need to do is (1) think inductively rather than deductively, (2) think exclusively in terms of probabilities, and (3) understand that when speaking of sufficient evidence what is meant is evidence plus reasoning based on that evidence. The requirement for sufficient evidence does not come from a deductive argument stemming from the first principles of philosophy. No, it comes by means of an inductive argument based on the results of science. So an inductive argument that leads to a probable conclusion about the need for sufficient evidence cannot be self-defeating. This conclusion might be wrong, as improbable as that is, but it's not self-defeating. If, in addition, we think exclusively in terms of probabilities rather than possibilities, we won't need to achieve certainty with regard to any proposition either. A good argument based on some evidence is good enough. This means that if we understand the requirement for sufficient evidence is based on evidence plus reasoning based on that evidence, there can be no objection to this requirement.

Who in their right mind would not want sufficient evidence for what they accept as true? The evidence for this requirement can be found everywhere, leading us to an exceedingly probable conclusion. Again, probability is all that matters. Christians cannot slip in the mere possibility that there are things they can believe without sufficient evidence when the total weight of evidence is against such a bald-faced assertion. We need only look to the alternative proposition that people are within their epistemic rights to believe without sufficient evidence in any other area. That's a recipe for disaster.

What about the possibility seen in the blockbuster movie The Matrix? The possibility that I'm presently living in a virtual, matrix world, rather than in the real world, cannot be taken seriously by any intelligent person. The story is extremely implausible. I see no reason why there would be any knowledge of the matrix by people living in it, since the matrix determines all their experiences. So how could taking a virtual red pill while in the matrix get someone out of it and into the real world in the first place? As far as Neo, the protagonist in The Matrix, knows, the red pill could have been nothing more than a hallucinogenic drug. And even if Neo came to believe a real world lies beyond his own virtual, matrix world, how could he know that the so-called real world isn't just another matrix beyond the one he experiences? Neo would have no good reason for concluding that he knows which world is the really real world at that point. The really real world could be beyond the one he experienced after taking the red pill, or beyond that one, or beyond that one, and so forth. If all we need to be concerned with is what is possible rather than what is probable we couldn't claim to know anything at all. We would end up as epistemological solipsists. So, as David Mitsuo Nixon has argued with respect to the matrix, "The proper response to someone's telling me that my belief could be false is, 'So what?' It's not possibility that matters, it's probability. So until you give me a good reason to think that my belief is not just possibly false, but probably false, I'm not changing anything about what I believe or what I think I know."[4]

In fact, believing we're in a matrix would be a much closer parallel for believing in God than Craig may realize. Craig is actually giving us a reason to doubt an ad hoc, unevidenced assumption like God. For if it's silly to believe in the matrix, it should be silly to believe in God. As I've argued before, Christians repeatedly retreat to the position that what they believe is "possible" or "not impossible." A possibility is not a probability. The inference does not follow. It's a huge non sequitur.

These questions are the stock-in-trade of Western philosophers who want to explore the boundaries of knowledge. But ask them if they seriously entertain them and they will almost to a person say no.

Take as another example the existence of a material world. Christian apologist and philosopher of religion Thomas Talbott argued that by examining religious faiths from the perspective of an outsider, with the *Outsider Test for Faith*, I don't have any basis for thinking there is a material world.[5] I find it amazing that apologists elevate bizarre hypothetical scenarios in order to object to a healthy amount of skepticism. I mean, really, for all of Talbott's verbosity he thinks, like I do, that there is a material world. I taught philosophy. I know what it's like to argue that there isn't a material world. I did it every semester whenever I taught my introduction to philosophy class. It was fun to do. It takes students by surprise as they struggle to find reasons why they think otherwise. It was, to use Talbott's own phrase, "a pedagogical device."[6] Apparently then, Talbott is stuck in a pedagogical mode, which he states as follows:

> As any good teacher knows, a less than fully accurate statement will sometimes reveal more to beginning students, or do more to nudge them in the right direction, than a fully accurate statement will when the latter would be unintelligible to them. As I have elsewhere put it: "Like many teachers, I often find myself saying things to beginning students that I would prefer them to reinterpret (perhaps even to discard) as they mature into more advanced students."[7]

Being pedagogical just won't do here. Either Talbott thinks there is a material world or he does not. If he does, then why bother with this objection at all? Christian apologist and philosopher of religion Mark Hanna thinks there is a contradiction in my reasoning:

> It is patently contradictory to say, on the one hand, as Loftus does, that the scientific method is our "only" sure way for assessing truth claims and to say, on the other hand, that we know certain things, such as the existence of a material world and the essential reliability of our senses, which are not the results but the pre-requirements of implanting "the scientific method."[8]

My reasons for thinking there is a material world are similar to Dr. Samuel Johnson's kicking a stone and declaring he had refuted George Berkeley's idealism. They are also similar to G. E. Moore's assertion that he's more assured he has a pencil in his hand than that the skeptical arguments to the contrary are correct.[9] There are plenty of other reasons. One of them is simply that it makes no difference at all if there isn't a physical universe. There ought to be some sort of difference between propositions if we are to make sense of them as different propositions. Ockham's razor does the requisite work after acknowledging this. Another reason is science itself. How can we conceive of it working without a materially existing world? Why do we need brains, a liver, lungs, and organs of any kind? Why does surgery save us from death if these organs are not real? How does a doctor prescribe a pill to heal us if there is no material body? What then causes us to be healed if the pill doesn't do it? Where's the mechanism for producing a healing effect from a nonphysical cause? To argue there is a spiritual reality that heals us means we do not need to take the prescribed pill at all. Why not just pray instead? Why bother with medicine or surgery at all?

Additionally, why do I have the experience of moving from place to place? Who is moving if I am not the one doing this? How can there be a change of scenery if I do not have a physical body that moves? And who or what guarantees that when I step outside my house day after day the house has the same physical characteristics when I return? Why should our experience be the same every time we look at a given object unless there really is a physical object and a physical world?

The burden of proof is therefore laid squarely on the back of anyone who denies this. But there is no way anyone can deny a material world, since one must presuppose it for the sake of the arguments. After all, these arguments require physical evidence of some kind, so where are we supposed to find this physical evidence if it doesn't exist? Why not just dispense with the physical evidence altogether and simply assert that an external material universe does not exist, since if this is the case, the physical evidence is irrelevant?

Even scientists who argue for a holographic universe, who think our experience is nothing but a hologram, do not deny that a physical universe exists, because they base their conclusions on the physical evidence. How is it possible to argue there is no material world from evidence that cannot exist without a material world? This would be contradictory. There must be some physical evidence for this conclusion. And if there is evidence, then the material world—at least some kind of material world—does exist. It may not be like the one we experience, but it still would exist.

How would such a nonmaterial idealist be able to exclude the possibility that there is a totally different kind of reality beyond the spiritual one, or another reality beyond that one, and so forth? That's why Ockham's razor stops these kinds of questions with the simplest explanation rather than adding on entities endlessly. The simplest explanation is that a physical universe of some kind exists. Talbott argues that

> with respect to his [Loftus's] belief in an external physical reality, the perspective of an outsider would be that of many Hindus, an idealist, a panpsychist, a panentheist, or perhaps even a philosophical skeptic such as David Hume. So if Loftus should subject his own belief in an external physical reality to the Outsider Test, then he would need to examine that belief at least as skeptically as an idealist or some other outsider might examine it. And yet, one searches in vain for the slightest hint of doubt on his part or even for a willingness to examine an outsider argument against physical realism (of which there are many).[10]

If Talbott thinks for one moment that, as an outsider, I must take an outsider stance to a healthy amount of skepticism based in science and reason, then he needs to show why the science I base my argument on is faulty and then propose an alternative that can solve the problem of religious diversity better. The bottom line is that idealism is religious in nature. It seems to me the only people who argue that there is no material world are believers, like George Berkeley, who used this as an argument to God's existence. He used it in an attempt to solve the mind/ brain problem, which would otherwise undercut his religious faith, by denying the existence of brains. Only religious people would think this, and only a philosopher of religion would use this argument, which is one reason so many people are beginning to eschew philosophy of religion as vacuous.

Talbott also argues that because David Hume was looking for and did not find certainty when it came to a material universe, I should likewise be skeptical that there is a material world. But Talbott should know that the quest for certainty died soon after Hume. Certainty is an unattainable goal. To Talbott or anyone else who may suggest that I might possibility be wrong about a material world, all I can say is, so what? Probability is the only thing that matters. Until he gives me a reason to think I am probably wrong, I'm not changing anything I think. We're always talking about probabilities, not certainties. And we're not in his introduction to philosophy class either. He should own up to what he really thinks on this issue. I have provided my reasons, just as I did about the matrix and demon hypotheses. That there is a material world passes the outsider test of an informed skepticism.

Consider next the reasons to think the world has existed for more than five minutes. We have memories that are usually correct. We know people with whom we can reminisce. We have baby pictures of ourselves and old shoes, clothes, and memorabilia from previous years. There are artifacts from previous eras, too, including archaeological evidence of our ancient past. There are rock formations that show the earth to be a few billion years old. We also have scientific evidence for the Big Bang. That the world has existed longer than five minutes is extremely probable. To someone who claims differently, I merely say again, so what? Possibility does not matter. No wonder I think scientifically uniformed philosophy is of little use. No wonder it has little or no respect among real scientists.

As one last example, when it comes to the question of whether I'm dreaming right now, Norman Malcolm, in his book *Dreaming*, and Bernard Williams, in his book *Descartes*, have made the case that there is a difference between dreams and our waking experience.[11] The fact that we can distinguish between them presupposes that we are aware of both states as well as the differences between them. It's only from the perspective of being awake that we can explain our dreams. Hence we can only make sense of this distinction if we are sometimes awake. And since this is the case, all our experiences throughout our entire lives cannot be made up merely of a sequence of dreams. I still may not know exactly when I'm dreaming, but it's highly probable that I'm awake right now as I type these words and as I read over them.

One thing I have personally found is that when it comes to reading a document of any kind I cannot do so in my dreams. I suspect it's because my dreaming mind has to simultaneously write whatever it is I'm reading in a dream, and writing is hard mental work, the kind that doesn't take place on the spur of the moment even when I'm awake. But when I'm awake I can read through a whole book. So I can know I'm awake whenever I'm reading a book.

Furthermore, I can have conversations with people during my waking hours that can be the basis for subsequent conversations the next day, after I've slept and subsequently risen from bed. I don't fall asleep while eating dinner and I don't wake up while running a race. I fall asleep in bed and wake up in the same bed I laid down in, except if I sleepwalk or someone picks me up and carries me to another bed while I'm sleeping. I sometimes wake up from dreams a couple of times per night. But I always wake up in the same bed in which I fell asleep. In my dreams I can have the experience of seeing or doing things that go against the laws of nature, like having the superhuman power of flight or seeing something transformed into something else. The best explanation is that we know when we are awake, even if our dreams can fool us.

I live my life based on short-term memories. If I were to doubt them and habitually fail to arrive for appointments I've made the previous day, I would fail in life, groping without a compass through a haphazard dream world of random choices. I would be an unreliable person. Life demands that I trust my short-term memories, that I know I am not now dreaming, that I arrive at appointments I made the previous day while awake. I should do so even if I am dreaming right now. It doesn't change a thing if I am. My point is that faith has nothing to do with this reasoning process. Probabilities are all that matter.

What Christian apologists are doing with all these bizarre scenarios is leveling the playing field between what they claim to know on faith and what we know based on experiencing the natural world. So David Eller has rightly argued that "knowing is not believing." He claims that if believers "can drag down real knowledge to their level and erase any distinctions between the true and the false, the known and the merely felt or believed or guessed, they can rest comfortably in their own undeserved self-certainty." According to him, "knowledge is about reason" while "belief is about faith." He says, "The two are logically and psychologically utterly different and even incompatible."[12] He simply refuses to play this religious language game.

* * * * *

This is what I know about faith: Faith has no method. Faith cannot settle differences between believers. Faith does not lead to new discoveries. Faith cannot solve any problems. Faith cannot explain anything. Faith depends on mysteries. Faith can and does lead to a denial of the evidence. Faith is pretty much immune from debunking. Faith is rooted in fear and ignorance. With faith as a foundation anything at all can be believed or denied.

The problem is that practically nothing is certain. But accepting some conclusion because it's merely possible is irrational. We should never do that. I suppose it's possible a man could jump off a building and fly, right? After all, he could instantaneously grow wings or a huge burst of air could keep him afloat or a supernatural force could propel him through the air. It's even possible that the man could be dreaming, and in the dream he can fly, or that there isn't a material world, and in the world of his mind he can fly. Okay, I understand all this. All these scenarios are remotely possible, I suppose, but because they are so remote I consider them virtually impossible.

By contrast, consider the opposite scenario. It's probable that if the man jumps off a building he will fall to the ground. How probable is this? Well, since it's possible he won't fall (per our examples above), we cannot say with certainty that he will fall. But it's virtually certain that he will. In between these extremes there are a lot of different odds for something, stretching from extremely improbable, very improbable, improbable, and slightly improbable to even odds, slightly probable, probable, very probable, and extremely probable. As I have said, we should think exclusively in terms of probabilities. We don't have a word to differentiate between the odds on that continuum stretching from virtually impossible to virtually certain. But does anyone really want to suggest the word faith applies to these different probabilities such that there is the same amount of faith required to accept any one of them? If so, that is being irrational.

If believers want to say that more faith is required to accept something that is virtually impossible and less faith is required to accept something that is virtually certain, what can they possibly mean? What is faith at that point? Faith adds nothing to the actual probabilities. Having more of it or less of it does not change anything. If it's possible to accept a virtually impossible conclusion by having more faith, that's irrational. And if we have a virtually certain conclusion then we don't need faith at all.

What about something that is only slightly probable, one might ask. What if we accept something that has only a 60 percent chance of being true? I still don't see where faith can change the actual probabilities. Faith cannot change a thing, you see. Faith adds nothing. Accepting faith as a basis for knowledge is irrational. Who would fill in the probability gap with anything more than what the probabilities actually show us?

Not me.

The only sense I can make of the way believers use the word faith is that it's an irrational leap over the probabilities. Believers fill in the actual probabilities with faith in order to call an improbable conclusion extremely probable, and that is quite simply irrational. A probability is a probability is a probability. When it comes to propositions about entities that exist or events that may have taken place, we must think exclusively in terms of probabilities.

* * * * *

Randal Rauser thinks it's easy to define faith. He defines it as "assent to a proposition that is conceivably false."[13] By doing so he's lowered the bar so far that everyone could be thought to have faith. On the basis of this self-serving definition he can go on to claim Christians are doing nothing more than what all other people do. Faith, then, is equally involved when it comes to trusting our short-term memories, our senses, and even scientific conclusions that are based on an overwhelming amount of physical evidence.

Now I don't doubt for a minute that all propositions are conceivably false. What I deny is that mere possibilities count as anything significant. The more something is considered conceivably false, the less we should pay attention to it, for if we were to treat every proposition as being equally likely to be false, simply because any fact is conceivably false, we would all be paralyzed and unable to accept any proposition as true. This is what I object to.

Let's just focus on one example, the fact that the sun will rise tomorrow morning over the horizon where I live in Indiana. Given that the sun has risen every day of the earth's existence, and given that the earth has existed for about 4.5 billion years, the odds that it will rise again tomorrow are about 1.643 trillion to 1. So when I say I know the sun will rise today I can say this with a great deal of certainty. The odds are virtually certain the sun will rise over the horizon (even if clouds might hide it from view).

The question is whether I need to be absolutely certain that the sun will rise tomorrow. I think not, obviously so. I don't need this gap to be filled. I don't need to be certain the sun will rise tomorrow. I am quite comfortable going with the odds, the probabilities. I could be wrong, but so what? Probability is all that matters. We should think exclusively in terms of probabilities. Faith adds nothing to my calculations at all. This goes for everything else I think is probably true.

Is faith used to calculate the very probabilities I use to conclude the sun will rise tomorrow? How so? That a great deal of background knowledge from personal experience is used to calculate the probabilities is granted, and most all of it could conceivably be false, too. So? This background knowledge has the weight of probability; at least, we accept it as more probable than not overall. We cannot do otherwise. What else do we have for judging our background knowledge except the probabilities? I trust my background knowledge not because of faith, but because it is built up based on the evidence of personal experience one layer at a time from birth. Trust is based on the probabilities, which are in turn based on the evidence of past experience, that's why faith is not the same as trust. If it were the same, Rauser would be equivocating on the meaning of the word faith, for faith would become equivalent to trusting the probabilities, which is the very thing for which I argue. Therefore, to say we need faith to think the sun will rise tomorrow is at best superfluous, completely unnecessary, utterly irrelevant, and at worst irrational.

Christians will typically respond that faith is what is required to uphold the things we believe are most probable. How does faith do that? Imagine flipping a quarter. The probability of getting heads is equal to the probability of getting tails. Where is faith? What does it do here? How does having faith change the odds? Imagine a lottery in which you have a 1 in 80 million chance of winning. Where is faith? What does it do here? How does having faith change the odds? Imagine a sports contest, say a boxing match. Gamblers place their bets on who will win based on the odds. Where is faith? What does it do here? How does having faith change the odds?

When it comes to providing scientific evidence that we should think exclusively in terms of probabilities we must think in Bayesian terms. The two hypotheses to be compared are: (1) science helps us arrive at the truth and (2) faith helps us arrive at the truth. Since faith has no method, solves no problems, and reaches conclusions contrary to probabilities that are calculated based on the evidence generated by objective observation and experimentation, the probability that it helps us arrive at the truth is extremely low.

The really intriguing cases have to do with a host of hypothetical scenarios. Am I really typing these words in September 2012? There is faith involved, they argue, since it's conceivable that I'm not. For all I know, it's currently 2032 and a mad scientist, having just extracted my brain, is now pouring chemicals over it so that I'm merely remembering that I typed these words twenty years in the past. There is a host of scenarios like these. Perhaps our universe is nothing more than a raindrop in a thunderstorm that's taking place in a much larger universe. Perhaps. Perhaps.

I have argued that none of these hypothetical scenarios are probable, but that's beside the point here. Let's call these scenarios possible explanations for our mundane experience of life. Rauser claims that anyone who assents to the proposition that they are probably false has faith. But what Rauser has failed to provide in his definition is the continuum by which he judges something as conceivably false. Is everything conceivably false to the same degree? Or are there some things that are more or less probable?

So he has a choice to make. Either (a) he must say there is no way at all to judge between the probabilities of these scenarios, including our mundane experience of life, which means all the scenarios are equally probable, or (b) he must admit he's thinking about all of them exclusively in terms of the probabilities after all. In either case, Rauser doesn't have a soapbox to preach on, for it follows that choosing (a) requires Rauser should be a skeptic, a real skeptic, a nonbeliever, and, beyond this, potentially an epistemological solipsist, while choosing (b) dispenses with the need for, and the value of, faith itself. So in the end Rauser is playing a Christian language game, one that no one needs to accept.

But wait! Don't change the channel. There's more.

Let's say we are living in the matrix or dreaming right now. It still doesn't change the fact that we should think exclusively in terms of the probabilities inside the matrix or the dream. If reality is up for grabs, with no way to assess any probabilities at all, then we might as well take a gun and shoot ourselves in the head. After all, perhaps there isn't a bullet in the gun? Perhaps the bullet won't fire even if it exists? Perhaps there isn't really a gun in our hand? Perhaps we'll miss if we pull the trigger? Perhaps it won't hurt even if it hits our head? Perhaps our head will heal instantly even if it hurts us? What's the probability we'll die? We might just be dreaming instead. And we might as well rob a bank, too. Hey, why not? What's the probability we might get away with it? What if we're merely brains in a vat and we already got away with it or we already paid the price in prison twenty years ago? What difference does it make now? So even if we're inside the matrix or we're dreaming or our brains are in a vat, we should still assess Christianity based on the probabilities. Probabilities are all that matter. Faith adds nothing to the probabilities, nothing at all. Rauser's definition of faith is therefore utterly irrelevant to whether Christianity is true. It's a Christian language game, pure and simple.

Notes

1.   William Lane Craig, "The Witness of the Holy Spirit," Reasonable Faith, http://www.reasonablefaith.org/the-witness-of-the-holy-spirit (accessed November 26, 2012).

2.   Randal Rauser, *The Swedish Atheist, the Scuba Diver, and Other Apologetic Rabbit Trails* (Downers Grove, IL: InterVarsity Press, 2012), chapter 6.

3.   See Michael Martin, *Atheism: A Philosophical Justification* (Philadelphia: Temple University Press, 1990), pp. 35–38.

4.   David Mitsuo Nixon, "The Matrix Possibility," in *The Matrix and Philosophy: Welcome to the Desert of the Real*, ed. William Irwin (Chicago: Open Court, 2002), p. 30.

5.   Thomas Talbott, "The Outsider Test for Faith: How Serious a Challenge Is It?" http://www.willamette.edu/~ttalbott/Loftus% 20OTF2. pdf (accessed November 26, 2012).

6.   Ibid, p. 24, n. 23.

7.   Ibid., p. 26.

8.   Mark Hanna, *Biblical Christianity: Truth or Delusion* (Xulon Press, 2011), p. 125.

9.   G. E. Moore, "A Defense of Common Sense," Digital Text International, http://www.ditext.com/moore/common-sense.html (accessed December 27, 2012).

10.   Talbott, "Outsider Test for Faith," p. 24.

11. See Norman Malcolm, "Dreaming and Skepticism," *Philosophical Review* 65, no. 1 (January 1956): 14–37; Norman Malcolm, *Dreaming* (New York: Routledge & Kegan Paul, 1976); and Bernard Williams, *Descartes: The Project of Pure Enquiry*, rev. ed. (New York: Routledge, 2005).

12. David Eller, *Natural Atheism* (Cranford, NJ: American Atheist Press, 2004), pp. 132–33. For more, read chapters 5 and 11 in his book *Atheism Advanced: Further Thoughts of a Freethinker* (Cranford, NJ: American Atheist Press, 2007).

13. See Randal Rauser's post "John Loftus Challenges Me to Define Faith," March 10, 2012, Randal Rauser, http://randalrauser.com/2012/ 03/john-loftus-challenges-me-to-define-faith/.

ABOUT THE AUTHOR

John Loftus is a former Christian minister and apologist who received an MA and MDiv from Lincoln Christian Seminary in 1982, and a ThM from Trinity Evangelical Divinity School in 1985. While in school he studied philosophy, theology, and the philosophy of religion and majored under Dr. William Lane Craig, today's leading evangelical apologist and debater. He also studied in a PhD program at Marquette University for a year and a half in the area of theology and ethics (1985–87).

Loftus is the author of *Why I Became an Atheist: A Former Preacher Rejects Christianity* (rev. ed. 2012), which he considers his magnum opus, and *The Outsider Test for Faith* (2013), both published by Prometheus Books. He has edited four important anthologies, *The Christian Delusion: Why Faith Fails* (2010), *The End of Christianity* (2011), *Christianity Is Not Great: How Faith Fails* (2014), and *Christianity in the Light of Science: Critically Examining the World's Largest Religion* (2016), also published by Prometheus Books. He cowrote a debate book with Dr. Randal Rauser, *God or Godless?* (2013), published by Baker Books, and wrote *How to Defend the Christian Faith: Advice from an Atheist* (2015), published by Pitchstone.

He has traveled the United States and Canada speaking to audiences in Indiana, Ohio, New York, Georgia, Louisiana, Texas, California, Colorado, Wisconsin, and many places in between, and has participated in seven public debates. He welcomes other such opportunities to speak and debate.

He is a board member of Atheist Alliance of America. He is also a licensed minister with the First Church of Atheism and the Universal Life Church, so he does weddings and funerals (but no baptisms, sorry!). His website is Debunking Christianity (www.debunkingchristianity. blogspot.com). His Twitter handle is @loftusjohnw and his email address is loftusjohnw@gmail.com.